A Reader's Guide to College Writing

John J. Ruszkiewicz
The University of Texas at Austin

Bedford/St. Martin's | BOSTON ◆ NEW YORK

For Bedford/St. Martin's
Publisher: Leasa Burton
Senior Developmental Editor: Joelle Hann
Senior Production Editor: Gregory Erb
Production Associate: Steven Dowling
Executive Marketing Manager: Molly Parke
Editorial Assistant: Rachel Childs
Copy Editor: Steve Patterson
Indexer: Mary White
Senior Art Director: Anna Palchik
Text Design: Marsha Cohen
Cover Design: Billy Boardman
Composition: Cenveo Publisher Services
Printing and Binding: RR Donnelley and Sons

President, Bedford/St. Martin's: Denise B. Wydra
Editor in Chief: Karen S. Henry
Director of Marketing: Karen R. Soeltz
Production Director: Susan W. Brown
Director of Rights and Permissions: Hilary Newman

Manufactured in the United States of America.

8   7   6   5   4   3
f   e   d   c   b   a

For information, write: Bedford/St. Martin's, 75 Arlington Street, Boston, MA 02116   (617-399-4000)

ISBN 978-1-4576-4258-6   (Student Edition)

Acknowledgments

Acknowledgments and copyrights appear at the back of the book on pages 249–50, which constitute an extension of the copyright page. It is a violation of the law to reproduce these selections by any means whatsoever without the written permission of the copyright holder.

For Kate

Reading maketh a full man; conference a
ready man; and writing an exact man.

—Francis Bacon, "Of Studies" (1625)

Like many of his generation, recent University of Texas gradu-ate Doug Taylor set off for a big city after commencement—in his case New York—landed a few enviable internships, and re-turned home with possibly more questions than he'd left with. Then, while substitute-teaching in another part of Texas, Doug snared a spring-break job back in Austin as a gofer at SXSW, the town's annual music/film/media blowout. That's where I come in. Doug needed a place to stay during the gig and I needed a house sitter. We worked it out, and my former student and I caught up over ribs and brisket at a barbecue joint. It was there Doug outlined his ambitious plan to raise his already-appreciable skills as a writer to a whole new level.

And to do it (mostly) on his own.

The internships, elementary- and secondary-school teach-ing, and even time as a wilderness guide had all convinced this former history/government major that, whatever career he set-tled on, nothing would bring him more satisfaction, power, or self-knowledge than full-bore expertise in writing. The course in Advanced Composition he'd taken from me some years ear-lier had been a start, but I discovered that Doug, like many Digi-tal Natives, doesn't tally education by fifteen-week semesters. He's open to unconventional paths of learning and discovery, as he explains in the draft of an essay he was eager to show me:

> Learning by discovery is . . . immersing yourself in material
> that will only sort itself out in your head. It's the opposite of
> instructional learning, and I would argue the more frustrating
> and fulfilling of the two. And for good reason: You're isolated
> from outside help, trying to navigate in the absence of a
> map—maddening during the journey, but gratifying and
> invaluable once complete.

On his own, Doug had already burrowed through a roster of writing mavens—Strunk and White, Richard Lanham, William Zinsser, Joe Williams, Annie Dillard, Stanley Fish—but it was the idea of self-education itself, inspired by The Great Courses, publicity surrounding MOOCs, even a brush with Mortimer Adler, that intrigued this recent graduate who was enthusiastically and ingeniously carving his own pathways to a career. Needless to say, I was impressed and more than a little pleased.

Whether he realized it or not, Doug was confirming my intuitions about the media-savvy students I'd been encountering in recent decades. Literacy skills supposedly lost to what Kevin Kelly calls these "people of the screen" are simply waiting to be reawakened or rediscovered *within* the new technologies. And smart learners want to know where those connections might be. Pointing them out is one goal of this volume, which offers the kind of insider advice that students enjoy finding on blogs, Web sites, and social media.

So, I did not create *A Reader's Guide to College Writing* in response to a perceived crisis in education or precipitous drop in student ability. Frankly, a lot of what appears in the book is exactly the stuff I wish I'd known myself about academic practices and culture when I started college more than forty years ago. But it *is* naïve to think that students today read, write, and maybe even think the same way their colleagues, unplugged and paper-bound, did a generation or so ago. They command powerful streams of data channeled by seductive and relentless media capable of instantly amplifying any ideas that trigger their interest. But many of these students (as well as their instructors) realize that habits as basic as reading at length, taking ideas seriously, or even just responding to them now seem as outmoded as typewriters and as retro as vinyl records. *A Reader's Guide to College Writing* seeks to counter that impression. A handbook to academic culture, it capitalizes on the very curiosity that drives students' media explorations to champion literacy skills they need and lack, but honestly covet. It could be essential reading.

What It Does

Highly personal and pragmatic, *A Reader's Guide to College Writing* aims to give students an insider's perspective on academic life—its ideals, expectations, preferences, and conventions. More important, it is designed to help them produce successful writing—from short response papers to personal narratives to full research efforts. It does so by offering open-ended rhetorical strategies for engaging with ideas. But it purposely does not define a specific curriculum or outline a sequence of genre-based assignments, leaving those choices to instructors or writers themselves.

Provides a flexible and engaging approach to teaching writing

With its focus on key academic skills, *A Reader's Guide to College Writing* fits any college course or program in which extended readings and texts steer a curriculum, initiate discussions, or prompt writing assignments. As such, the book is a logical companion for many common reading programs or first-year seminars; for writing-intensive or writing-across-the-disciplines programs; for humanities courses with extended reading lists; and, of course, for composition classes, especially those built around topics or based on readings. *A Reader's Guide to College Writing* can be assigned chapter by chapter, but I've imagined it as a set of lessons appealing enough to win readers without much prompting and helpful to instructors, well-seasoned or just starting out. (After forty years in the classroom, I know what a tough audience students can be.)

Focuses on critical academic skills that students need

A Reader's Guide to College Writing covers ground that instructors hope students already know but suspect they do not. It deals with "big picture" strategies, such as figuring out the contexts that surround assigned books and articles. It introduces students to the worlds of authors and publishers, examines how they use source material, and—crucially—discusses in detail the aims and methods of serious writers, especially academics and public intellectuals. But the book also provides down-to-earth advice on how to summarize and synthesize information, as well as how to frame source material for maximum impact. There's even a full chapter that explains to students exactly how to join class discussions, and what essential college and life skills they stand to gain from the experience.

Features meaty examples from writers taught across the university

A Reader's Guide to College Writing teaches by example, with instruction that is anchored in the kinds of writing that students are routinely assigned across college campuses. Passages, drawn from acclaimed works of contemporary nonfiction and fiction by writers such as Malcolm Gladwell, Stanley Fish, Diane Ravitch, Barbara Ehrenreich, Luis Alberto Urrea, Annette Lareau, Nicholas Carr, and Dave Eggers, are meticulously analyzed to show exactly how and why they work.

Uses marginal notes to highlight moves that matter in academic writing

Annotations throughout the book make it easy for readers to see at a glance how to apply advice to their own writing. These brief guidelines provide cues to help readers navigate the book and remember what they've read. Selected passages from writers are also annotated to expose their most clever or artful rhetorical moves or to draw attention to specific features such as how a strong opening idea can lead to an effective closing statement.

Engages students with end-of-chapter exercises

All chapters conclude with exercise prompts designed specifically to apply or extend what has been presented in the chapter. There's no busywork in these activities. Instead they push students to try out or even challenge what they have learned.

Provides helpful reference materials to support college success

Chapter 18, "Clarity and Economy," offers a baker's dozen of dos and don'ts for strong writing. The principles can be taught in the classroom or used as a reference—and should prove valuable in college and beyond.

Further, in Appendix B, *A Reader's Guide to College Writing* briefly reviews MLA and APA documentation guidelines, providing excerpts from sample Works Cited and reference lists that students will find helpful for learning or recalling key concepts. It also presents a bibliography of major texts discussed or mentioned within the book.

Students will, I hope, find the volume useful not just as an introduction to college reading and writing, but as a guide worth keeping for years beyond since, for many, education truly begins on graduation day.

How It Is Arranged

Part One of *A Reader's Guide to College Writing* is entitled "You, the Reader." Its six opening chapters slow down a process that many students rip through from years of reading Facebook updates, blog posts, text messages, and Twitter feeds. The section challenges students to set books and articles in specific contexts, assess their intended audiences, examine their structures, and evaluate their sources and use of evidence. Only then are students in a position to respond to texts purposefully.

Replying to texts is the matter of Part Two, "You, the Respondent." Here, *A Reader's Guide to College Writing* introduces students to the powerful tools of traditional rhetorical analysis, offering them a closer look—sometimes line by line—at exactly how writers make claims, address their subjects, or rebut potential critics. Students can take these techniques away from the classroom and apply them in any situation requiring language and persuasion. The section concludes with an innovative and detailed chapter on class discussions: how to prepare for them, what to say in them, and how to achieve successful results.

Finally, Part Three of *A Reader's Guide to College Writing* is "You, the Writer." The seven chapters here are a succinct course in composition, based upon principles and insights that have guided the first two parts of the book. The advice is tight, frank, and pragmatic, covering everything from overcoming writer's block to framing ideas and quotations effectively. A final chapter focuses on the important matter of clear style—precisely what writers need in school and thereafter.

Who Helped

A Reader's Guide to College Writing began when, almost joking, I asked, "What do we do next?" after completing a hefty volume for Bedford/St. Martin's entitled *How to Write Anything*. Publisher Leasa Burton took up the challenge and quickly offered an array of possibilities, one of which—with her insight and sure-footed guidance—evolved into this new and, for me, somewhat unexpected book. I am deeply grateful to Leasa and to the full team at Bedford—especially Denise Wydra and Joan Feinberg—for the encouragement and freedom they gave me to pursue a fresh idea and to do it in a style somewhat outside the academic mainstream. It's easy to be creative when the people you work with have a lock on that market.

My developmental editor, Joelle Hann, came onto the project at precisely the moment when I was wrestling with major structural tangles in some of the most crucial chapters. She cut that Gordian knot and then went on to guide me through a number of lesser dilemmas, especially what to trim as our little book grew thick around the waist. I think I adopted all but one of her major suggestions; anyone who has worked with editors will appreciate how much insight and skill a record like that represents. Thank you, Joelle, for making *A Reader's Guide to College Writing* a smarter and much more graceful text.

Early in the project I had assistance from Megan Eatman and Stephanie Odom at the University of Texas at Austin and Alyssa Demirjian at Bedford/St. Martin's in identifying books that college students across the country were reading: my sincere thanks. Julia Green at Front Street Books in Alpine, Texas, helped me to find many of those items, sending me down Holland Avenue with stacks of new and used books that I'm still reading. I'm grateful to you and to Front Street Books. Thanks, too, to former colleague Justin Hodgson for permission to reprint portions of the syllabus from his course in Serious Games. I'd probably flunk the class, given my limited understanding of gaming technologies. But I'm sure I'd enjoy it.

A special nod, of course, to Doug Taylor, mentioned in this preface, and to another former student, Bryan Cory, who, after I explained this project to him, directed me to Pierre Bayard's delightful *How to Talk about Books You Haven't Read*—which plays a significant role in Chapter 16. In fact, I owe a debt of gratitude to a great many former students who have inspired me over the years by their enthusiasm and talent. Let me thank a few by name: Jordyn Brown, Jeremy Burchard, Molly Casey, Stefan Casso, Marissa Dahlstrom, Manasi Deshpande, Andrew Juraschek, Sean Kamperman, Phillip Lacey, Terrence Maas, Jon Mannhaupt, Anthony Mannino, Shane McNamee, Tempestt Moore, Eric Ormsby, Lily Parish, Taylor Pearson, Jennifer Pier, Matt Portillo, Brian Riady, Reagan Tankersley, Katherine Thayer, Suzanne Tobias, Susan Wilcox, and Holly Wu. I'd probably have retired already if I didn't so much enjoy working with fine people like these semester after semester at the University of Texas at Austin—which itself deserves some thanks for putting up with me for so long.

You Get More Choices

Bedford/St. Martin's offers resources and format choices that help you and your students get even more out of the book and your course. To learn more about or order any of the following products, contact your Bedford/St. Martin's sales representative, e-mail sales support (sales_support@bfwpub.com), or visit the Web site at bedfordstmartins.com/readersguide/catalog.

Let students choose their format

Bedford/St. Martin's offers a range of affordable formats, including the portable, downloadable *Bedford e-Book to Go for A Reader's Guide to College Writing* at about half the price of the print book. To order access cards for the *Bedford e-Book to Go* format, use ISBN 978-1-4576-6849-4. For details, visit bedfordstmartins .com/readersguide/formats.

Choose the flexible Bedford e-Portfolio

Students can collect, select, and reflect on their course work and personalize and share their e-Portfolio for any audience. Instructors can provide as much or as little structure as they see fit. Rubrics and learning outcomes can be aligned to student work, so instructors and programs can gather reliable and useful assessment data. Every *Bedford e-Portfolio* comes pre-loaded with *Portfolio Keeping* and *Portfolio Teaching*, by Nedra Reynolds and Elizabeth Davis. *Bedford e-Portfolio* can be purchased separately or packaged with the book at a significant discount. An activation code is required. To order *e-Portfolio* with the print book, use ISBN 978-1-4576-7620-8. Visit bedfordstmartins.com/eportfolio.

Watch peer review work

Eli Review lets instructors scaffold their assignments in a clearer, more effective way for students—making peer review more visible and teachable. *Eli* can be purchased separately or packaged with the book at a significant discount. An activation code is required. To order *Eli Review* with the print book, use ISBN 978-1-4576-7613-0. Visit bedfordstmartins.com/eli.

Select value packages

Add value to your course by packaging one of the following resources with *A Reader's Guide to College Writing* at a significant discount. To learn more about package options, contact your

Bedford/St. Martin's sales representative or visit bedfordstmar
tins.com/readersguide/catalog.

- **_EasyWriter_, Fifth Edition, by Andrea Lunsford,**
  distills Andrea Lunsford's teaching and research into
  the essentials that today's writers need to make good
  choices in any rhetorical situation. To order _EasyWriter_
  packaged with _A Reader's Guide to College Writing,_ use
  ISBN 978-1-4576-8232-2.

- **_A Pocket Style Manual_, Sixth Edition, by Diana
  Hacker and Nancy Sommers,** is a straightforward, in-
  expensive quick reference, with content flexible enough
  to suit the needs of writers in the humanities, social
  sciences, sciences, health professions, business, fine arts,
  education, and beyond. To order _A Pocket Style Manual_
  with _A Reader's Guide to College Writing,_ use ISBN 978-1-
  4576-8231-5.

- **_LearningCurve for Readers and Writers,_** Bedford/St.
  Martin's adaptive quizzing program, quickly learns what
  students already know and helps them practice what
  they don't yet understand. Game-like quizzing motivates
  students to engage with their course, and reporting tools
  help teachers discern their students' needs. An activation
  code is required. To order _LearningCurve_ packaged with
  the print book, use ISBN 978-1-4576-7654-3. For details,
  visit bedfordstmartins.com/englishlearningcurve.

- **_Portfolio Keeping_, Third Edition, by Nedra Reynolds
  and Elizabeth Davis**, provides all the information students need to use the portfolio method successfully in a
  writing course. _Portfolio Teaching,_ a companion guide for
  instructors, provides the practical information instructors and writing program administrators need to use
  the portfolio method successfully in a writing course. To
  order _Portfolio Keeping_ packaged with the print book, use
  ISBN 978-1-4576-7580-5.

Try Re:Writing 2 _for fun_

What's the fun of teaching writing if you can't try something
new? The best collection of free writing resources on the Web,
Re:Writing 2 gives you and your students even more ways to

think about, watch, practice, and learn about writing concepts. Listen to Nancy Sommers on using a teacher's comments to revise. Try a logic puzzle. Consult our resources for writing centers. All free for the fun of trying it. Visit bedfordstmartins.com /rewriting.

Instructor resources

You have a lot to do in your course. Bedford/St. Martin's wants to make it easy for you to find the support you need—and to get it quickly.

- **Teaching Central** (bedfordstmartins.com/teaching central) offers the entire list of Bedford/St. Martin's print and online professional resources in one place. You'll find landmark reference works, sourcebooks on pedagogical issues, award-winning collections, and practical advice for the classroom—all free for instructors.

- **Bits** (bedfordbits.com) collects creative ideas for teaching a range of composition topics in an easily searchable blog format. A community of teachers—leading scholars, authors, and editors—discuss revision, research, grammar and style, technology, peer review, and much more.

- **Bedford Coursepacks** (bedfordstmartins.com /coursepacks) allow you to easily download digital materials from Bedford/St. Martin's for your course for the most common course management systems—Blackboard, Angel, Desire2Learn, Web CT, Moodle, or Sakai.

CONTENTS

PART TWO
You, the Respondent

PART THREE
You, the Writer

CHAPTER 14 Structure 167

CHAPTER 15 Evidence 185

CHAPTER 16 Frame Ideas and Quotations 195

> The new slogan seems to be "Don't
> trust anyone over 140 characters."
> —Ron Charles

"I just don't read," a young woman explains to me and to a dozen or so classmates sitting around a large table. "I prefer communicating one-on-one. I'm a people person."

With warm eyes and a friendly smile, she makes a plausible case, though she seems uneasy about offering so candid an admission to her instructor—and at the very first meeting of Advanced Writing no less. Advanced writing! Why take a course for aspiring authors, I wonder, if you don't care what fellow writers do? It's like being a chef who won't dine out.

Some classmates look uncomfortable, even embarrassed for her, but others nod.

Probably not readers either, I guess.

Of course, I know that this young woman and her sympathetic colleagues do, in fact, read, and they write too, at least as much as members of any recent college generation. They spend hours daily bent over screens checking e-mail, updating Facebook, keeping up with Twitter feeds, and mining dozens of blogs and Web sites to stay current on things that matter to them: the Red Sox, dubstep, hot singer-songwriters, foreign movies, maybe even a political cause or two.

On pads, pods, phones, and laptops, people who don't consider themselves readers today are actually obsessing over words and generating them in great heaps just about everywhere—on the bus, in the gym, at lunch, and, yes, during many a humdrum classroom lecture. But most of it comes out as small plates: e-mails, tweets, social network chatter. Neither the reading nor the writing from these fits of literacy is sustained or filling, enduring or consequential.

And that's likely what my student in Advanced Writing means when she confesses that she just doesn't read. Like many of her generation, maybe including you, she finds it tough to spend time with full-length books or serious articles that require staying power. A colleague recently described a student who confessed that she lacked even the *technical* skills to read a book cover to cover. Pages in sequence simply befuddle this collegian, much as hi-tech environments unnerve people not raised on screens and keyboards. And, approaching graduation, she realizes that she's been deprived of a basic cognitive ability, one she fears she may never acquire. Who knew that words on a page could be as daunting as Excel or Photoshop?

But what about *The Hunger Games, The Twilight Saga,* and those seven Harry Potter volumes, each thicker than the one before? Don't they prove that college (and middle and high school) students still read? *Washington Post* book critic Ron Charles doesn't think so, phrasing his complaint memorably, if unkindly: "On today's college campuses, you're more likely to hear a werewolf howl than Allen Ginsberg." Where Charles will take his argument is predictable, his hair turning grayer with every clause:

> Where are the Germaine Greers, the Jerry Rubins, the Hunter Thompsons, the Richard Brautigans—those challenging, annoying, offensive, sometimes silly, always polemic authors whom young people used to adore to their parents' dismay? Hoffman's manual of disruption and discontent—*Steal This Book*—sold more than a quarter of a million copies when it appeared in 1971 and then jumped onto the paperback bestseller list. Even in the conservative 1950s, when Hemingway's plane went down in Uganda, students wore black armbands till news came that the bad-boy novelist had survived. Could any author of fiction that has not inspired a set of Happy Meal toys elicit such collegiate mourning today?

This might be termed a "Where are the snows of yesteryear?" argument, a rhetorical move that compares a dissolute present to a time when things seemed much better.

But that nobler era didn't have search engines: You'd probably figure out pretty quickly exactly how you're being insulted in this passage (if you're not in Charles's generation) simply by Googling the unfamiliar allusions, let's say, Allen Ginsberg, Germaine Greer, Jerry Rubin, *Steal This Book,* and so on, maybe even my own reference to "snows of yesteryear," and then snapping the pieces together. It might take you all of five minutes, maybe ten. The process is called *annotating a text*. You do it unprompted and intuitively if you're media savvy, and it is an essential reading skill, clever in its own way—and, as you'll discover, a key strategy in the book you are holding.

But let's be clear. Ron Charles and many teachers, employers, and public officials (as well as researchers tracking measurable declines in the scholastic achievements of college students) are not *wrong* to point out the reluctance of many people today to engage in serious, challenging, and sustained reading. Ask veteran college teachers how their students have changed over the past twenty or thirty years, and chances are they'll say they've gotten heavier and they don't do the assigned readings. And yet good reading and writing skills are almost universally regarded as a ticket to success in school and in subsequent careers. Even students believe this is so, according to "Writing, Technology and Teens," a 2008 study by the National Commission on Writing: "[F]ully 98% [of teens surveyed] agree that writing is at least somewhat important for their future success. Of these, more than half (56%) think that writing is 'essential,' 30% think that it is 'important, but not essential' and 12% see it as 'somewhat important.'"

The reading and writing connection is so crucial that many colleges (and some high schools) have doubled down their requirements in both areas. Lots of schools distribute reading lists to prospective students before they arrive on campus, or they choose a single book for all freshmen to read, discuss, and write about in introductory seminars or first-year-experience courses. Many first-year writing classes now focus on book-length readings too, which students have to review, summarize, and then spin arguments from. And—no change here—most college courses still come with lengthy reading lists.

So how does a generation of non-readers survive in school?

In middle and high school, many students simply lean on those classmates who actually do the reading assignments—easy people to spot—and then use one form of needling or another to win their cooperation. Alternatively, lots of would-be scholars, I'm told, rely on SparkNotes for the summaries or analyses they need of *Lord of the Flies*, *To Kill a Mockingbird*, or *1984*; this online resource tool even features animated summaries of literary classics and plenty of diversions for when times get tough: "Chelsea Dagger interviews Chris Hemsworth, Kristen Stewart, and more!"

Worst-case scenario? Admit it: In a pinch, you've relied on friends who've done no more than browsed the SparkNotes or CliffsNotes themselves, and you just hope for the best. At that point, you're two steps removed from the original assigned material—but what could go wrong?

In college, such tactics *might* still work sometimes, but the problem is that by then you're likely paying for your own education, and you face the possibility of leaving school not much smarter than when you arrived (one controversial study suggests that's the case for many students). With little to show for your "effort" except loan payments, you've got to hope there's a better way.

There is. It starts with doing whatever it takes to boost your core literacy skills—reading and writing—in middle school, high school, and college. The not-so-negligible payoff for such labor is becoming an adult equipped to make your way in the world. Sure, some people fake it all their lives, make a career of their ignorance, and earn themselves reality shows on subpar TV networks. But good luck with that career plan.

Your self-esteem, as well as your ambitions, whatever they may be, *will* be better served if you stop looking for shortcuts and take your academic life seriously. Winning the long game will take backbone, but the effort needn't be onerous once you realize that strategies that enhance your reading and writing skills neatly parallel those you use whenever you find yourself consumed by a subject, pastime, skill, or avocation. When it comes to stuff you care about, you already have high standards for yourself and others.

And we all have such passions. It may be the Civil War, rock climbing, collecting jazz on vinyl, playing a violin (or first base), birding, making video mash-ups, or photographing nineteenth-century courthouses. When you care about a subject or activity—serious or frivolous—you do all it takes to understand it, master it, become proficient. You meet with fellow enthusiasts, learn the lore and literature, follow leads and connections, and do what's necessary to make yourself legit, realizing how easy it is to discriminate between experts and poseurs. By then, no one has to convince you that knowledge and skill matter. And you take real pleasure in your expertise: You begin teaching others to scale walls. You share your jazz collection with enthusiasts. You put up a photo essay about those courthouses, and people actually look at it and respond positively.

You know where this is going.

You don't become an expert on any but the most frivolous concerns by following Twitter celebrities or browsing Web comments. With academic subjects that evolve into professional careers, at some point you must read serious work by knowledgeable people—sometimes formidable, well-documented fully researched articles; sometimes full-length books; sometimes works of literature with their original, demanding words, not translated into more readable English or turned into video plot summaries. You must identify experts and authorities, communicate with them, assess them, and learn to argue with them. Then you must write something yourself that moves the conversation along.

Reading and writing well will help make you an adult ready to be taken seriously. And they are certainly the academic skills propaedeutic to most of the others you'll acquire in higher education. (And I'm still grateful to the philosophy professor who taught me the word I hope you're looking up.)

And guess what? Taking literacy seriously gives you deep and lasting satisfaction—even pleasure. I taught Shakespeare for many years and so I recently checked the SparkNotes on one of that playwright's greatest (and most commonly taught) works, the tragedy *Hamlet*. Perhaps you've experienced it in video or "no fear" form on the Web site. SparkNotes explains what happens in the play competently, and its summaries, analyses, and thematic discussions even require considerable attention if you hope to turn them into a paper. But SparkNotes or your best friend's crib sheets aren't *Hamlet*—not even close. There's no glee in such material, no chills down the spine. You gain nothing from the surrogate exposure, except maybe a satisfactory quiz grade. It's turkey bacon, non-alcoholic beer, lip-synch fails —maybe less. Until you experience the *Hamlet* Shakespeare made (or the Pemberton that Jane Austen created or the manifesto that Marx and Engels professed), you won't know the pleasures that come from authentic encounters with consequential work. Who can be satisfied with SparkNotes' "God controls everything—even something as trivial as a sparrow's death" when Shakespeare actually wrote, "There's a special providence in the fall of a sparrow"?

This book may not teach you to untangle Shakespeare, but it will give you specific and portable advice for managing the kinds of reading you'll typically do in college courses. Think of it as an insider's guide to college literacy. Part One, entitled "You, the Reader," makes difficult texts less intimidating by pulling back the curtain on the world of books and publishers and walking you through the strategies that skillful academic readers use routinely. The chapters also outline key rhetorical principles — such as audience, purpose, and genre — to give you frames of reference to use whenever you're asked to read unfamiliar authors and texts. The section even explains how to use Web skills to make your academic reading more productive.

The second part of *A Reader's Guide to College Writing* is "You, the Respondent." I use "respondent" here specifically to describe someone expected to react to texts and other speakers in some public forum — that's *you* in many situations in school. For many students, discussing books and reading assign-ments and the arguments they tender is scary. You realize soon enough that it just won't do to say, "I like the piece," or, maybe, "I disagree with it." The people you speak or write to expect *why*s and *wherefore*s to follow. So the chapters in this section offer insights into responding to texts of all kinds — beginning with basic techniques for sizing up and replying to them. They look beneath the surfaces of books and articles to discover what holds them together and how they serve their audiences. The section ends with specific advice for entering discussions, mov-ing them along, and making them productive.

Predictably, the final section of *A Reader's Guide to College Writing* is "You, the Writer." Building upon what the book has said about reading and responding, these chapters try to offer a fresh perspective on composition, a subject you've doubtless encountered already in high school and college English courses. You'll find these chapters succinct and specific, designed to help you with assignments of all kinds, whatever your field or major. They show how to use what you read to give substance to what you write.

Though obviously connected, the chapters of *A Reader's Guide to College Writing,* like any typical "guide," have been composed (mostly) to stand on their own so you can pick and choose those that address your concerns. Many of the chapters are written like personal essays, full of examples, anecdotes, and colloquialisms that might seem out of place in academic writing. This informal style is a tactic to keep you interested in topics not high on every student's reading list. In recent decades, the most admired books on writing have been short and personable. I'm confident, at least, that this one is short.

Finally, one bit of advice before we start. In life, it has been observed, showing up is half the game: Cal Ripken Jr., the poster boy for diligence, got himself into baseball's Hall of Fame by playing shortstop and third base for the Baltimore Orioles in 2,632 consecutive games. If, however, you think that the academic equivalent of "showing up" is attending class, you're wrong: It's doing the reading. To stand out these days and give instructors a line to use in letters of recommendation, *do the reading*, every day and every time. You'll be surprised by what you learn and, decades later, even remember.

ONE

You, the Reader

Read not to contradict and confute; nor to believe and take for granted;
nor to find talk and discourse; but to weigh and consider.
— Francis Bacon, "Of Studies" (1625)

A decisive moment in the lives of many students occurs when they first crack open a book or scan a syllabus in college. A core skill they thought they'd mastered years earlier suddenly seems deficient: *reading*. Assigned texts seem calculatedly difficult, idiosyncratic in their moves, and almost foreign in their vocabularies—as if they're written for people from a different planet. In a way, they are.

Part One of *A Reader's Guide to College Writing* introduces you to the world of academic reading, that is, to the people, audiences, publishers, contexts, and assumptions behind a great many of the texts you'll be meeting in college. The practical skills and insights offered in these chapters reflect what can be a comforting truth: *We never stop learning to read*. Most of us spend our lives mastering the ways our communities, disciplines, and professions communicate. It's just that some of this learning happens at lightning speed in school.

You need to be prepared.

1

We think too small, like the frog at the
bottom of the well.

— Mao Tse-tung

Contexts

Chinese revolutionary leader Chairman Mao Tse-tung
(1893–1976) drew on an ancient tale to make a philosophical
point possibly as applicable to readers and writers as to political
insurgents: "We think too small, like the frog at the bottom of
the well. He thinks the sky is only as big as the top of the well.
If he surfaced, he would have an entirely different view."

When you pick up a book or an article, your instinct will be to
examine it from your own point of view. You apply what you know
or have experienced to interpret what you read and then respond
to it. That makes sense. All the electronic communications you
juggle (e-mail, text messages, tweets) connect to specific aspects
of your life—you were the one, after all, who gave Starbucks
and Bose your e-mail address—and the elective reading you do
reflects what you know and care about. You breeze through the
latest issues of *Sports Illustrated*, *Vogue*, *Time*, *Game Informer*, *Women's Health*, or *Wired* for a reason, and you get most of what you
find there. They are part of the sky at the top of your well.

But that may not be the case with much of the academic reading you'll face, starting even before Day One when you get a
reading list from a prospective school or find out you must finish
The Omnivore's Dilemma, *Freakonomics*, or *One Nation, Underprivileged* before the first class day. Okay, no big deal. These may
not be titles you'd pick up on your own, but you anticipate reading a lot of new and challenging stuff in college. That's the whole
point of getting an education. And, again, you'd be right.

But then you start browsing and just a few pages into a
book you wonder *Why am I reading this stuff?* What does it

have to do with me—a music major, or mechanical engineer, or, at this point, "liberal arts, undecided"? Why exactly should I be invested in reading three hundred pages about, let's say, poverty?

> This book is intended to provide a radically different perspective on American poverty. It will be argued and empirically demonstrated that poverty is the result of systemic failings within the U.S. economic and social structures, that a majority of Americans experience poverty during their adult lifetimes, and that poverty is an issue of vital national concern. In short, the purpose of this book is to lay out and detail a paradigm for thinking about U.S. poverty that is entirely different from the manner in which we have traditionally thought about this issue. Such a paradigm shift is essential to constructing lasting and effective changes that will reduce the severity, magnitude, and injustice of American poverty.
>
> —MARK ROBERT RANK, *ONE NATION, UNDERPRIVILEGED*

Why such a formidable assignment? Whose idea was it, and, honestly, what's the big deal? Everybody knows poverty is bad—why make a federal case out of it? And, oh, yeah, what's a *paradigm shift*?

You might feel similarly baffled and overwhelmed, if in different ways, when you scan the syllabi of your actual courses, usually distributed at the first meeting—if you haven't already checked them out online. You sign up for an elective rhetoric/writing course called Serious Games because you're into online gaming and figure you'll ace this subject. But then you're hit with a reading list with titles that might alarm Sheldon Cooper:

> Marshall McLuhan, *Understanding Media: The Extensions of Man* (1964)
>
> Richard Lanham, *The Economics of Attention: Style and Substance in the Age of Information* (2006)
>
> Gregory L. Ulmer, *Electronic Monuments* (2005)
>
> Gregory L. Ulmer, *Teletheory: Grammatology in the Age of Video* (1989)
>
> Paul D. Miller (a.k.a. DJ Spooky), *Rhythm Science* (2004)
>
> Lars Von Trier & Jørgen Leth, *The Five Obstructions* (film, 2003)
>
> Selected essays, hypertexts, Web sites, e-books, podcasts, and videos; additional readings

Wait! This was supposed to be fun, and now it looks like serious *work*. (Maybe an apprenticeship in plumbing and pipe trades isn't such a bad idea?)

The actual hurdle in situations like these is not the prospect of intellectual heavy lifting, but figuring out how to make encounters with unfamiliar texts less scary. A first step is to put intimidating reading assignments in context. *Context* can be an intimidating word in school because it conjures up dusty layers of history, fact, circumstance, and background information that just seem to complicate life — as if you can't figure anything out until you already know everything. To appreciate a book like *One Nation, Underprivileged,* you might examine it in the context of Lyndon Johnson's War on Poverty, as well as civil rights and antiwar struggles of the sixties and even earlier progressive movements spurred by the Great Depression in Europe and the United States. Where to begin?

To make readings manageable, put them in context.

When you read or write about any weighty issue, you're plunging into a moving river full of currents, eddies, rapids, and even some swamps and sandbars. But you needn't jump in unprepared.

Get the Backstory: Who's Assigning What?

Start by exploring the background for any major reading project, from campus-wide booklists to common reading assignments to that syllabus full of unfamiliar books and articles. Don't hesitate to ask administrators and faculty questions about them, or use the online tools you already manage so well to learn whatever you can about such programs and courses. You'll be surprised how much you can discover.

Common Readings

Let's start with one of those books assigned by a school as part of a common reading program (CRP). One option is just to accept the assignment and thumb your way through the first chapter. Or you could spend half an hour exploring the rationale and context for such programs (in which first-year students read and discuss the same book in one or more introductory courses). Find out who supports them and who runs them. What are their history, stated goals, and entailments (that is,

Find out who assigned the book in your CRP.

what you'll be doing *in addition to* reading a book)? For your effort, you'll be better prepared to read critically.

Did you know, for example, that faculty and academic departments run some common reading programs while others are managed by student services or orientation units? Academic departments might favor books that mirror the intellectual aspirations of a school while administrators look for readings to support goals like community spirit, diversity, or service learning. Books can serve both objectives, of course, fostering both intellectual engagement and a sense of community. But isn't it to your advantage to know who selected your common reading and for what reasons?

An answer may be in the letter or e-mail that announced the assignment, if one was sent before classes started. Check who signed the message, how the reading assignment is framed, and what exactly is expected from you. Lots of students simply care about the bottom line: the identity of the book or the items on the reading list. Somebody wrote the accompanying materials attentively, so pay attention yourself. You'll likely find out something about the program's history and procedures.

Note, too, whether the common reading is a school-wide effort, part of first-year orientation, or alternatively, attached to a particular first-year composition, English, or other course. And if no explanation of the program is provided, you might easily (and quickly) do a Web search, perhaps to find out what books were assigned in previous years. What would a list of previous selections tell you? A lot, actually. You'll learn whether the program emphasizes political or social themes—war, poverty, sexism, education, immigration, environmentalism, technology, academic integrity—thereby discovering something about the values of the institution. You might even discover how the books are selected, by whom, and whether students have input into the choice. Good stuff to know: You might want to weigh in yourself in the future.

Find out what books were assigned in previous years.

How special is the book you are reading? Chances are that students at many other places are facing the same selection. Search "common reading" on the Web and you'll be into the thick of things quickly and able to compare what your school is doing with what other institutions are striving to accomplish. As you browse to deepen the context of the assignment, you'll find yourself moving from clueless grunt to active participant in a literacy movement with national roots and implications. You'll be better positioned to assess and appreciate any activities that support the book program on your campus—guest speakers, discussion groups, service projects, or media projects. I use "assess" deliberately in the previous sentence: Understanding the context for programs like these gives you precisely the kind of critical perspective common reading programs are supposed to foster. It's a good thing to be both appreciative and skeptical.

Find out what campus activities support the CRP.

Course Syllabi

When it comes to the readings on a course syllabus, you have both fewer and more opportunities to put the works assigned in context. But the effort is usually worthwhile.

You can perhaps find less about the immediate history and rationale for items in a syllabus than for books in a common reading program—unless the syllabus is from a multisection course required of many students on campus, such as introductory mathematics, psychology, or history courses. Then a committee or an administrator may define the textbooks, readings, and assignments; and individual instructors may be restricted in their choices. This is often the case with first-year composition courses that also require a common book. Check departmental or school Web sites for information about any multisection required courses and see what you can discover about policies, requirements, and assignments. Once again, examine any readings common to all these classes and try to connect them to the themes and goals of the course.

With more distinctive courses, like Serious Games mentioned earlier in this chapter, you can set the context quickly with some Web searching. Most important, as I'll explain in Chapter 2, find out all you can about authors on the syllabus and the types of writing they do. Also check dates of publication for assigned readings to gain a sense of what the course will cover: Will it survey important works from the past, focus on a specific era, or concentrate on just the latest research? In the case of Serious Games, notice that several of its readings cluster around the years 2003 to 2006. That's not exactly current, but the class is clearly about recent thinking in a relatively new academic field. Yet the inclusion of a 1964 book by media guru Marshall McLuhan suggests some historical perspective as well. Already, you've gained a sense of trajectory for what you'll be reading and learning.

The titles of the works on a syllabus also foretell the level and type of instruction to expect in a course. The materials assigned in Serious Games, for example, suggest some abstract and theoretical content. You aren't going to be fiddling with *World of Warcraft* in the seminar (at least not exclusively). Instead, you'll be introduced to sophisticated thinking about gaming. Are you ready for a high-powered course in theory? Obviously, you need to make a judgment about the appropriateness of this class.

Moving on from the works actually named on a syllabus, check out how those readings will be used as prompts or models for specific projects and assignments. Are you expected to prepare frequent summaries and response papers in the course, or maybe a full research paper or media project at its conclusion? That's vital information for you at the outset of a semester, particularly when it comes to time management. Read it right and a syllabus prepares you for what to expect.

Game on.

A syllabus reveals the approach of a course. Is it for you?

Locate the Text: Canonical or Contemporary?

Again, you could begin reading whatever has been assigned without knowing anything more than the title of the course, such as Rhetoric and Composition 101 or Problems in Management. With some materials, starting clean might be bracing. But the world is complicated and your time is limited. In most cases, you'll read more productively if you know what you are getting into. In subsequent chapters, we'll discuss major rhetorical considerations, such as authorship, place of publication, and audience, which will influence how you understand and interpret works. For now, here are some landmarks by which to orient yourself quickly at the outset of your reading, especially when facing book-length assignments.

First, establish what kind of text you are reading. *Not everything is a story.* Reserve that term for fictional tales or nonfiction narratives without political or social agendas imbedded in them (which make them arguments).

Find out if the text is "canonical."

You *will* sometimes be assigned to read substantial pieces of fiction and other canonical works of literature, philosophy, political theory, and so on. *Canonical* is a relatively recent term for books regarded as essential reading—what used to be called "classics," except that many academics regard that term as exclusionary. Whatever. From high school, you probably remember *The Scarlet Letter, Huckleberry Finn,* and *The Tragedy of Julius Caesar.* In college, you could encounter Plato's *Republic,* John Stuart Mill's *On Liberty,* or Charles Darwin's *The Origin of Species.* Canonical works have their status for some reason, you'd guess, so go to them with at least one question in mind: Why do some people admire this book so much?

However, much of what you'll read in college will be less renowned and more contemporary. A lot will be factual stuff, running a gamut from purely informative to aggressively persuasive. If you're assigned articles from scholarly journals — that is, the kind of limited-circulation publications published for credentialed experts in a specific field — you should expect data, technical language, complex reasoning, and laborious documentation. The going won't be easy. If readings come from sophisticated popular magazines like the *Economist, Foreign Policy,* or the *New York Review of Books,* the material may seem more accessible, but the concepts will still be demanding. Books in common readings programs (and even in many upper-division college courses) tend to be aimed at more mainstream audiences. They'll be more approachable because their authors need to keep readers interested if they hope to inform or persuade them. Such works still require close attention, but they likely won't intimidate you. And then there are your course textbooks, tough slogging in some cases, but specifically designed to present material systematically and thoroughly. Give them the attention they deserve.

> **Find out if the text is current, specialized, popular, or academic.**

Scan the Text: Meet the Supporting Elements

When facing a book-length reading assignment, expect a nicely designed paperback (for cost reasons) published by a major publisher. Pay attention to its title, naturally, though the real tip-off for you may be in the subtitle, which describes what the work is *really* about. Here's a classic combination:

> **Take titles and subtitles seriously.**

The Tipping Point: How Little Things Can Make a Big Difference

Or consider how much you learn from this title/subtitle from a volume analyzing the causes of the Great Recession of 2008. Don't miss the signal that the "$" sends.

*Reckles$ Endangerment: How Outsized Ambition, Greed, and
Corruption Led to Economic Armageddon*

**Read the back-
cover blurbs.**

Back and front covers of an assigned book deserve scrutiny, too.
They explain what the work is about, trumpet its significance,
quote favorable reviews, and profile the author:

"A fascinating study." Malcolm Gladwell

"Essential reading for anyone trying to understand the
culture." Frank Rich, *New York Times*

"Read it and weep. Read it and vow: *Never Again!*" Bill Moyers,
journalist

AESA Critics' Choice Award, American Educational Studies
Association

Puffery? Sure. But a moment of online research will confirm
that the kudos aren't just kind words from Grandma: Many of
these books have earned credibility with important critics or
professional organizations.

Scan TOCs.

Next, scan the table of contents (TOC), paying attention
to the sequence of the topics within the book. You'll gain perspective on the entire work, an accurate road map of its terrain.
When you start reading, you'll know what the argument is and
how it will unfold. (For reports and journal articles, headings
can be almost as helpful.) Or, if the work is an anthology—
that is, a collection of essays by different authors on a single
theme—you'll discover what topics are covered and what opinions are represented. (I once criticized an anthology for a first-year
writing course by pointedly asking a colleague who supported the
book if she could point to any two pieces in the political collection that disagreed with each other. She couldn't.) Sure, studying
a TOC this way removes any suspense from the project, but you
don't read academic books for their surprise endings—though
what you find in a TOC may make you more interested in the
book. Simple point: Tables of contents are your friends.

**Read
prefaces and
introductions.**

Prefaces, introductions, and even acknowledgments are also
your friends: Never skip them. Authors are as up-front about
their intentions, motives, hopes, and expectations in these sections (or in their first chapters) as they are anywhere in the
book. If they prepared their own SparkNotes, they'd probably
borrow material from these sections. Here are some examples.
They are dead giveaways:

"I've written this book out of a belief that people should know what lies behind the shiny, happy surface of every fast food transaction."

— ERIC SCHLOSSER, *FAST FOOD NATION*

"We have witnessed stunning transformations of society, politics, communication, and even selfhood. . . . To understand them, to judge them well, we need steady and penetrating reminders of the changes they have wrought. The writers included here provide just that."

— MARK BAUERLEIN, *THE DIGITAL DIVIDE: ARGUMENTS FOR AND AGAINST FACEBOOK, GOOGLE, TEXTING, AND THE AGE OF SOCIAL NETWORKING*

Introductory matter does a remarkably good job of putting materials in context by identifying the arguments a work is addressing, explaining explicitly what's at stake in a piece, naming the people or ideas the writer intends to address or refute, and providing you with GPS-like responses to questions such as *who, what, where, when, how,* and *why.* Think of introductions and prefaces as orientation sessions for readers.

If you are wondering what help an author may have had in producing a book, look to the acknowledgments sections, usually quite brief. A writer may simply thank relatives, close friends, and careful editors. But he or she may also give a nod to organizations and institutions that supported the project, identify people who offered advice and criticism or reviewed the manuscript, and so on. Read carefully, and the acknowledgments may reveal interesting contextual facts about how the book was conceived and written. In college reading assignments, you may not worry too much about the info here. But it's worth a quick look.

Browse the acknowledgments.

Finally, before you plunge in, check out three more items at the back of most serious books: the notes, bibliography, and index. The more academic a work, the more detailed these "scholarly" add-ons will be. (We'll cover notes in more detail in Chapter 5.) But expect the authors of even "popular" works to make an effort to document sources and inventory their topics. Notes and bibliographies tell you what a writer has read, or at least browsed. Is the book based on academic research, respectable journalism, or "pop" sources? It helps to know. The index is a different kind of TOC,

Scan notes, bibliographies, and indexes.

providing a topographical guide to a project, a quick survey not just of a book's big themes, but of its details as well. Spend a few minutes in the book's back alleys and, before you read a paragraph, you'll smoke out the interests of the author and, maybe, surmise how your view of the world is about to be enlarged.

Read Reviews — Intelligently

An especially astute way to come up to speed with assigned works is to read book reviews — and here I mean *serious and professional* evaluations of the sort you'd find in respected journals, magazines, or newspapers. You do not want unfiltered, anonymous, and largely unedited opinions like those on Amazon. com or lesser sites. Admittedly, reviews on Amazon might be spot-on when you're trying to decide whether the next 700-page George R. R. Martin tome is worth a month of your life. But for academic or serious nonfiction works, get reviews from people at least as credible as the author being reviewed, when that's possible.

A professional review will supply layers of contexts for a work you are reading, framing the issue it addresses, providing background information about its subject, assessing the author's credentials, outlining the scope and significance of the project, and, of course evaluating it. Too easy? Possibly. Reading reviews of classics in any field from Plato to Freud is time well spent if the studies are academic, original, and scholarly, not just quick summaries of the Cliffs-Notes variety.

But some instructors may discourage you from reading reviews of contemporary works (*A Long Way Gone: Memoirs of a Boy Soldier, Too Big to Fall, Now You See It*) or unfailing book-list favorites (*Nickel and Dimed, The Kite Runner*), even when they have appeared in the best publications and are splendidly argued. Maybe *especially* if they are splendidly argued. Their reasoning is that you might make the review a substitute for reading the original text, which would be plain academic laziness. More seriously, a good review, some teachers fear, could influence you too much, discouraging you from fresh and original thinking. Who are you to weigh in after the *New York Review of Books* has rendered its verdict?

In fact, once you've done your homework, you are indeed ready to bring original perspectives to assigned texts. But, realistically, a critic's insights may overwhelm or prejudice you, especially if you consult a review before you read a book. You will gain lots of knowledge and probably save yourself some misreading and misinterpretation. But you may also find yourself irresistibly buying the assumptions and assessments the reviewer has offered, seeing the same things and coming to identical conclusions. But, no doubt about it: Reviews *are* valuable. So here's a rule of thumb. Unless an instructor vetoes the use of outside assessments entirely, commit yourself to reading *several* reviews or none at all. That way, you'll have a chorus of voices in your head when you encounter the text on your own.

Read several reviews — or none.

YOUR TURN

1. What are college students reading in common reading programs? Use the Web (or other resources, such as research librarians) to create a list of books commonly assigned on campuses today. Better, see if you can find a study that provides that information for some recent period or year.

2. Once you have identified a few lists of popular campus readings, study them (alone or in a group) and see whether you can categorize the choices. Look for patterns in what is covered by these works and think, too, about what sorts of works are excluded. Draw conclusions about their content, subject matters, or political, cultural, and social orientations.

3. Take a look at a reading you've been assigned or a course syllabus you have on hand. What can you determine about it before you start in-depth reading? Use the strategies in this chapter to prepare a one- or two-page summary of your findings that you think a future student would appreciate.

4. Determine how useful it would be to read reviews of a book already assigned. In your opinion, are you likely to be more influenced if you read reviews *before* or *after* you read the text? Write a paragraph explaining your choice. If possible, test your theory on books you read this term.

2

No man but a blockhead ever wrote
except for money.

— SAMUEL JOHNSON

Authors and Publishers

Samuel Johnson (1709–1784), an essayist, critic, lexicographer, and conversationalist who dominated the cultural scene of London in the eighteenth century, claimed "No man but a blockhead ever wrote except for money." A poor man who endured tough times, Johnson eventually won a government pension for his literary contributions, including the first major dictionary of the English language and an important edition of Shakespeare's works. Predictably, three centuries later, matters of money, commerce, influence, and power still frame the reading you do in college, though in ways that may seem unfathomable and, maybe, unimportant. But they're not. By Johnson's definition, many of the people you'll be reading and quoting from while in school are blockheads — they aren't motivated by money but by a desire to contribute to a never-ending conversation about what we think and know.

Appreciate Scholars and Their Work

Many students scanning a course syllabus in college or facing their first serious research projects don't understand exactly why their instructors seem so smitten by jargon-ridden books full of endless notes or equally demanding articles published in "journals" very few people have ever heard of. At first glance, these readings can seem like an impediment to learning, especially when you're just gaining traction in a major or field.

But as you move along in your studies, you'll discover that the materials described as "scholarly" represent why you are going to school in the first place. Teachers, researchers, librarians, and even fellow students who aspire to academic careers value academic books and articles above all others because they are offered as pure, disinterested research, undertaken to increase the stock of human knowledge. At least, that's the ideal. Written by experts for experts, scholarly works are carefully and blindly reviewed by other academics for their insight, innovation, acuity, accuracy, timeliness, and rigor (whew!), and published without concern for sales and profitability.

Scholarly writing expands knowledge.

That's fortunate, because by some estimates the average scholarly book in the humanities rarely sells more than a few *hundred* copies, and those mainly to libraries. No commercial press can survive on print runs that small—and so academic books are subsidized by publishers affiliated (like the authors and reviewers themselves) with colleges, universities, or research institutes: Oxford University Press, University of Arizona Press, Yale University Press, and several hundred others in the English-speaking world.

Scholarly journals, which are far more numerous than presses, represent the "magazine" side of the academic market, publishing research articles, reviews, and other short pieces by college and university faculty in just about every academic field, subfield, and cubbyhole. (One study tallies more than forty thousand such professional research journals.) The best of them share the rigorous standards of the book publishers, the same highly specialized readers, and the same minuscule audiences compared to those of commercial magazines: An edition of *College English* has a circulation of six thousand; *Car and Driver*, a niche magazine for auto enthusiasts, reaches 1.3 million subscribers. Predictably, many scholarly journals have recently moved online to lower their costs, but unlike commercial and popular magazines—even prestigious ones like the *Economist, Scientific American,* or *American Heritage*—research journals don't expect to earn a profit or even aim to. Their role is, once again, to identify and circulate the latest and best research in every academic and professional field, from kinesiology to nuclear engineering.

Recognize scholarly presses and journals.

Rankings among these academic presses and journals matter as much as any in NCAA sports. There's a top tier in every field, and utility players, and some also-rans. Publish a book with Yale or Oxford University presses or place an article or two in the *Lancet, American Historical Review,* or *Shakespeare Quarterly,* and your academic career is on a roll. And that is the payback for the authors of such material: prestige, possible promotion in academic rank, and a bump in salary. Royalties don't matter.

Why do you need to know all this? On most subjects, scholarly books and articles are the most authoritative and credible sources available, built upon original research drawn from primary data or equally credible and ruthlessly documented academic studies; in the case of scientific papers, they may themselves become primary sources. As you move forward in school, you'll find that citing such blue-ribbon items in your own work will carry the most weight and be the most persuasive.

You'll certainly encounter scholarly articles or chapters from scholarly books in advanced or topic-driven classes and seminars, especially when instructors prepare packets for their courses or assign specialized anthologies. Expect to read these pieces slowly and carefully. Only rarely will you be asked to read a full scholarly book in a college or university course. In a common reading program, for example, the assigned book will likely be one or two tiers down from scholarly. But, as you'll see, there's no shame in that.

Recognize Popularizers, Experts, and Public Intellectuals

In the academic world, the term *popularizers* refers to professors who decide to repackage their scholarly work for general audiences to make it more widely available and potentially more influential. Beth Luey defines popularizations as "the books that explain complicated subjects and ideas to non-expert readers." To a remarkable degree, popularizers do precisely that by trading on their academic credentials to become trustworthy narrators who turn intellectual subjects or problems **Popularizers** into highly readable stories full of memorable and documented details. Indeed, popularizers, like classroom teachers, tend to take on broad subjects to give readers a wide view of a topic, synthesizing not only their own research but also the more specialized work of dozens, sometimes hundreds, of other scholars. The books they produce are usually carefully sourced and supported by lengthy bibliographies, but they also make exactly the adjustments you might expect to help readers who are not themselves experts in, say, history, government, physics, or astronomy. These popularizations are rich in background information; they offer clear-cut accounts of key concepts; they contain a minimum of technical terms and avoid jargon when possible; and so on. While purely academic works are often very well written, books and articles in this crossover genre make good style a priority, and the authors (and publishers) are sometimes rewarded with best sellers.

Who are we talking about here? In the sciences, people like the late Stephen Jay Gould, an evolutionary biologist at Harvard; Stephen Hawking, a mathematician and physicist at Cambridge; and the late Carl Sagan, an astronomer at Cornell. In the humanities, Harvard historian Laurel Thatcher Ulrich has won a wide general audience, as have Elaine Pagels, a professor of religion at Princeton; Stephen Carter, a professor at Yale Law School; Sherry Turkle, professor of the social studies of science and technology at MIT; and Paul Krugman, professor of economics at Princeton. Chances are you have heard of at least a few of these academics and maybe sampled their books, articles, or newspaper columns.

Only marginally different from popularizations by academics are books by *experts* without academic affiliations, though usually with credentials earned at school, in the field, or in jobs as researchers, editors, or journalists. Authors in this category tend to specialize; that is, they cultivate one area of expertise — it may be history, anthropology, or technology. Indeed, people today theorizing about the impact of computers, technology, gaming, and such — writers like Douglas Rushkoff and Marc Prensky — worked in those fields before academic departments started paying attention to them. And people are sometimes surprised that widely respected historians such as David McCullough and the late Barbara Tuchman, or even Doris Kearns Goodwin, don't have professorships attached to their names. Neither does internationally famous primatologist and best-selling author Jane Goodall. With her own institute (and a PhD from Cambridge), a formal academic position might only have hampered her work with chimpanzees. And though it might be argued that experts rely on the spadework of more traditional scholars, it's hard to fault them for writing books — many of

Experts

them widely read in academic programs—that so clearly demonstrate their passion for a subject or issue.

Yet another type of serious work you'll encounter in school—and especially in common reading and first-year writing programs—is produced by people who might be characterized as *public intellectuals,* a loose category of individuals, many of them journalists or freelance writers willing to explore weighty issues in society and culture in detail and at length. Some write for magazines (or even a few blogs willing to post lengthy posts) and many publish books. The tie-in to journalism is important: Writers and works in this category tend to be investigative rather than research oriented. The writer takes on an issue and explores it from every angle, scouring the existing research, interviewing people involved, walking neighborhoods, workplaces, or institutional hallways. Perhaps more often than academic popularizers or experts, public intellectuals frame their studies dramatically, hoping to awaken public attention to a looming crisis, an unrecognized injustice, or, maybe, a fascinating phenomenon. And there is usually a market angle to these books. After all, these authors aren't blockheads; they make a living by writing.

Public intellectuals earn their considerable status (and presence in college courses) by the breadth of their intelligence and by keeping readers glued to the page. Barbara Ehrenreich, an exemplar of the public intellectual, is probably best known for *Nickel and Dimed,* in which she explores blue-collar working conditions by becoming a laborer herself; the book has been required reading on many American campuses for years. But Ehrenreich has written books critiquing American culture on topics ranging from joy to war. An ability to identify important issues and give them currency in the public sphere is characteristic of freelancers and public writers.

Consider Malcolm Gladwell, an ingenious and inventive writer, who parlayed the intriguing concept of "the tipping point" into common speech and a best-selling book of the same name. He then followed up with *Blink* (on decision making) and *Outliers* (on success). As an essayist, he's tackled a huge range of subjects, always finding a new or unexplored angle. The opening lines of "Troublemakers," a *New Yorker* piece on stereotypes and profiling, suggest how far Gladwell is removed from the constraints of academic writing:

Public intellectuals

One afternoon last February, Guy Clairoux picked up his two-and-a half-year-old son, Jayden, from day care and walked him back to their house in the west end of Ottawa, Ontario. They were almost home. Jayden was straggling behind, and, as his father's back was turned, a pit bull jumped over a back-yard fence and lunged at Jayden. "The dog had his head in its mouth and started to do this shake," Clairoux's wife, JoAnn Hartley, said later. As she watched in horror, two more pit bulls jumped over the fence, joining in the assault. She and Clairoux came running, and he punched the first of the dogs in the head, until it dropped Jayden, and then he threw the boy toward his mother. Hartley fell on her son, protecting him with her body. "JoAnn!" Clairoux cried out, as all three dogs descended on his wife. "Cover your neck, cover your neck."

Don't you want to keep reading? The drama certainly grabs you. (And the entire article is available online.)

But understand that Gladwell is not doing traditional research; instead, he's exploring an idea powerfully and origi-nally in an *essay*—which amounts to a serious and informal thought experiment. That's what public intellectuals do and what makes them valuable. They make us think.

I should note that the neat categories in this section—scholar, popularizer, expert, and public intellectual—leak worse than a sieve. Writers follow their own agendas and find new and creative ways to explore subjects and use source materials. But **Authors cross categories to reach different readers.** appreciating the distinctions between the groups may help you sort out who authors are, in general, and what they are up to in specific books and articles. Occasionally (well, more accurately, *rarely*) an academic book such as Allan Bloom's *The Closing of the American Mind* (1987) becomes a *New York Times* best seller. And sometimes a formidable scholar and thinker will use the prestige of academic work to claim the mantle of public intel-lectual. Perhaps the most famous example is Noam Chomsky, likely the greatest linguist of the twentieth century, who has spent decades as a political activist. Or consider Michael Pol-lan, a professor of journalism, widely regarded today as an expert on the culture and politics of food, or the team of Uni-versity of Chicago economist Steven D. Levitt and journalist Stephen J. Dubner that produced *Freakonomics: A Rogue Econ-omist Explores the Hidden Side of Everything*—which now has evolved into a radio show and podcast. I won't, however, say much here (though more later) on the welter of books patched together by non-expert talk-show hosts or politicians—or their ghostwriters—pretending to speak authoritatively to issues of the day. Suffice to say that they don't generally meet the standards for handling arguments and evidence seen in the categories of books discussed here and, hence, only rarely appear on academic reading lists.

Understand Bloggers, Tweeters, and Citizen Reporters

Authors you encounter on various media platforms (tablet, phone, computer, notebook) play an undeniable role in your life—particularly when you are reading or writing about popular culture, current events, and politics. With some exceptions, though, their postings fall a notch or two below journalism in terms of authority and clout in academic work. But they are far from worthless, especially when you need to reflect on the world as it is today: Where else can you go for such news?

Writing about an ongoing presidential campaign, for example, you can't wait for the relevant books to be published *in a few years*. And to be honest, what happens online these days sometimes *is* the news. In writing about pressing events—such as the unfolding of the ultra-destructive Hurricane Sandy in 2012 or political upheavals in various parts of the globe—most of the up-to-the-minute information and reporting now comes from small local news outlets or even individuals communicating via social networks with their data published online.

In academic circles, bloggers, tweeters, YouTubers, tumblrs, and commentators on social networks get about the same measure of respect as Wikipedia: Everyone (including your instructors) uses the indispensable site, but few would mention it in the same breath as, say, the *Encyclopaedia Britannica*—now an online product itself, but one regarded as more rigorous, more thorough on the subjects it covers, and, ultimately, more persuasive in academic writing. Appraisals of this kind aren't entirely prejudiced: When it comes to electronic discourse, what's published almost instantaneously usually isn't vetted, fact-checked, or edited. And, let's face it, almost anyone can post online.

Approach instant news cautiously.

And yet almost all reputable news organizations (*Wall Street Journal, New York Times*) and serious publications (*Atlantic*

Monthly, New Republic) now have strong Web presences, disseminate information and commentary electronically, and support interactive discussions via blogs, Facebook pages, and Twitter sites. Online resources supported by reputable organizations do make mistakes, but they tend to correct them with lightning speed. While you will still encounter mostly time-honored sources, reputable books, and conventional articles in your academic work, expect to encounter new voices working in novel environments as well. Becoming a skilled critical reader will help you navigate between what's sketchy and what's trustworthy. That's the world we are in.

Appraise Individual Authors

Writers almost always bring their biographies, professional credentials, life experiences, and sometimes agendas into the books and articles they produce. And, as the preceding sections hint, the world of books and authors has as many cliques as a high school lunchroom and as many entertaining personalities. So you will simply be better equipped to read a book or article once you know about the backstories of its authors.

Finding such information used to take work. Today, a few keystrokes on a computer can usually generate enough data about authors to embarrass them. (There are pictures, too!) But don't ignore material right in the reading itself. Professional articles or essays often include a brief note about the writers or researchers, identifying their institutional affiliations or describing their careers. Similarly, book covers typically carry blurbs about authors, and the writers may volunteer additional biographical details in their prefaces or introductions. This material is helpful because it often connects the lives of writers to their specific projects or acknowledges people and institutions that have influenced them. You gain insight into why someone has tackled a lengthy or difficult job.

Explore authors' credentials.

If you are searching for biographical information on your own, what's relevant? Certainly anything you can find about life experiences related to an author's specific project. It matters, for example, that Khaled Hosseini, author of *The Kite Runner*, a best-selling novel about a troubling childhood in Kabul, did indeed grow up in Afghanistan and Iran. But pay attention to academic training, experiences, and positions. The fact that Diane Ravitch, author of *The Death and Life of the Great*

American School System, is a research professor of education at New York University, gives her credibility. And when you are dealing with academics like Ravitch, know that you can often find career data or a full curriculum vitae (CV) on college and university Web sites. Such a document will tell you what they have published, what courses they have taught, what lectures they have delivered, and what academic and administrative positions they have held. That may be more data than you want, but consider all the context it offers for an article or book you will read. When time comes for discussion, you will be prepared. (For more on participating in class discussions, see Chapter 11.)

The careers of experts, freelancers, and public intellectuals are open books as well; many of these authors even have their own Web sites. But just what have authors done to qualify them to write about religious extremism, urban farming, or life in Borneo? Pay attention to the jobs they've held, the places they've lived and worked, and the positions they've held. Most writers are happy to acknowledge awards and prizes; whatever you might think about Paul Krugman's politics, he writes under the halo of the Nobel Prize for Economics he won in 2008. But look to personal difficulties or failures, too, that may explain why an author is concerned by burgeoning diagnoses of autism or regulatory abuse in our financial institutions. What is an author's personal stake in the issue? Such insights may influence the way you read a book or article.

Connect authors' lives to their work.

In the hotbed of contemporary politics and ongoing culture wars, you may want to know something about a writer's allegiances, alliances, and affiliations. Understand that no reasonable viewpoints should disqualify writers from your consideration. Blacklists are for bigots. But you don't want to be naïve either, especially when so many books selected in common reading programs or for first-year writing classes support specific agendas, often both local and national. Part of your responsibility as a reader is to figure out how writers perceive the world or use data to reflect their understandings of it. Sometimes a writer will help you, as William Patry does with the disclaimer he offers in *Moral Panics and the Copyright Wars,* which calls for sensible copyright reforms:

> Although I serve as Senior Copyright Counsel to Google Inc., the views in this book are entirely mine, and should not be attributed to Google. The book is not Google's book, nor

did I write it as a Google employee or to advance Google's interests, as much as I identify with and value those interests. Instead, I wrote the book on my own initiative to make *personal* observations—observations that come from being a fulltime copyright lawyer for 27 years, 24 of which occurred before I joined Google.

Patry is anticipating the objections of readers who know that he works for an employer with a huge stake in copyright laws. He recognizes how heavily a writer's "affiliations" will weigh with critical readers—like you. (You'll learn more about conceding and replying in Chapter 9.)

One more recommendation: Figure out what *else* a writer has written. You can generate a list of books easily enough from library catalogs or even Amazon.com (where authors also sometimes have Web pages); articles may be harder to find, but the library databases in an author's field may lead you to relevant titles. For academic authors, check that online CV again, which will list all major publications. Try to get a feel for books and articles surrounding the one you are reading. Is the writer pursuing a fresh topic or following up on themes developed in earlier work? Quick summaries of some of these materials might provide useful context. Is the author clearly an expert on the subject, with multiple studies to his or her credit? Or does the latest project represent a new direction?

Consider what else a writer has written.

Take the time to scope out authors and you'll have a leg up on readers who don't have a clue.

Know Publishers and Their Platforms

Do you pay much attention to who publishes what? Probably not. But magazines, journals, presses, and publishing houses have brand labels (and logos) as expressive as Apple, BMW, or Family Dollar. They work hard to establish a link between what they stand for and the materials they publish. Some publishers earn a reputation for offering cutting-edge and distinguished fiction and nonfiction; others specialize in technical or scientific work; still others focus on educational materials, textbooks, and platforms.

Reading lists for academic courses may have outliers—for instance, classes in media and pop culture may list film reviews from Web sites like Rotten Tomatoes or bizarre items from tabloids. (Tabloids are small-format newspapers with sensational stories; you find them especially at grocery checkout counters.) But you can be confident that course syllabi will usually lean on "respectable" academic journals, solid academic presses, and first-rate trade publishers. Any newspaper articles assigned will come (I'd wager) from the *New York Times*, *Wall Street Journal*, or *Washington Post* at least half of the time.

As should be evident by now, such choices aren't accidental. Serious readers get to know publishers at least as well as they know shoe companies or software makers. Reputable publishers have good editors who select first-rate work and stand by it through the production process, right down to the design and copyediting. Although they may serve different markets, journals, magazines, and newspapers all earn their reputations by the quality of the writing they present, the writers they feature, and the audiences they consequently attract. They establish a track record that readers count on. As you move forward in a college program or major, ask your instructor about the lead journals and publishers in your field and get to know them.

Get to know publishers' specialties.

Nonetheless, you should still remain a critical consumer. Publishers and scholarly journals alike have their points of view and perspectives. Some book publishers even establish *imprints* to promote specific kinds of work such as progressive, conservative, feminist, environmentalist, gay and lesbian, and so on. This book, for example, is published by Bedford/St. Martin's, a press that specializes in college textbooks in the humanities, and is an imprint of the international publisher Macmillan.

Newspapers, too, as you must already know, have biases in their editorial pages and, to some extent, in their news reporting. That's the nature of the business. It's up to you to detect the preferences and slants and make appropriate adjustments, counter-weighing their perspective with other knowledge you have. It's called critical reading.

Consider slants and biases in news.

Your savvy as a reader should extend to electronic environments, too. As we discussed on pages 21–22, many traditional publishers — the *New York Times*, *Time*, *Christian Science Monitor* — have moved at least some of their operations online, carrying their reputations with them. But as newspapers and publishers become media companies, interacting with social networks, expanding into interactive blogging and reporting, and finding new streams of income driven by interactive advertising, they change their basic products, too, or at least the way we encounter them. For instance, *Newsweek*, a once mainstream weekly magazine available on every newsstand, merged with the Web platform *The Daily Beast* in 2010 and now comes in tablet form only. Just as interesting, online platforms such as Google and Amazon have entered the world of writing and publishing through innovations in technology and marketing. Consider how the convenience of Amazon's Kindle e-reader and Kindle Fire mini-tablet affects readers and authors alike, altering our relationship with words and texts. We want our books now! And authors of fictional series, such as Lee Child and Craig Johnson, for example, find they have to write faster to satisfy that demand or even offer short stories to tide readers over until the next full novel is ready. We'll see more changes in a future that seems fully wedded now to screens.

And here you thought all you had to worry about was reading a book.

YOUR TURN

5. Go through the syllabus for two courses you are taking this semester to determine what kinds of authors are on the reading list. Are they scholars, experts, popularizers, or public intellectuals, as defined in this chapter? What do you know about them? Then write a one-half to one-page summary of the kind of class you are taking based on what you know about the authors you will read in it.

6. What are the top scholarly journals in your major or in a field that interests you? See if you can discover a list or ranking online—and pay attention to the criteria used to determine quality. Then ask for advice about top journals from a reference librarian or professionals in the field, such as a teacher, graduate student, or lab assistant. Do their rankings agree? What might account for variations?

7. Choose one of the authors named in this chapter and spend an hour finding whatever you can about him or her either in the library or online. Turn your discoveries into a paragraph-length blurb for the back of a book jacket.

3

It is the mark of an educated mind to be able to entertain a thought without accepting it.

—ARISTOTLE

Audiences and Publics

Early in childhood, about the time you figured out which parent or relative was the soft touch—"Grandpa, will you buy me some candy?"—you also discovered the rhetorical concept of "audience." As the example suggests, our words, spoken or written, are usually targeted to specific individuals (or groups) and tailored to win their approval. Yet explaining fully just how speakers might persuade specific audiences led the Greek philosopher Aristotle to write what amounted to the first treatise on human psychology and emotions, a book called *Rhetoric*— way back in the fourth century BCE. Turns out that, then as now, people were complicated creatures and, for that reason, so is the notion of audience. Think of each text you read as a trendy dance club: Your task is figuring out who's being invited in and who's left outside behind the velvet rope—and why.

Rhetoric **is the art of using language to persuade.**

Define the Audience: Who's a Text For?

A surprising number of celebrities decide to write children's books. What better way to jump-start a drooping career or get five minutes on *Fox and Friends*? Children's books don't require all that many words, an artist handles the pictures (that's most of the book), and how hard can it be to appeal to kids?

Ah, but wait a minute. Will that story be for girls, boys, or a mixed table? Five-year-olds or nine-year-olds?—because there's a difference. Upper-crust preteens with posh city flats and attending cooks and nannies? Or maybe blue-collar and ethnic youngsters stuck in after-school programs until a parent gets home? And, oh, as J. K. Rowling discovered, much to her delight, adults might read the books, too, if the stories are good enough. Just think of the possibilities.

The simple project just got a lot more complicated.

Truth be told, it's usually an advantage if a writer works for a narrow, well-defined demographic. A friend of mine is an expert on spinning and weaving. When she writes for a specialty magazine (*Spin-off*) about crafting fine yarn or making a scarf, she has a precise notion of what readers need. That's usually the situation, too, for academic writers producing books and articles for experts in their fields. They are writing for *peers*. Though they still may have to justify a project, they can assume a level of expertise that minimizes any need to explain or enliven it. Readers like you don't stumble upon works like *Gender and the Negotiation of Daily Life in Mexico, 1750–1856* or *Sea Turtles of the Eastern Pacific: Advances in Research and Conservation* by accident. Instead, the titles themselves summon the books' highly selective audiences. Hence, when you're assigned an academic book or article, you may have to imagine what intended readers would know and how they might think. Then you have to come up to speed by taking advantage, for instance, of the tips in Chapter 1 such as surveying a book's TOC and reading its front and back matter. You may not get into the coolest club that night, but at least you can peek in at the dance floor.

Specific audiences know the key terms already.

You'll usually have an easier time reading materials written by popularizers and public intellectuals (described in the previous chapter) because, from the get-go, they want to reach the "general public" or "educated readers," usually across a range of professions and occupations. So they make adjustments to explain themselves more fully, define key terms carefully, and use less technical language. That's the case even when their works — for example, books about business, management, or technology — target specific subcultures within society. Even then, the audience challenges remain formidable, especially when an academic work shows potential to cross over into a wider market, as was the case with Annette Lareau's provocative study of parenting among working-class families, *Unequal*

General audiences need more explanations.

Childhoods: Class, Race, and Family Life. Lareau acknowledges the problems she faced, describing critical reactions to her manuscript prior to publication:

> Some reviewers worried that given the contested character of race relations in the United States, the behavior patterns described in this book might reinforce negative stereotypes of certain groups. The results could be taken out of context and exploited by others, particularly political conservatives. Some early readers encouraged me *not to report* results that might be used to reinforce negative images of, for example, poor Black families. The fact that the manuscript includes portraits of poor white families as well as Black families did not completely assuage these concerns. A key problem is that most readers will be middle class or, as college students, on the road to becoming middle class, even if they had working-class or poor origins. As readers, they will have their own childhoods and their own lives as parents or future parents as a base for what they consider appropriate.

Acknowledges readers' reactions

Imagines readers' reactions

Here you see an author imagining and assessing the reactions of potential readers both within the academy (college students) and outside of it (middle-class readers, political commentators). Pay attention to such comments because they may point out issues beneath the surface of reports and arguments you would not notice on your own.

How Writers Appeal to Readers

The fact is that writers have many strategies for *inviting* readers to join their audiences or making them believe that they're already part of it. How do they manage that trick? Media theorist Steven Johnson, for one, about to defend the oddball thesis that "popular culture is actually making us smarter," pushes readers to admit that they've suspected as much themselves:

> I hope for many of you the argument here will resonate with a feeling you've had in the past, even if you have suppressed it at the time—a feeling that the popular culture isn't locked in a spiral dive of deteriorating standards. . . . The sky is not falling. In many ways, the weather has never been better. It just takes a new kind of barometer to tell the difference.
>
> —EVERYTHING BAD IS GOOD FOR YOU

Invites readers to react to the thesis

Does Johnson strike a chord? If so, you are pulled into his circle of readers. Or consider the more general invitation Gretchen Morgenson offers for her book *Reckle$$ Endangerment* to just about anyone who feels less secure today than before the 2008 financial crisis, about which she and Joshua Rosner write:

> Even now, more than four years after the cracks in the financial foundation could no longer be ignored, people remain bewildered about the causes of the steepest economic downturn since the great depression. And they wonder why we are still mired in it. . . . The American people realize they've been robbed. They're just not sure by whom.

If you believe early on that *Reckle$$ Endangerment* offers answers, you might sign up for its full three hundred pages.

Going one step farther, authors often use the convenient first-person plural pronoun *we* (or even second-person *you*) to draw readers into a conversation or argument, sometimes even guilting them into agreement by challenging their fitness to join an audience. You can see the technique on display in the following paragraph from Walter Benn Michaels's *The Trouble with Diversity: How We Learned to Love Identity and Ignore Inequality*, in which he tries to convince people on the political left—traditional champions of cultural diversity—that they are fighting the wrong battle:

Helps readers identify where to stand politically: *you*

Names outlier groups: *they*

Encourages appropriate collective action: *we*

If you're worried about the growing economic inequality in American life, if you suspect that there may be something unjust as well as unpleasant in the spectacle of the rich getting richer and the poor getting poorer, no cause is less worth supporting, no battle is less worth fighting than the ones we fight for diversity. While some cultural conservatives may wish that everyone should be assimilated to their fantasy of one truly American culture, and while the supposed radicals of the "tenured left" continue to struggle for what they hope will finally become a truly inclusive multiculturalism, the really radical idea of redistributing wealth becomes almost literally unthinkable. . . . But we don't need to purchase our progress in civil rights at the expense of a commitment to economic justice. More fundamentally still, we should not allow—or we should not continue to allow—the phantasm of respect for difference to take the place of that commitment to economic justice.

The argument is a tough one to make politically, but Michaels hopes few liberals, progressives, or Democrats can resist the call: If *you* worry about economic inequality, if *you* resent the rich getting richer, this is what *we* need to do. The movement from *you* to *we* is not accidental—and it's precisely the kind of audience maneuver that you want to catch and maybe comment on in a discussion group or response paper. A maneuver like this one matters.

Authors aren't the only people concerned with audiences or clever enough to attract them this way. Popular media, too, are fully invested in *demographics*, the ruthless effort to define audiences by analyzing characteristics that predict their choices—as voters, consumers, or viewers. Just about every time you offer up information online, for example, algorithms process your Web behavior (what you look at; what you click) and your identity markers (age, gender, economic level) to pinpoint products or services to tempt you. So it's only fair to push back with analyses of your own. Here's one such reading of the cable network TNT, in which a writer embeds an audience assessment in her review of the revival of the TV series *Dallas*:

> TNT is all about satisfying most of the people most of the time, and the channel does a good job of churning out the kind of crowd-pleasing, reliably decent, not-too-challenging fare that the networks used to air two or three decades ago. That's not a dig; it's just a statement of fact to say that when you tune in to a TNT program, you know what you're getting and it'll probably be reasonably competent (which is more than I can say for a fair number of broadcast network shows, especially in the summer).
>
> —Maureen Ryan, *"Dallas* Review"

Media audiences are comprised of demographics.

"Crowd-pleasing, reliably decent, not-too-challenging fare"? Do you want to be in this network's demographic? Or maybe you already are?

As you see, questions about texts, media, and their audiences can lead to rewarding insights. Hence, such queries ought to be part of your repertoire whenever you're asked to read or analyze texts—and that includes visual fare such as TV series or video games and the networks and platforms that support them.

Your Background as a Reader

Sometimes you'll find your relationship to a work especially thorny when it involves matters of "difference," that is, how we

Acknowledging
difference

are all shaped by the categories into which we are born—our gender, race, economic class, religion, sexual orientation, physical natures, and so on—and how these markers of identity affect relationships with others. It seems self-evident that being, let's say, a working-class, straight female in rural Iowa likely makes you different as a reader, writer, and person than a young gay man living in New York City's Chelsea neighborhood who is building his career on Ivy League connections.

Many works, both nonfiction and fiction, deliberately foreground such group differences in identity and culture and explore the consequences. As mentioned in Chapter 2, Barbara Ehrenreich, a PhD and an already successful writer, rather famously decides in *Nickel and Dimed: On (Not) Getting By in America* to find out firsthand what life is like for blue-collar laborers in America by taking a string of low-paying jobs: as a waitress in Florida, a housemaid in Maine, a clerk at a Minnesota Wal-Mart. Predictably, she learns a lot from her experiences, notably that wages barely cover minimal expenses (especially rent) for the working poor, trapping them in cycles of poverty and inequity. In her conclusion, Ehrenreich invokes an audience she assumes has the power to do something about the problem:

> But now that the government has largely withdrawn its "handouts," now that the overwhelming majority of the poor are out there toiling in Wal-Mart or Wendy's—well, what are we to think of them? Disapproval and condescension no longer apply, so what outlook makes sense?
>
> Guilt, you may be thinking warily. Isn't that what we're supposed to feel? But guilt doesn't go anywhere near far enough; the appropriate emotion is shame—shame on our *own* dependency, in this case, on the underpaid labor of others.

Unless you are a laborer yourself, the *we*'s and *our*'s in these paragraphs should unsettle you—just as Ehrenreich intended. Nor can you respond to a text like this without considering other audience issues Ehrenreich raises, including how the blue-collar laborers she describes in *Nickel and Dimed* might respond to her attempt to live among and write about them.

Other authors don't have to role-play to understand difference. They live it, and so make it an objective to share a version of their world with those unfamiliar with it, reaching across cultural boundaries and physical borders to explain, often defend, unfamiliar practices and beliefs. Leslie Marmon Silko does this for the Native American culture she shares in a novel entitled *Ceremony* (1977), her protagonist a mixed-race World War II veteran, Tayo, returning home to find white men still assailing native peoples, this time by mining uranium in their sacred lands:

> He lay there and hated them. Not for what they wanted to do with him, but for what they did to the earth with their machines, and to the animals with their packs of dogs and their guns. It happened again and again, and the people had to watch, unable to save or to protect any of the things that were so important to them.

A tale like Silko's asks readers, mostly from outside groups, to ponder where they stand in relationship to people different from themselves; it invites them to address issues that shape their own lives, too. Such readings may disturb you when they tread close to your own prejudices or assault your sense of identity. But it is important to read works that put you on the fringe or make you feel like the outsider—whatever your home communities might be. You will learn something.

Welcome to the Academic Community: A Fish Story

Every year, I begin a survey course I teach called The Rhetorical Tradition by requiring not only that students read a lengthy, densely printed essay by critic, theorist, and public intellectual Stanley Fish entitled "Rhetoric," but also write a short paper about it prior to in-class discussion. I warn my students that Fish's article may be the most difficult selection they encounter all term, and that all I expect is an honest response to whatever parts of the essay they understand. It is usually not very much, especially for any newly declared rhetoric majors.

"Rhetoric" opens with ten lines from John Milton's epic poem *Paradise Lost* describing the fallen angel Belial in Hell, followed by this commentary from Fish:

> For Milton's seventeenth-century readers this passage, introducing one of the more prominent of the fallen angels, would have been immediately recognizable as a brief but trenchant essay on the art and character of the rhetorician.

> Indeed, in these few lines Milton has managed to gather and restate with great rhetorical force (a paradox of which more later) all of the traditional arguments against rhetoric.

Got that? As you can see, Fish assumes that his readers are familiar with the details of *Paradise Lost* as well as with the traditional arguments against rhetoric. That's a lot to demand. But did you notice the unexpected and slightly helpful bit of authorial intervention in the parentheses—what we'll define as "meta-discourse" in the next section? Perhaps the essay won't be all that difficult?

You'd be wrong. Within a few pages, Fish is in full academic mode, his style almost impenetrable to the non-specialist. Here are two sentences chosen almost at random from fairly early in the essay—and did I mention that "Rhetoric" runs for almost thirty pages?

Reading academic prose requires practice.

> It is the view of the anti-rhetoricians that this double task of inner and outer regulation can be accomplished by linguistic reform, by the institution of conditions of communication that at once protect discourse from the irrelevancies and contingencies that would compromise its universality and insulate the discoursing mind from those contingencies and irrelevancies it itself harbors. Wilkins proposes to fashion a language that will admit neither *Superfluities*—plural signifiers of a single signified, more than one word for a particular thing—nor *Equivocals*—signifiers doing multiple duty, single words that refer to several things—nor *Metaphor*—a form of speech that interposes itself between the observer and the referent and therefore contributes "to the disguising of it with false appearances."

As you might expect, the position papers I receive from most students are grim. The writers latch onto a comprehensible line or two and then spin out personal narratives from it, related to their own experiences with deceitful language. Or, if they're more adroit, they'll paraphrase what they discover about Fish in the introduction to "Rhetoric," provided conveniently by the editors of the anthology in which the essay is reprinted. Why, you might wonder, don't students just drop the class in droves? Because I frame the assignment with this promise: We're going to read "Rhetoric" again for our last class meeting and by then you will understand it.

For them, learning to read "Rhetoric" becomes a fifteen-week exercise in joining an academic audience and community. They struggle with the original assignment not because "Rhetoric" is impenetrable—Fish is a writer who routinely speaks to the general public, for example, in essays and blog entries for the *New York Times*—but because the "traditional concepts" of the field aren't second nature to them yet. They don't know exactly what rhetorical theory is or what rhetoricians do, what the core issues in the field might be, what its key vocabulary terms mean, who its major figures are, and what positions they represent. Reading "Rhetoric" for my students is like changing the oil in a car for the first time; what takes a skilled mechanic ten minutes (if that) burns a whole afternoon for the newbie because every move is unfamiliar and unpracticed. There is no muscle memory.

> The academic community is comprised of standards, issues, terms, and key players.

Yet in fifteen weeks, a great many students in The Rhetorical Tradition do move from amateur to player. They pick up the assumptions and jargon of the field; they read Plato (opponent of rhetoric) and Aristotle (ally) and a smattering of Wilkins, too. Sweeping through twenty-five centuries of intellectual history, they realize at the end that Fish's essay is a precise outline of the course they've just about completed—chronicling the unending tale of conflict between proponents of rhetoric and critics who find the art inimical to truth and science. The most serious and hardest-working students have earned places in an academic audience—maybe somewhere near the back but definitely in the auditorium.

And that's what you'll be doing every day in school, sometimes without realizing it: assimilating the culture of a world likely not native to you, but very much within your grasp.

So what exactly are the expectations of academic audiences? They really are different from the standards operating among the general public—which is why students struggle with them. Academics don't need or admire razzle-dazzle. Instead, they expect from their colleagues original research that advances (at least a bit) the ideas, theories, and perspectives under consideration in their field. As professor of cell biology Daniel Colón–Ramos explains, "My job is to chart out new areas of knowledge and add them to a 'knowledge map' that my colleagues, past and present, have been charting for years."

> Academic audiences expect writing to contribute new ideas.

Predictably, scholars expect writing that shows mastery of conventions: the concepts, methods, vocabulary, and publication standards of the discipline. In effect, people in academic departments create ways of speaking to each other efficiently; the ability to use that language makes you part of the intended audience for their books or articles. Helen Sword, for one, defends the value of such specialized language:

> Academics turn to jargon for a wide variety of reasons: to display their erudition, to signal membership in a disciplinary community, to demonstrate their mastery of complex concepts, to cut briskly into a continuing scholarly conversation, to push knowledge in new directions, to challenge readers' thinking, to convey ideas and facts efficiently, to play around with language. Many of those motivations align well with the ideals of stylish academic writing.
>
> —"Inoculating against Jargonitis"

What scholars produce can be narrow and seem incomprehensible; in general, they feel no obligation to make their research more available to wider audiences. But academics (like all serious writers) do understand the civic and cultural ramifications of their work, and hence many interact with various "publics," that is, people and groups that share common concerns. Consider the words of retired scholar Nell Irvin Painter: "As an historian, I would take your hand, and I tried to make things clear so readers could go from A to C. Clarity was my great strength." Academics in a wide range of fields remain notably committed to efforts to improve general education. They are part of that conversation. In school, as you grow familiar with academic language, you too will gain expertise that ultimately prepares you for greater public engagement. If there is an ivory tower, it's one surrounded by a crowd.

Accommodate Readers: Keep Them Interested

How, then, do writers attract and hold onto as many members of an audience as possible—even when a subject is formidable or not immediately appealing? They have dozens of strategies for adjusting the comfort zone between readers and themselves. Authors can be warm and inviting when they need to keep readers happy, and they can turn as grim and hard-nosed as TSA agents when circumstances warrant total seriousness.

Meta-discourse helps to include readers.

Writers eager to help less expert audiences often use what's called *meta-discourse* to explain what they intend to do. The author's voice intrudes and speaks directly, helpfully, and sometimes even cordially to readers: *Here's what comes next* or *here is my reason for telling you all this*. Following, for example, is meta-discourse from an essay that asks what can be done about obnoxious people who ask rambling, self-indulgent questions after lectures or at public forums (especially at colleges):

> Clearly we need help. This isn't a matter of a deficit in "critical thinking." It is a problem of recovering a lost art. Television and radio producers acknowledge this by filtering questions in advance or asking would-be questioners to submit their interrogatories in writing. We lose something important in this filtering. The questions that get asked are the ones moderators pick out to make their own points. We would be better served if people could ask their own coherent and pertinent questions. Here's how.
>
> —Peter Wood, "How to Ask a Question"

Author's voice

Author's voice

The short underlined sentences provide just the nudge you need to recognize Peter Wood's intentions. But meta-discourse can be even more explicit, sometimes running for many paragraphs:

> The next chapter describes the schools that most of the children in the study attended and where we visited during the year. It also briefly discusses different approaches to understanding why inequality exists. The book then proceeds by . . .
>
> —Annette Lareau, *Unequal Childhoods*

Such intervention by authors can be invaluable to you when it genuinely helps clarify a work. But you may also find it fussy or self-indulgent; if so, ask yourself *why* and identify the reasons. Maybe you don't trust the *ethos* of pushy writers or you doubt their control of the material: Well-designed highways don't need incessant signage.

Ethos: the character a writer conveys in a work.

Meta-discourse is related to an even simpler technique for cuing readers, the familiar transitional words or phrases (*however, nevertheless, on the other hand*) that you forgot about in middle school. Writers use transitions to slide readers from sentence to sentence, paragraph to paragraph. Reduce the number of those transitions, and the language becomes tougher to handle. (For more on transitions, see Chapter 14, p. 174.)

Writers also make important choices at the sentence level to frame their relationships with readers. Usually, we think of long and complicated sentences as scaring readers away from topics. So the conventional advice is to produce shorter sentences with concrete subjects and active verbs. Yet some readers do want more—sentences that entertain them with structures as rich and expressive as the ideas they convey. Talented writers can, in fact, spin sentences that move so easily that readers barely notice how complicated they are. (See Chapters 17 and 18 for more on style.) Lean or labyrinthine, straight-shooting or subtle, concise or indulgently long—every sentence represents choices writers make to accommodate readers and yet also do justice to a subject. You ignore style at your peril. You may be charmed into agreeing with ideas by the seductiveness of well-turned phrases; you may miss worthy notions because a writer can't make them sing. Either way, there are rhetorical points waiting for you to make in a discussion of the text.

Sentence-level choices matter.

Words matter, too. Specialized and formal vocabularies of the sort you'll encounter in academic writing appeal to readers who appreciate information delivered precisely and efficiently. Yet, in context, almost any words can be made expressive, colloquial, and connotative, rich in unspoken meanings and associations; such usages appeal to readers when ideas need to be shaded with feelings. Even technical language can work in emotive narratives such as *The Immortal Life of Henrietta Lacks*. Here, the author describes the cancer afflicting her protagonist:

Vocabulary choices matter.

> Cervical carcinomas are divided into two types: invasive carcinomas, which have penetrated the surface of the cervix, and noninvasive carcinomas, which haven't. The noninvasive type is sometimes called "sugar-icing carcinoma," because it grows in a smooth layered sheet across the surface of the cervix, but its official name is *carcinoma in situ*, which derives from the Latin for "cancer in its original place."
>
> —Rebecca Skloot

So there's no neat continuum, no simple cutoff between technical, difficult, and what some might call "sophisticated" word choices and those that are more common, accessible, and "easy" for an audience. Consider the opening sentences of a highly technical essay in a scholarly book on the concept of historical memory—the imposing vocabulary raises few impediments to the non-specialist reader interested in the subject:

The field of history is premised on the idea that knowledge of our past can inform our behaviors in the future. Indeed, this idea is central to many assumptions within personality, developmental, and clinical psychology. Implicit in this thinking is that history is somehow made up of immutable facts that are set in stone in society's memory. Who, after all, could doubt the accuracy of America's role in World War II, the facts surrounding the discovery of the New World by Columbus in 1492, the bravery and upstanding characters of the men who defended the Alamo in 1845, or the profound effect of the Magna Carta in 1215? These events, of course, are not as straightforward as we were taught in grade school.

Opening sentence introduces the concept.

Examples explain the concept.

—James W. Pennebaker and Amy Gonzales, "Making History: Social and Psychological Processes Underlying Collective Memory"

The technique is quite simple here: The concept of knowledge described in abstract language is immediately illustrated through particular and (in this case) comfortably familiar examples. But it's important to appreciate exactly how a writer manages to be both precise and clear—especially when it's by employing a technique you can use yourself.

Complicating a writer's verbal options are levels of style, as palpable as different zones of comfort at a party (for more on style, see Chapter 17). In formal styles of language, writers stand at the equivalent of a podium in front of their audience, lecturing in highbrow and technical terms, while avoiding first- and second-person pronouns (*I, we, us, you*), most contractions, and just about all eye contact. In contrast, colloquial styles are like hugs between friends, full of shared experiences, idiomatic and idiosyncratic language (*dude*), and the rhythms of spoken language—right down to its exclamations and sentence fragments. And there's a full range of options (called a "middle style") between the extremes of formal and colloquial language. It's important to appreciate these differences because the style of a piece signals how writers feel not only about an audience, but also about their subject. Tune out the signals sent by a writer being ironic or satiric and you could misread an entire work—as some students do every year with Jonathan Swift's "A Modest Proposal."

Using a high, middle, or low style matters.

Consider the way even length affects audiences. At a time when people have gotten used to on-screen messages honed to a nub, writers choose carefully what to include in articles or even books, balancing how much detail readers will tolerate with how much coverage a subject requires. Maybe it's not actually possible to explain particle physics in a paragraph. But a tactic as simple as using headings and subheads can make material more palatable. Even a timely paragraph break makes life easier for readers.

Multimedia options keep readers interested.

Writers now have the option, too, of offering plenty in the way of eye candy. For scientists or business writers, visual options include the ability to generate handsome charts or graphics that convey data efficiently in a written text or to make presentations using slides (via PowerPoint or Keynote) or other kinds of media (Prezi). For bloggers, embedded photos, videos, or audio files often work well. For other writers, a simple line drawing or cartoon underscores a point already made in words.

"Well, all of this is pretty obvious," I hear you say. And you'd be right—to an extent. Writers have never had so many options for adapting language—textual or visual—to specific subjects and audiences. And yet how often do you struggle with prose that could be more helpful? (I still resent my high school physics textbook, which, in five hundred pages, never once acknowledged its audience of befuddled seventeen-year-olds.) You recognize immediately when writers either try too hard to ingratiate themselves or alienate you with the first boneheaded idea they use. It takes talent for writers to partner with readers, something to recognize whatever side of the author/audience divide you are on. So feel free to comment on any author/audience relationships you find intriguing or problematic. Other readers certainly will.

> **YOUR TURN**
>
> **8.** Huffington Post and Arts & Letters Daily are two wide-ranging Web sites covering news, arts, entertainment, and culture that serve vastly different (if occasionally overlapping) audiences. Study the home pages of each site and then read through some of their articles. When you have a feel for each site, write a paragraph about them, describing their intended audiences.

9. Describe an audience of specialists in which you could claim membership. Maybe you're far enough along in an academic major to feel like part of the field. Or perhaps you have expertise in a non-academic area with its own specialized knowledge, specific tools or technologies, or shared vocabulary and jargon. Explain this world to others who are not familiar with it.

10. Choose a relatively short piece of assigned reading (an article or a section from a book, or perhaps even its front matter). Look for any special strategies it uses to reach what you regard as its intended readers: Consider devices such as meta-discourse, transitions, sentence-level adjustments, vocabulary choices, length, and use of visuals or media. Then in one page, assess its success in attracting and holding readers. What does it do well? How might it be improved?

4

I write what amuses me. . . . I never
in my wildest dreams expected this
popularity. There's no formula.
— J. K. ROWLING

Genres

In rejecting formulas, J. K. Rowling, author of the incredibly successful Harry Potter series, follows in the tradition of many fiction writers with fearless attitudes toward blank pages. Ray Bradbury, author of *Fahrenheit 451,* shows similar bravado when talking about composing: "Your intuition knows what to write, so get out of the way." But lest you think imaginative daring comes without costs, novelist Ernest Hemingway offers a famous caveat: "There is nothing to writing. All you do is sit down at a typewriter and bleed." It's enough to make mere readers feel unworthy in the presence of such willingness to take creative risks unfettered by patterns, rules, or templates.

And yet there *are* formulas for composing that are useful to you both as a reader and as a writer, and most especially in school. They are called *genres,* and grasping them makes a writer's work seem a trifle less mysterious. Consider for a moment that many students (I mentioned this in Chapter 1) describe everything they read as "stories." But writers of fiction and nonfiction alike know that the word *story* is just not specific enough to describe the options open to them. It's like having no term but *music* to label forms as different as rock, indie, rap, reggae, country, classical, and all the other genres on your iTunes list. Many writers do, in fact, compose stories, but they likely think of them as novels, or fables, or crime fiction, or fantasies, or even *short* stories. Other authors write reports, technical articles, book reviews, news stories, movie reviews, editorials, blog posts, and so on. If you kept a list of all of the verbal and visual texts you create in a week, you'd likely be surprised by the variety of what you produce and discover that only a few of your texts are actually "stories."

Experienced authors may start with empty pages or screens, but they aren't blank slates themselves. Instead, they are doing their composing within traditions they've learned by reading voraciously and watching what other writers do. They appreciate what a short story looks like, how a news article is organized, what readers expect in a blog posting; in short, they know the moves and options available to them when they work within a specific genre and they expect their readers to respond to them. They have the ability—as you do—to grasp the specific purpose and structure of written texts they're reading and examining.

Just as important, writers intuitively treat genres not as fixed categories but as real-life responses to ever-changing situations: They have to figure out what to do to achieve some goal. So they adapt a familiar form of writing to a specific moment, context, audience, and purpose. These moves turn writing into rhetorical action that accomplishes something: Narratives tell stories; reports convey information; arguments convince people, and so on. When you've figured out the genre of a text, you gain insight into its author's strategies. You learn too what features the work should display. Then you can kick back and watch how well a writer follows the formula—or purposefully deviates from it.

Understand genres to appreciate writers' strategies.

When writing in school, you likely produce subgenres of narratives, reports, or arguments. You won't produce a generic evaluation or story; you'll write a book review of an assigned reading or a personal narrative about a true-life experience. You won't compose an open-ended report; you'll write a history term paper or sports column about college recruiting. In effect, like any writer, you'll adapt genres to an assignment's specific needs. And you'll encounter new genres all the time: position papers, lab reports, seminar papers, ethnographic projects, a senior thesis. They won't come with hard-and-fast rules for writing; more likely, you'll be shown models, be encouraged to study them, and then produce something similar.

Writers adapt patterns to their needs.

Understand, though, that many readings—especially lengthier ones—borrow features from more than one genre: For instance, a book may open with a series of narrative chapters, which in turn furnish the evidence necessary for an argument.

In the remainder of this chapter, I'll briefly describe three key genres you'll encounter in your reading assignments and the features that may make them especially compelling.

Read Narratives

Children know to expect a story when they hear the phrase "Once upon a time." Then they wait for something to happen; that's what narratives do. They describe an action that writers want readers to experience, from deeply personal events to the sweep of armies across continents. Narratives also control time, recording just the blink of an eye, or if the teller of the tale is a geologist or astronomer, entire eons. Works in this genre can be exciting tales, full of twists, turns, and surprises; or they can be as boring as an account of a city council meeting. Infinite in variety, narratives typically try to enlighten or entertain readers, but as we'll see, they slip with ease across genre boundaries. Narratives come in so many forms simply because people respond well to them: Storytelling is in our DNA.

Your first question about a narrative is likely to be "Is this fact or fiction?" That makes sense. You need to know whether what you are reading—let's say Rudolfo Anaya's *Bless Me, Ultima*, a story about a Chicano boy growing up in a small New Mexican town—is an imaginative tale or an autobiography. Of course, it can be a little bit of both, as it is with Anaya's novel and Sherman Alexie's tale discussed later in this chapter. That's because narratives can deliver information or make their points in intricate and wildly varying ways. Charles Dickens used the novel *Oliver Twist* to expose sordid conditions in nineteenth-century London's slums; the writer Marjane Satrapi turns the story of her childhood in Iran into a graphic novel; an investigative journalist may explain the appeal of gang life by focusing on the lives of a few at-risk kids.

> Narratives can be fact, fiction, or something else.

With pure fiction you'll usually be satisfied by *verisimilitude*, an impersonation of reality with its own internal logic. (Consider the world of Harry Potter again—wholly fictional but operating by complex rules.) Nonfiction narratives are, by definition, more responsible to the fact-checker. You expect the authors of biographies, autobiographies, and histories to tell faithful tales—but be aware that all authors select and shade their materials. Sometimes you can detect those subtle perspectives even in book titles of personal stories and memoirs:

> George Dawson and Richard Glaubman, *Life Is So Good: One Man's Extraordinary Journey through the 20th Century and How He Learned to Read at Age 98*
>
> Carlotta Walls LaNier, *A Mighty Long Way: My Journey to Justice at Little Rock Central High School*

In both cases, you'd rightly expect narratives framed by incidents that show their authors dealing successfully with lives of considerable difficulty.

Narratives almost always have narrators. "Call me Ishmael" is the famous opening line of Herman Melville's novel *Moby-Dick*. Immediately, you should be asking, "Who is this guy with the biblical name and why does he want to tell me this story?" Be no less inquisitive about nonfiction narratives—though their authors are often more than eager to introduce themselves, as naturalist and writer Redmond O'Hanlon does at the start of his account of a harrowing expedition:

Locate the narrator and his motives for telling a story.

> As a former academic and natural history book reviewer I was astonished to discover, on being threatened with a two-month exile to the primary jungles of Borneo, just how fast a man can read.
>
> Powerful as your scholarly instincts may be, there is no matching the strength of that irrational desire to find a means of keeping your head upon your shoulders.
>
> —*INTO THE HEART OF BORNEO*

From just these few lines you can guess where this first-person narrative is going and how O'Hanlon intends to tell his story.

Other narratives, both fiction and nonfiction, are told less personally, from what is called a third-person point of view: The narrators describe events without seeming to be part of the story. But that's often a ruse. Writers pick and choose the materials they present and decide what slant to give events, and you always have to keep both in mind. That is especially true of the so-called "omniscient" narrators of novels who stand outside the stories they tell, like disinterested observers—though, be advised, they rarely are.

Third-person narratives can still have agendas.

Many stories are just that, tales for entertainment without axes to grind. Yet just as many narratives—especially those assigned in school—make social, cultural, even political statements. Precisely because stories have a way of stirring our emotions to *feel* ideas rather than just think about them, the genre is perfect for writers supporting a cause or agenda. For instance, rather than offer a point-by-point argument about problems with Mexican-U.S. border policies, Luis Alberto Urrea illustrates them in a 200-page account of twenty-six Mexicans struggling to cross into Arizona, more than half of whom die:

> The men had cactus spines in their faces, their hands. There wasn't enough fluid left in them to bleed. They'd climbed peaks, hoping to find a town, or a river, had seen more landscape, and tumbled down the far side to keep walking. One of them said, "Too many damned rocks." *Pinches piedras*, he said. Damned heat. Damned sun.
>
> —*THE DEVIL'S HIGHWAY: A TRUE STORY*

Narratives can make a statement.

Point made? And notice the subtitle of the book. You can (and should) imagine the issues such a book might raise with an American public concerned about the human dimensions and costs of current immigration policies.

Authors of nonfiction narratives do sometimes lay their cards right on the table for you to see. What, for instance, moves author and editor Jon Krakauer to write the biography of Christopher McCandless, a young man who starved to death in the Alaskan wilderness? The tale itself is riveting (and was even made into a movie), but the narrative has other dimensions, as Krakauer explains in a valuable author's note:

> In trying to understand McCandless, I inevitably came to reflect on other, larger subjects as well: the grip wilderness has on the American imagination, the allure high-risk activities hold for young men of a certain mind, the complicated, highly charged bond that exists between fathers and sons.
>
> —*INTO THE WILD*

Agendas can be subtle or overt.

These are certainly themes you'd want to look for in reading the narrative. And you'd want similarly to consider motives other writers have for telling you a story.

Your responses to narratives also depend on how they are told. You know from watching films how many different ways stories can unfurl. Movies complicated by inversions—flashbacks, dreams, and memories—are almost routine. And storytellers invented all these devices. In reading nonfiction, notice when authors weave multiple stories to make a single point or simply embed narratives within what are essentially reports or arguments. Eric Schlosser uses that device when he presents a different story in each chapter of *Fast Food Nation*, his popular exposé of the "dark side of the all-American meal" (the book's subtitle), layering his critique of the fast food industry with wildly varying human experiences:

> [Chapter 1] Carl N. Karcher is one of the fast food industry's pioneers. His career extends from the industry's modest origins to its current hamburger hegemony. . . .

> [Chapter 6] Hank was the first person I met in Colorado Springs. He was a prominent local rancher, and I'd called him to learn how development pressures and the dictates of the fast food industry are affecting the area's cattle business. . . .

> [Chapter 8] One night I visited a slaughterhouse somewhere in the High Plains. The slaughterhouse is one of the nation's largest . . .

Narratives can be embedded in reports and arguments.

Journalists use the technique too, if on a different scale, in articles and magazine features.

Finally, understand that narratives have special features that support the craft of storytelling. They are often rich in descriptive and figurative language. Admire the carefully orchestrated passages when you find them, and then consider the impact they have on you. Note, for example, when locations are drawn in such detail that they become, in effect, characters in the narrative with an impact on people in the story—and by extension, the reader. Illustrating the point here is a paragraph from Tracy Kidder's *The Strength in What Remains*, a nonfictional account of the life of Deo, a young man from Burundi forced by civil war and genocide to flee his country. He finds his way to New York City, where, impoverished and working for meager wages, he struggles to understand the disparity of wealth he sees around him, embodied by outrageously priced items in a children's clothing store:

Narratives use evocative language.

> It was clear to be a New Yorker could mean so many things that it meant practically nothing at all. He had studied the graffiti on the outer walls of subway cars, noting especially the crude, sexually explicit drawings and vulgar words that his dictionary did not contain. He had come to think of these as messages, sent from people uptown in Harlem to people downtown who shopped in places like that children's clothing store. A

phrase he'd put together out of his dictionary kept coming to him. "A different planet." New York had many planets. Better, he thought, to be in Burundi, if Burundi were at peace, than to live on the wrong, impoverished planet in New York. This place made you feel like you were simply not a human being. How could you be a human being like everyone else, if your circumstances were this different?

Narratives also routinely use dialogue, a subtle and powerful tool to make points and reveal character. Dialogue captures habitual ways of thinking and speaking, and thereby adds texture and authenticity to incidents. For example, near the end of Sherman Alexie's semiautobiographical *The Absolutely True Diary of a Part-Time Indian,* the author presents a conversation between Junior, the first-person narrator and his alter ego in the book, and a tough guy best friend (Rowdy) who at long last figures out why Junior decided to go to school off the reservation:

> "So, anyway," he said. "I was reading this book about old-time Indians, about how we used to be nomadic."
> "Yeah," I said.
> "So I looked up nomadic in the dictionary, and it means people who move around, who keep moving, in search of food and water and grazing land."
> "That sounds about right."
> "Well, the thing is, I don't think Indians are nomadic anymore. Most Indians, anyway."
> "No, we're not," I said.
> "I'm not nomadic," Rowdy said. "Hardly anyone on this rez is nomadic. Except for you. You're the nomadic one."
> "Whatever."
> "No, I'm serious. I always knew you were going to leave. I always knew you were going to leave us behind and travel the world. I had this dream about you a few months ago. You were standing on the Great Wall of China. You looked happy. And I was happy for you."
> Rowdy didn't cry. But I did.
> "You're an old-time nomad," Rowdy said. "You're going to keep moving all over the world in search of food and water and grazing land. That's pretty cool."
> I could barely talk.
> "Thank you," I said.
> "Yeah," Rowdy said. "Just make sure you send me postcards, you asshole."
> "From everywhere," I said.

Narratives may use dialogue.

As a reader, you recognize that this isn't idle chatter. It's the cruder Rowdy stumbling upon insights—and a sense of loss—that the more sensitive Junior never anticipated. It's Junior (and author Sherman Alexie, perhaps?) wrestling with the consequences of living between two communities, white and Spokane Indian. It's the discovery of a word (*nomadic*) that makes such a choice defensible. What a narrative gives up in simple explanation it gains in texture and nuance. Who needs an explicit claim when readers are already choking up?

Read Reports

Reports make up one of the broadest genres of writing. If you use Google to search the term online, you will turn up an unwieldy 4.5 billion items, beginning with the Drudge Report and moving on to sites that cover everything from financial news to morbidity studies. Just as interesting is what appears if you click the "images" option: report cards, credit reports, government studies, and lots of charts and tables. If you didn't know it already, reports are about facts, facts, and more facts. Even the titles of books and articles in this genre tend to be remarkably informative, and they are almost always accompanied by illustrative subtitles: *1491: New Revelations of the Americas before Columbus; The Big Burn: Teddy Roosevelt and the Fire That Saved America;* "The Trouble with Gay Rights: Race and the Politics of Sexual Orientation in Philadelphia, 1969–1982."

Reports focus on hard data.

If a clear title isn't enough, almost any article or report from a scholarly journal opens with an abstract, which is a compact summary of an essay or research paper prepared by its authors. (You should never skip it.) Here's an abstract of an article on doping from the *American Journal of Psychology* by Michael B. Johnson:

Always read a report's abstract.

> Human behavior occurs within a system, and as such, so do behaviors in performance-related domains (e.g., athletics, academics). Doping is a performance enhancement behavior that can be problematic because of the negative physical and psychological effects associated with the use of some substances and the common argument that doping is unfair. However, doping continues and may be increasing. Because a firm theoretical or empirical understanding of doping does not exist, this article proposes a conceptual, comprehensive, and innovative systemic model of doping behavior. The model is built from relevant empiricism supporting the idea that contemporary

doping behavior is a function of systemic transactions between historical doping practices, the present environment, current antidoping interventions, one's genetic makeup, developmental milestones, social factors, and epigenetics.

— "SYSTEMIC MODEL OF DOPING
BEHAVIOR"

Abstracts like this may not be enough to make highly technical pieces easy to navigate, but at the least you now have a map and flashlight.

You'll be assigned reports to read in all kinds of classes to discover what you don't know or confirm what you do. Not all reports will be as forthcoming about their content as those in scholarly journals, but most will state a clear thesis or raise a series of questions and then promise answers, as Pietra Rivoli does early in her book on the economics of world trade:

Year in and year out, American cotton farmers, as a group, are on top. What explains American cotton's success as an export commodity in a country that has experienced a merchandise trade deficit in each year since 1975? And what explains U.S. cotton producers' ability to export such a basic commodity to much poorer countries? Why here? Why was my Chinese T-shirt born in Texas?

— THE TRAVELS OF A T-SHIRT IN THE GLOBAL
ECONOMY

If there is any genre that makes a point of declaring its mission early and often, it is the report.

Reports are also time sensitive, especially in the sciences where a review of literature in chronological order is a routine element of any article. Readers of such material want to be sure they are examining the most current research. When reading reports, you, too, want to deal with timely and accurate information. So check out the dates not only of assigned books or articles but also of the sources *they* use. (Occasionally, you'll be introduced to an older study regarded as a classic: Charles Darwin's *Origin of Species*, published in 1859, for example, is on many reading lists.)

Reports are straightforward and time sensitive.

If academic reports generally present new and original material, reports penned by experts or public intellectuals will often repackage data from already-published sources or pull available facts together in new patterns. This is not a problem so long as the authors themselves don't rely on seriously

Reports by
non-academics
repurpose
research from
scholars.

outdated information. Quite often, they are able to give material a fresh spin. Note how science writer Charles C. Mann explains his rationale for writing *1491* after listening to panelists at a conference discussing exciting discoveries about the size and sophistication of Native American civilizations prior to Columbus's voyages:

> Gee, someone ought to pull all this stuff together, I thought. It would make a fascinating book.
>
> I kept waiting for that book to appear. The wait grew more frustrating when my son entered school and was taught the same things I had been taught, beliefs I knew had been sharply questioned. Since nobody else appeared to be writing the book, I finally decided to try it myself. Besides, I was curious to learn more. The book you are holding is the result.

This brief passage highlights many of the elements you should look for when examining any report: an excitement over new data and an appreciation for its value, a commitment to sharing knowledge, and a determination to learn more. It offers you a rationale for writing reports of your own.

At the heart of any report are reliable sources that provide information or confirm it—whether they are the "high government officials" quoted anonymously in news stories or the scholarly articles dutifully listed in the bibliographies of your term papers. So, when you pick up any report, take a look at the notes and bibliography: They should be ample, wide-ranging, and from credible journals or recognizable publishers. Pay attention to sources identified within the text whenever you read journalism or articles from popular magazines like the *Atlantic* or the *Economist*. If you don't see a record of research (or it seems that an author's sources are all unnamed or unwilling to speak on the record), proceed with caution and raise questions in discussions. Don't trust *until* you can verify. (For more on sources, see Chapter 5.)

Quite often in school, the information in reports is generated by careful experiments and observations—and reported in formal research articles, which you'll be writing yourself someday if you major in a scientific or technical field. Naturally, such writing differs significantly, field by field. Articles in mathematics and the hard sciences (biology, chemistry, physics) tend to be the most specialized genre and are perhaps the least comprehensible to

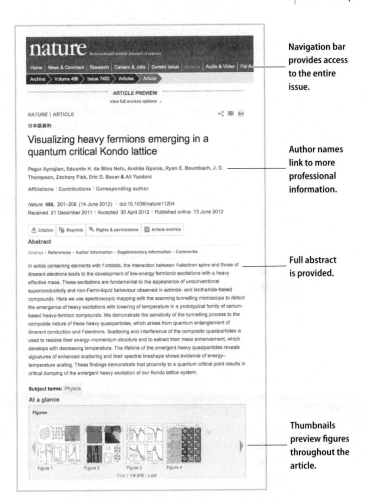

Navigation bar provides access to the entire issue.

Author names link to more professional information.

Full abstract is provided.

Thumbnails preview figures throughout the article.

non-experts—even though the material, especially as available online, is logically and sometimes beautifully produced. Above is a screenshot from an article in the weekly journal *Nature: International Weekly Journal of Science*. The original is rendered in full color.

Notice all the genre features aimed at making the research useable by other scientists: the abstract, the menu of printing and distribution options, the "figures at a glance," and so on. Every part of the item is functional. Don't, however, be dismayed if you find the reading intimidating. If this is where you'll spend a career, you'll master the territory soon enough.

Writers and institutions (such as newspapers or government agencies) know that they'll lose credibility if their factual presentations seem incomplete or biased. So expect at least a nod to objectivity in most reports or a rationale for any obvious biases. Of course, smart readers understand that reports on contentious subjects—global warming, stem-cell research, or conditions of the working poor, for example—may lean one way or another. You may, in fact, read a report with strong biases of your own. But since readers of reports prefer to draw their own conclusions, expect a competent report to encourage open-ended thinking. If it doesn't, perhaps it should—and you can raise the point in a discussion, citing passages where the item loses its credibility. (For more on discussions, see Chapter 11.)

In reading factual material, expect it to be arranged (and perhaps illustrated) purposefully and conveniently. Review the table of contents for a plan or scan through the headings and subheadings. Academic reports aren't mystery stories: They gain no points for surprises, twists, or suspense. However, such tactics are not uncommon in books and articles directed to the general public. Still, when you do research, you'll come to appreciate reports that give away the game on the first page, announcing not only a thesis but also perhaps their major conclusions.

Reports are efficient, formal, and technical.

Expect technical language in reports; that's part of the genre. But, as you well realize by now, writers routinely make audience-sensitive moves to expand their potential readership, particularly when they see an opportunity to expand public knowledge of a serious or complicated subject. So watch how a report defines any new terms, illustrates key principles, or uses graphics to convey concepts that benefit from visual explanations.

Academic reports are typically written in a formal or high style—free of emotional language that might make them sound like arguments. The formal style is one of those nods to impartiality, signaling that the writer's opinions are (or, at least, should be) less important than the facts reported. Scientific style can even feel clinical in its detachment from its subject matter, typically avoiding most personal references as well as devices such as contractions and dialogue. But you'll find reports in newspapers, magazines, and even encyclopedias to be less formal: You *might* even detect a person behind the prose. Yet the moment you suspect a writer of moving away from facts to push an agenda, you'll lose some faith in the report.

Read Arguments

As the coauthor of a book entitled *Everything's an Argument*, I may have a bias here: Almost everything you read in school will, in one way or another, be trying to persuade you of something. Even the most detached and impersonal lab report or research article is, consciously or not, laboring to convince you that its numbers are correct or its claims reliably demonstrated. Still there is a genre of writing that is, to its core, all about full-throated persuasion or principled advocacy. The writer's agenda is to change your mind (or confirm a position you already have) and then to move you to take action.

Arguments persuade readers to do something.

Some books in this genre — even a few that land on the *New York Times* best-seller lists — don't make it into college reading lists or syllabi because their mandate to persuade overrides traditional academic concerns, especially for close reasoning, original research, and sound evidence. Moreover, the authors of such works, chiefly media celebrities or would-be senators or presidents, rarely have done the legwork necessary to become experts on their subjects: Their books and articles seem crafted from newspaper clippings. Nonetheless, titles of this sort, alone or in clusters, do sometimes steer the national conversation, especially in the arena of politics. And passionate arguments — called *polemics* — written to jump-start discussions within specific communities occasionally become classics, ranging from Tom Paine's *Common Sense* (1776) urging American colonists to separate from Great Britain to Rachel Carson's assault on the use of pesticides in *Silent Spring* (1962). Precisely because arguments can be so influential, you have to approach this genre with critical faculties turned up high.

Public arguments and polemics might not meet academic standards.

After all, it doesn't take much to start an argument these days — a casual remark, a political observation, a dumb joke that hurts someone's feelings. Loud voices and angry protests follow, leaving observers upset and frustrated, wishing that we could all just get along. But arguments aren't polarizing or hostile by nature, not when offered by people more interested in generating light than heat, that is, in explaining the good reasons for a course of action rather than merely riling people up. Ideally, arguments you read should make you smarter and better able to deal with problems in the world.

Persuasive pieces come in many forms and borrow techniques from other genres. Arguments may feel like narratives or reports for dozens of pages, intriguing you with life stories or burying you under pages of data (much of it pointing in one direction). Eventually, though, authors will tip their hands. Generally, scholars, experts, and public intellectuals aren't shy about telling you what's on their minds. Here's Barry B. LePatner explaining exactly why he has written an entire book about the nation's failing bridges:

Arguments often include techniques from other genres.

> The risks of continuing to ignore our ill-maintained national infrastructure are almost unimaginable. We can no longer fail to devote massive amounts of money to repair our aging roads and bridges. We must begin to set a national policy that goes beyond the myopic vision of state and local politicians who prefer to use federal transportation funds on pork-barrel projects. We will need to reorganize our priorities for years to come, or risk the lives and well-being of our fellow citizens.
>
> —*Too Big to Fall: America's Failing Infrastructure and the Way Forward*

This consequential policy recommendation full of hot-button words and phrases—*risks, massive amounts of money, national policy, myopic vision, pork-barrel projects, lives and well-being*—points fingers at lots of people. Now what's the author got to do in the remaining two hundred pages? Prove that bridges are falling down and that his proposals to save the infrastructure are on target at a time when governments at every level are flat broke. (We'll return to LePatner shortly.)

Arguments make claims and then prove them.

Sometimes you'll have to work harder to figure out not only what the argument of a book or article might be, but also whether the author even intends to offer a straightforward claim. Recall that we discussed Luis Alberto Urrea's *The Devil's Highway* earlier as a *narrative* that calls for a rethinking of border and immigration issues. But its author doesn't lay out specific recommendations. Instead, he leaves it to readers to examine the painful details of the deadly border crossings that are the subject of his book and to consider what might be done to prevent such tragedies. Here are some lines from the final chapter of *The Devil's Highway*, reflecting on the deaths of fourteen men:

If only Mexico paid workers a decent wage.

In Iowa City, Omaha, Nutley, Waycross, Metairie, those [Mexicans] who survive the northern passage can earn in an hour what it took a long day's work in radioactive chemical Mexican sludge to earn before.

Consul Flores Vizcarra says it isn't the desert that kills immigrants. It isn't Coyotes. It isn't even the Border Patrol.

"What kills the people," he says, "is the politics of stupidity that rules both sides of the border."

Thunderbird [the American Graduate School of International Management] learned that Arizona "gets $8 billion in economic impact annually from the relationship" with Mexico. That's profit, not costs. Mexico makes $5.5 billion. Reymundo and his son would have been stunned to know they were dying under a high tide of money. Critics [of illegal immigration] will be stunned to learn that the United States makes more money in the deal than those wily Mexicans.

There's more of course, but you doubtless get the point. No explicit claim is made in these paragraphs, but there *is* an argument. And that's not atypical of many readings you will do in college courses.

When you do find yourself disagreeing with an author's arguments or objecting to the direction a reading is taking, don't stop reading. Instead, take a deep breath and admit that, in any subsequent discussion or writing assignment, you won't be able to counterargue coherently until you can honestly paraphrase the claims and logic offered in the offending text. In addition, you will seem smarter and fairer (and you'll learn more) if you admit the possibility of legitimate points of view different from your own. However, you never have to accept stupidity or bigotry; just be prepared to address irrational claims calmly, but firmly. (For more on disputing, see Chapter 9.)

Authors of consequential arguments actually expect you to challenge their opinions: Refutations and counterarguments are key elements of the genre. Remember Barry LePatner a page back, who wants to spend boxcars of money fixing roads and bridges he claims are on the verge of collapse? Just another corporate lawyer looking to push contracts to his clients in construction? Here's his response, before you even wondered:

Objections, counter-arguments, and rebuttals are part of *argument*.

For those who would seek to dismiss the facts that support the thesis of this book, I ask them to consult the many professional

Invokes experts

engineers in state transportation departments who face these problems on a daily basis. These professionals understand the physics of bridge and road design, and the real problem of ignoring what happens to steel and concrete when they are exposed to the elements without a strict regimen of ongoing maintenance.

—*Too Big to Fall: America's Failing Infrastructure and the Way Forward*

You can see (underlined) what a shrewd move this is, invoking the authority of expert engineers in the public sector who know their steel and concrete. We'll listen to writers this earnest.

Yet it is likely that we've all been seduced by frivolous claims just because they are stylish, hip, or repeated by so many talking heads that they begin to seem true. Such ideas can become a *meme*, a notion repeated so relentlessly (usually online) that it draws attention to its simplistic claim even as it is challenged: "the war on women," "class warfare," "pay their fair share." But lame advertising techniques count for nothing in academic reading. Expect higher standards and ask tough questions, like the following, when reading an argument critically:

Guidelines for responding to arguments

What does the writer claim—or want me to believe or do?

What specific reasons support this claim?

Do these reasons make sense? Are they genuinely connected to the claim?

On what premises or values does the argument rest?

Are these underlying assumptions reasonable and do they apply in this case?

What solid and verifiable evidence supports the claim?

Is the evidence trustworthy?

Can I trust the author?

Read critically and relentlessly.

There's a whole course in argumentation in these questions (and we'll work more on your critical thinking skills in Chapter 6). But for now, you see what the genre requires: close and relentless critical reading of all texts—maybe especially those you find yourself instinctively agreeing with. Don't let anyone off easy.

But what's this business about trusting the writer? People who study persuasion use the term *ethos* to describe the character that writers create for themselves within an argument—the voice and attitude they choose to give their appeal. It is a powerful concept, worth remembering. Surely you recognize when writers are coming across as, let's say, ingratiatingly confident or stupidly obnoxious. And don't you respond in kind, giving ear to the likable voice and dismissing the malicious one?

A few audiences — like those for political blogs — may actually prefer writers who come across as edgy or snarky. But in academic situations you'll likely find yourself attending more closely to authors who present themselves as reasonable, knowledgeable, and fair — neither insulting those who disagree with them nor making people who share their views embarrassed to have them on their side. But be careful: An ethos, like an argument itself, is a construction. Watch how authors you read fashion their images by adjusting their style, tone, and vocabularies: Contractions, for instance, can make them seem friendly (or too casual); an impressive vocabulary suggests that writers are smart (or maybe just pompous); lots of name-dropping makes writers seem hip (or perhaps pretentious). All of this primping, too, may be an effort to soften you up for a sales pitch.

Academic arguments strive for fairness.

Finally, pay attention to style. Writers use lots of verbal cues to frame their intentions. It's no accident that unsigned editorials in newspapers so often sound formal and overbearing: It's the voice of the *New York Times* or *Wall Street Journal* you hear. Other arguments are written full throttle, marshaling a complete range of rhetorical devices, from deliberate repetition and parallelism to dialogue and quotation to hammer home a point. Metaphors, similes, and analogies fit right in, too. The trick is to create sentences with a texture rich enough to keep you hooked, yet lean enough to advance an argument. In the following concluding paragraph from a book review, a fairly specialized form of argument, note how author Alison Gillmor, writing for the Canadian magazine *The Walrus*, uses remarkably simple and yet evocative images to make us appreciate how absurdly writers try to make our beloved pets into something they cannot be:

Writers use *style* to advance their arguments.

In a very real, evolutionary sense, dogs were made by people. Once wide-ranging wolves, they have been domesticated into the warmer, softer creatures that lie next to our beds at night. We are still shaping dogs today, making them into what we want and need them to be and accepting precious

Contrasts images of dogs past and present

little responsibility for doing so. The dog-book writers in North America—with noteworthy exceptions—set up <u>dogs</u> <u>as soul-mates, spirit guides, and savants.</u> If dogs could read these inflated images, they would probably <u>look sad-eared and</u> <u>embarrassed, the way they do when their owners dress them</u> <u>up for Halloween.</u> Fortunately, <u>dogs</u> remain unaware of their current celebrity status: they just carry on <u>doing what they do.</u> It's the <u>humans,</u> as usual, <u>making all the fuss.</u>

Contrasts canine obliviousness and human obtuseness

—"It's a Dog's Life: They're Not Just Pets Anymore"

You may not think of this paragraph as an argument, but Gillmor clearly intends to win readers over to a more sensible view of dogs than what she's found in the books she reviewed. Don't dismiss good style or be afraid of it. Just learn to appreciate the way it seduces you.

> **YOUR TURN**

11. Show that you understand the concept of *genre* by making a list of genres or subgenres in a field other than writing. Revisit the chapter's opening section that breaks down genres of music (p. 43). Begin with a category that is something people create (sports, buildings, governments), and not found in nature.

12. Identify and describe a narrative you have read or seen recently that has a purpose beyond entertaining you. Identify its goal, and explain how you detected it in the story. Did you have to interpret the narrative in some way to find this purpose or was it simply hard to miss?

13. Write a paragraph on a topic you know well, framing it as a factual report full of information and details. Then write a second paragraph based on the first, but now compose an argument instead. What specific changes did you make to turn your report into an argument?

14. Browse several online newspapers until you find a recent editorial or op-ed column with which you strongly disagree, preferably one long enough to develop its argument or offer supporting evidence. Rather than offer your objections to the argument, explain what you have learned from the piece.

5

Sources

Here's a small case study in just how tough it can be to establish facts, even trivia. People old enough to remember the dead-pan TV (and radio) crime drama *Dragnet* are also likely to recall Sgt. Joe Friday's signature phrase, "Just the facts, ma'am." Supposedly, Sgt. Friday aimed his line at female witnesses over the course of the long-running show. Except Joe Friday never said that exactly, at least not according to Wikipedia, which cites Snopes.com, which cites Michael J. Hayde, author of *My Name's Friday: The Unauthorized but True Story of* Dragnet *and the Films of Jack Webb* (2001). It seems that Sgt. Friday, with his tough, wooden dialogue, was parodied by comic Stan Freberg in a 1951 phonograph recording that went "viral" in 1953. In his book, Hayde quotes briefly from the script of the parody and then explains how the signature phrase evolved from it:

> *Little Blue Riding Hood:* Why Grandma, what big ears you've got!
>
> *Sgt. Wednesday:* All the better to get the facts. I just want to get the facts, ma'am.

> As this exchange entered the American subconscious, it soon found itself truncated to "Just the facts, ma'am." From that point on, every press release, every Web interview, every newspaper and magazine article that had anything to do with *Dragnet* made use of the phrase. For the next year it so dominated media coverage of the show that finally, inevitably, the line was credited to Sgt. Friday, as if he'd been saying it all along. His actual phrase— "All we want [to know] are the facts, ma'am"—bit the dust.

So, it seems that a famous line about facts is a fake— assuming that Hayde's very plausible account is accurate.

Hayde doesn't credit any sources for this incident, but then *The Unauthorized but True Story of* Dragnet doesn't sound like a work written for scholars. Hmmm. A lesson in how vigilant writers need to be when working with facts and research materials.

But you probably know how tangled sources can be since you've been documenting research papers since middle school. So I'll keep this chapter brief and won't bore you with the minutiae of in-text notes and works cited pages—there's a section in Appendix B for that. Instead, we'll take a different approach, examining what sourcing reveals about the authors and works you're reading—useful information whenever you're facing a serious assignment. We're going to peel back the curtains a crack: Think of this as the academic equivalent of snooping on authors.

How Academics Establish Credibility

For the most part, academics have little to hide when they publish books and articles with pages of notes and references. When presenting research or supporting a hypothesis, scholars leave an extensive paper trail, building their arguments or demonstrations one citation after another. Early citations often provide what's called a review of literature: The writer establishes *where the argument stands now*, identifying major articles and books that set the new research in context. Then just about any subsequent claim in the article is linked to sources that gloss it. Citations point to articles that contain data and evidence, methodology, precedents, supportive studies, contrary views, and on and on. Reading a scholarly paper, especially in a field new to you, can seem like having dinner with a name-dropper, except less interesting. But this welter of notes represents the way academic research works: It builds information in small, traceable, reproducible steps so that other scholars can track every movement of the argument.

Sources in STEM Fields

In what are now routinely called STEM fields (science, technology, engineering, mathematics), the handling of sources is conspicuously efficient, rigorous, and disinterested—especially in online journals. Click an in-text note within an article published there, and you are whisked to the full item in the reference list.

Click a reference list entry and you jump to the place the item is cited in the article. Some online journals even generate bibliographies of authors' related works when you click on their names; other links pull up abstracts, citation lists, indexed keywords, and much more. A scientific article today is what most scholarly reading will be like in the future, an intricate network of relevant data instantly available.

Such notes and documentation embody the no-nonsense, impersonal, unbiased nature of research in STEM fields—its ethos. Even researchers' first names are reduced to initials. Browse a reference list, like the partial bibliography on page 64 (just A–E) from an article in *Psychological Bulletin,* 2010, and you get an accurate read on where the research comes from, how thorough it is, and how disciplined the field might be. However, you don't get much sense of the people involved; there's no need for a human voice here. This reference list is from Sara M. Linberg, Janet Shipley Hyde, and Jennifer L. Petersen's "New Trends in Gender and Mathematics Performance: A Meta-Analysis." (For more on APA documentation style, see Appendix B, p. 239.)

Sources in the Humanities

Formal academic research in the humanities is just a tick less tight because its subject matter bends more toward people and ideas than facts and data. Yet articles in the humanities are as rigorously sourced as those in the STEM fields. Look at the opening pages of research essays in history, philosophy, classics, and English, and you will typically find a review of the literature introducing the subject, mapping its contours, and arguing its relevance. You can see these conventional moves in the opening page (p. 65) from an article on Shakespeare's rarely performed tragedy *Coriolanus;* half of the page is made up of citations, each directing scholars to materials that offer a context for the discussion. These items become required reading for anyone *seriously* interested in the topic.

As the argument develops, citations continue, thick and fast. Many of them are of the "bibliographic" variety common in scientific writing; that is, they clearly identify the books and articles referenced in the essay. But arguments in the humanities also commonly include "explanatory" notes that give authors more room to maneuver. In such notes, they can add remarks, which, though related to the main argument, are just

References

Reference list in APA style

For a complete list of studies included in the meta-analysis in Study 1, go to http://dx.doi.org/10.1037/a0021276.supp

Entries are alphabetical by author.

Ambady, N., Shih, M., Kim, A., & Pittinsky, T. L. (2001). Stereotype susceptibility in children: Effects of identity activation on quantitative performance. *Psychological Science, 12,* 385–390. doi:10.1111/1467-9280.00371

Anastasi, A. (1958). *Differential psychology* (3rd ed.). New York, NY: Macmillan.

Arms, E. (2007). Gender equity in coeducational and single-sex environments. In S. Klein (Ed.), *Handbook for achieving equity through education* (pp. 171–190). Mahwah, NJ: Erlbaum.

Journal articles are cited by author, year of publication, title of article, followed by publication information.

Au, W. (2007). High-stakes testing and curricular control: A qualitative metasynthesis. *Educational Researcher, 36,* 258–267. doi:10.3102/0013189X07306523

Bandura, A. (1986). *Social foundations of thought and action: A social cognitive theory.* Englewood Cliffs, NJ: Prentice-Hall.

Bandura, A. (1997). *Self-efficacy: The exercise of control.* New York, NY: Freeman.

Ben-Zeev, T., Fein, S., & Inzlicht, M. (2005). Arousal and stereotype threat. *Journal of Experimental Social Psychology, 41,* 174–181. doi: 10.1016/j.jesp.2003.11.007

Bouchey, H. A., & Harter, S. (2005). Reflected appraisals, academic self-perceptions, and math/science performance during early adolescence. *Journal of Educational Psychology, 97,* 673–686. doi:10.1037/0022-0663.97.4.673

Journal articles include a DOI (digital object identifier) for easy electronic access.

Bureau of Labor Statistics. (n.d.). *National Longitudinal Surveys: The NLSY 97.* Retrieved from http://www.bls.gov/nls/nlsy97.htm

Bussey, K., & Bandura, A. (1999). Social cognitive theory of gender development and differentiation. *Psychological Review, 106,* 676–713. doi:10.1037/0033-295X.106.4.676

Cadinu, M., Maass, A., Rosabianca, A., & Kiesner, J. (2005). Why do women underperform under stereotype threat? Evidence for the role of negative thinking. *Psychological Science, 16,* 572–578. doi:10.1111/j.0956-7976.2005.01577.x

Cohen, J. (1988). *Statistical power analysis for the behavioral sciences.* Hillsdale, NJ: Erlbaum.

Dwyer & Johnson's work is an essay published within a collection.

Dwyer, C. A., & Johnson, L. M. (1997). Grades, accomplishments and correlates. In W. A. Willingham & N. S. Cole (Eds.), *Gender and fair assessment* (pp. 127–156). Mahwah, NJ: Erlbaum.

Eccles, J. S. (1994). Understanding women's educational and occupational choices: Applying the Eccles et al. model of achievement-related choices. *Psychology of Women Quarterly, 18,* 585–609. doi:10.1111/j.1471-6402.1994.tb01049.x

Else-Quest, N. M., Hyde, J. S., & Linn, M. C. (2010). Cross-national patterns of gender differences in mathematics and gender equity: A

The Controversial Eloquence of Shakespeare's Coriolanus—an Anti-Ciceronian Orator?

MICHAEL WEST

University of Pittsburgh

MYRON SILBERSTEIN

University of Chicago

The title marks the article as scholarly, not for general readers.

Authors are listed with academic affiliations.

For the past four decades, *Coriolanus* has been interpreted as a play about language, but with curiously contradictory results. "Coriolanus has a natural antipathy to eloquence," claims one critic; "he is emphatically 'no orator.'" "Lacking the verbal resources and the confidence in language required for effective argument, he remains taciturn whenever possible," adds another, while a third terms him "the only central character in Shakespeare who is an inadequate speaker."[1] In an influential essay arguing that for Coriolanus "the circulation of language is an expression of cannibalism," Stanley Cavell likewise finds "the words of this particular play . . . uncharacteristically ineloquent" and claims that insofar as Coriolanus can't express desire he "cannot speak at all."[2] "Coriolanus is antirhetoric," echoes one critic.[3] His bodiliness "is utterly unrelated to Volumnia's life of speech," another agrees.[4] Reviewing such linguistic studies, one recent article concurs

First paragraph reviews existing literature on the paper's subject.

---

1. Maurice Charney, *Shakespeare's Roman Plays* (Cambridge, MA: Harvard University Press, 1963), 34–35; James L. Calderwood, "*Coriolanus*: Wordless Meanings and Meaningless Words," in *Essays in Shakespearean Criticism*, ed. James L. Calderwood and Harold E. Toliver (Englewood Cliffs, NJ: Prentice-Hall, 1970), 551; John Porter Houston, *Shakespearean Sentences: A Study in Style and Syntax* (Baton Rouge: Louisiana State University Press, 1986), 163. For similar pronouncements, see Carol Sicherman, "*Coriolanus*: The Failure of Words," *ELH* 39 (1972): 191, 199; Leonard Tennenhouse, "Coriolanus: History and Crisis of the Semantic Order," *Comparative Drama* 10 (1977): 334; Lawrence Danson, *Tragic Alphabet: Shakespeare's Drama of Language* (New Haven, CT: Yale University Press, 1974), 142.

2. Stanley Cavell, "'Who does the wolf love?' Reading *Coriolanus*," *Representations* 1 (1983): 12, 17, 6.

3. Bruce Krajewski, *Traveling with Hermes: Hermeneutics and Rhetoric* (Amherst: University of Massachusetts Press, 1992), 52.

4. Jarrett Walker, "Voiceless Bodies and Bodiless Voices: The Drama of Human Perception in *Coriolanus*," *Shakespeare Quarterly* 43 (1992): 182.

Footnotes point to additional sources.

Viewed online, the notes link to the cited sources when possible.

far enough removed from it to be sent to the bottom of the page or the end of the essay. In such comments writers might even express opinions or occasionally tweak a nose. Below are two such notes from the *Coriolanus* essay.

Opinion
expressed

35. Philip Brockbank's judicious gloss on this passage (200) has obviously been misunderstood by Bryan Reynolds when he perversely argues that here Cominius is agreeing with Sicinius rather than with Coriolanus, in "'What Is the City But the People?': Transversal Performance and Radical Politics," in his *Performing Transversally: Reimagining Shakespeare and the Critical Future* (New York: Palgrave Macmillan, 2003), 100–101.

Provocative
claim made

49. See esp. Brian Vickers, "The Power of Persuasion: Images of the Orator, Elyot to Shakespeare," in *Renaissance Eloquence: Studies in the Theory and Practice of Renaissance Rhetoric*, ed. James J. Murphy (Berkeley: University of California Press, 1983), 411–35; also his *Shakespeare: "Coriolanus"* (London: Arnold, 1976), and "Teaching *Coriolanus*: The Importance of Perspective," in *Teaching Shakespeare*, ed. Walter Edens et al. (Princeton University Press, 1977), 228–70. Vickers's interpretation of the play seems implausible in several respects: e.g., in viewing the hero as a modest man ruled by love and in treating all the play's oratory as "evil eloquence." But his sensitivity to rhetorical issues encourages a healthy skepticism about other characters' self-serving descriptions of Coriolanus that lets us begin to recapture the tragic dimension of the drama. On the political and moral biases that sway reactions to the hero, see also Houston, *Shakespearean Sentences*, 178.

One appeal of remarks like these is that they enable you to see how authors make judgments about their sources and the positions they support. You can almost feel the weight on them to make a good decision. The comments don't exactly gambol, but they breathe.

When you're under pressure to finish a reading assignment, it's all too easy to skip the apparatus that accompanies scholarly writing. However, the handling of sources in academic books and articles reveals the respect authors have for research and discovery. What seems remote, fussy, and pedantic from a distance proves, up close, to be logical, helpful, even admirable.

Don't skip the
notes!

But the academic way is not the only path to knowledge.

How Experts and Public Intellectuals Earn Authority

Writers outside of the academic world often treat their notes as an alternative channel of communication with readers, often less formal than the actual texts of their books or articles, sometimes like a conversation over a fence. Whether mimicking the style of formal documentation or carving another path, these items have an openness not suited to academic writing. In public writing, authors not only acknowledge their sources, but sometimes celebrate or even question them. What, for example, do you hear in this paragraph from the introduction to a popular book, Rebecca Skloot's *The Immortal Life of Henrietta Lacks*?

> This is a work of nonfiction. No names have been changed, no characters invented, no events fabricated. While writing this book, I conducted more than a thousand hours of interviews with family and friends of Henrietta Lacks, as well as with lawyers, ethicists, scientists, and journalists who've written about the Lacks family. I also relied on extensive archival photos and documents, scientific and historical research, and the personal journals of Henrietta's daughter, Deborah Lacks.
>
> —"A Few Words about This Book"

This is clearly a description of the author's research procedures, which creates an ethos for her of hard-earned expertise. But the paragraph also affirms what Skloot calls "a decadelong [sic] adventure," one that culminated in a much-admired work about a heretofore forgotten woman who played an unexpected role in medical science. Documentation at the end of the volume speaks with the same confident informality.

CHAPTER 2: CLOVER

> Several books helped me reconstruct the era and places in which Henrietta lived, including *Country Folks: The Way We Were Back Then in Halifax County, Virginia*, by Henry Preston Young, Jr.; *History of Halifax*, by Pocahontas Wight Edmunds; *Turner Station*, by Jerome Watson; *Wives of Steel*, by Karen Olson; and *Making Steel*, by Mark Reutter. The history of Turner Station [where Lacks moved with her husband] is also chronicled in news articles and documents housed at the Dundalk Patapsco Neck Historical Society and the North Point Library in Dundalk, Maryland.

Notice that Skloot does not give full publication information for the books she mentions the way academic authors would. She's more methodical with articles, always supplying journal titles and dates, though page numbers appear only rarely. But the documentation affirms what readers need to know: that Skloot has read widely enough to write with authority about Henrietta Lacks's early life. Moreover, Skloot seems to invite readers to follow up on her discoveries if they like, right into those libraries in Maryland.

Sociologist Annette Lareau, an academic who expects her detailed study of working-class childhoods to reach a general audience (see Chapter 3, p. 28), documents *Unequal Childhoods* in a way to satisfy both sociologists and common readers. The notes and bibliography, which cover sixty-five pages, include items like these from Chapter 12, "On the Power and Limits of Social Class":

Explanatory note

30. Middle-class families did not live problem-free lives. The point here is that middle-class families have more varied occupational experiences; their superior educational training also gives them access to jobs with more economic returns.

Academic note

31. Katherine Newman, *Declining Fortunes*, and Donald L. Barlett and James B. Steele, *America: What Went Wrong?*

Academic note

32. Erik Olin Wright, *Class, Crisis, and the State*, chapter 1.

Explanatory note

33. Not all middle-class parents we interviewed approved of this scenario, either. Many thought it was wrong to force a child to take piano lessons that he did not enjoy. Still, unlike working-class and poor parents, many stressed the importance of "exposure."

Here you see two academic-style citations (somewhat modified) linked to fuller entries in the bibliography (not shown) and two explanatory notes only slightly more formal than Skloot's notes. The items clearly signal that both academic and non-specialized readers are welcome.

Sixty pages of notes also accompany novelist Jonathan Safran Foer's passionate and aggressive argument in *Eating Animals*; his notes might seem eccentric to a scholar like Lareau, and maybe to you. Keyed to particular lines in the book, some notes cite conventional studies and articles while others point to Web sources of varying authority (accompanied by dutifully reproduced URLs, some five and six lines long). There is a pragmatic frankness to some of these items, as in these two consecutive notes:

Public authors may use sources in academic and non-academic ways.

258. ***Hitler was a vegetarian* ...** The legend of Hitler's vegetarianism is quite persistent and widespread, but I have no idea if it's true. It is especially doubtful given various references to his eating sausages. For example, H. Eberle and M. Uhl, *The Hitler Book* (Jackson, TN: PublicAffairs, 2006), 136.

259. ***"one must take a position ..."*** This Martin Luther King Jr. quote is widely cited on the Internet; for example see Quotiki.com, www.quotiki.com/quotes/3450 (accessed August 19, 2009).

As a reader accustomed to academic writing, you may find Foer's admission surprising: *I have no idea if it's true.* But spend time browsing his citations and you quickly appreciate how strongly he feels about killing animals for food, how widely he has read on the subject, and how inclusive his sources are. Clearly not a scholarly treatise, *Eating Animals*—like many public arguments—is indebted to materials readily available to any concerned writer and citizen.

Notes can even give you surprising and useful insights into an author's writing process. Erik Larson's *The Devil in the White City* tells side by side the stories of Chicago's triumphant 1893 World's Columbian Exposition, celebrating the four hundredth anniversary of Christopher Columbus's voyage to the New World, and serial murderer Dr. H. H. Holmes's macabre connection to that event. In the following paragraph from his "Notes and Sources," Larson explains how he struggled to maintain the realism of his account while describing two of Holmes's crimes:

> Notes can establish the authority, attitude, and ethos of authors.

> Clearly no one other than Holmes was present during his murders—no one, that is, who survived—yet in my book I re-create two of his killings. I agonized over how to do this and spent a good deal of time rereading Truman Capote's *In Cold Blood* for insights into how Capote achieved his dark and still deeply troubling account. Sadly, Capote left no footnotes. To build my murder scenes, I used threads of known detail to weave a plausible account, as would a prosecutor in his closing arguments to a jury. My description of Julia Conner's death by chloroform is based on expert testimony presented at Holmes's trial about the character of chloroform and what was known at the time about its effect on the human body.

Larson's next paragraph is no less interesting and may even influence a reader's research habits:

> I do not employ researchers, nor did I conduct any primary research using the Internet. I need physical contact with my sources, and there's only one way to get it. To me every trip to a library or archive is like a small detective story. There are always little moments on such trips when the past flares to life, like a match in the darkness.

What is the lesson here? You're going to miss something if you don't at least browse the notes that accompany your readings. The documentation is always part of the story; it reveals not only what authors have read, but also what they think about their sources, their subjects, their audiences, and their jobs as writers. One could argue, academic materials aside, that notes reflect the character of their writers, demonstrating their obsessions, methods, and so on. Some authors are formal and disciplined, others freewheeling and downright chatty. And their notes can be sincere invitations to read more, to follow up on what they have discovered, perhaps even to write something of your own one day.

Notes provide special insight into authors and texts.

How the Other Guys Do It

Much of what you read—probably most—doesn't come with documentation, notes, or bibliographies of any kind. Such appendages would just clutter up news stories, articles in popular magazines, or other forms of everyday reading, which use different conventions for sourcing. You tolerate it when journalists don't show all their cards because you expect them to live up to a professional code of ethics that mandates adequate sourcing, objectivity, fairness, and so on. The Web, however, has revolutionized the delivery of news, news reporting, and editorial opinions. Anyone with a blog can transmit and comment on stories and maybe even do some firsthand reporting. When everyone is a journalist, everyone is also a critic. And today everyone, it seems, has access to an audience.

So you have important reasons to pay attention to the way nonfiction pieces are sourced, understanding the challenges writers face. Consider a nonfiction narrative like Dave Eggers's *Zeitoun*, a 300-page account of what Abdulrahman Zeitoun and his family endured in New Orleans in the wake of Hurricane Katrina—a harrowing sequence of disaster, police abuse, and false imprisonment. Eggers tells his story like a novel, describing scenes through his characters' eyes and taking us into their minds. Here's the Syrian American Zeitoun in the city after the levees have been breached:

Pay attention to how all writing uses sources.

> When he had eaten, he felt restless, trapped. The water was too deep to wade into, its contents too suspect to swim through. But there was the canoe. He saw it, floating above the yard, tethered to the house. Amid the devastation of the city, standing on the roof of his drowned home, Zeitoun felt something like

inspiration. He imagined floating, alone, through the streets of his city. In a way, this was a new world, uncharted. He could be an explorer. He could see things first.

   He climbed down the side of the house and lowered himself into the canoe. He untied the rope and set out.

Lovely scene. But how does Eggers know all this? How can he describe what Zeitoun is seeing and thinking at that moment? As a reader, you have the right to wonder. And yet wouldn't an intrusive parenthetical note or even a footnote number spoil the passage?

As you must expect by now, *Zeitoun* opens with an explanatory section:

> This is a work of nonfiction, based primarily on the accounts of Abdulrahman Zeitoun and Kathy Zeitoun. . . . Dates, times, locations, and other facts have been confirmed by independent sources and the historical record. Conversations have been recounted as best as can be remembered by the participants. Some names have been changed.
>
> — "Notes about This Book"

If the note is not enough (and it probably isn't if the work is to be taken seriously as a historical account of a major event), Dave Eggers fills four very tightly printed single-spaced pages at the back of *Zeitoun* with the names of dozens of researchers, journalists, books, reports, and agencies whose work either confirms or contributes to his remarkable Hurricane Katrina narrative. Eggers then follows up with an author's note on his "process and methodology." Due diligence has been given.

But what about the many serious pieces you've read, in school and out, that are wholly without explanations, notes, footnotes, or bibliographies? Why do you, for the most part, trust the arguments and the stories they tell? The explanation is right in front of you, presented so deftly that you barely notice. Their authors rely on informal documentation, that is, credit lines offered just as they are needed and without distracting glances to the bottom of the page or back of the book.

For example, a journalist as admired and honored (three Pulitzer Prizes) as Thomas L. Friedman doesn't offer more than a few pages of acknowledgments to support the almost five hundred pages of analysis and argument in *Hot, Flat, and*

Crowded: Why We Need a Green Revolution—and How It Can Renew America. You'll look in vain for formal notes or a bibliography, and even his acknowledgment pages seem mighty chatty, more about people and adventures than the sources he used:

No documentation? Look for informal notes and credits.

> My primary teacher when it comes to the issue of biodiversity has been Glenn Prickett. Glenn and I have traveled from the Atlantic rain forest in Brazil to Shangri-La in Chinese Tibet and from the wilds of Southern Venezuela to the southern tip of Indonesia. . . . Bill Gates and Craig Mundie, from Microsoft, had me out for a lengthy discussion about all aspects of the energy issue. . . . John Doerr was a delightful traveling companion, from the rain forests of Peru to the sugarcane fields of Brazil.

Take this approach with your next research paper and see where it gets you. Your professor may not be so impressed.

But Friedman didn't earn those Pulitzers for his signature mustache. As a journalist he knows how to interview people and take notes. Then the notes and a great deal of reading find their way into the book, cleanly and unobtrusively. Watch how he identifies his sources in just one page-and-a-half section of *Hot, Flat, and Crowded* entitled "Energy Efficiency and Resource Productivity" (underlines added):

Source 1

Here's a scary statistic (*Time*, January 12, 2009): "Only 4 percent of the energy used to run a typical incandescent light bulb . . ."

Source 2

As the U.S. Department of Energy notes on its official Web site, . . .

Source 3

"We can't just focus on innovation on the energy supply side," says Diana Farrell, director of the McKinsey Global Institute.

Source 4

A study by the McKinsey Global Institute (February 2008) concluded . . .

Source 5

. . . we need to do everything we can, as Jim Rogers, the president and CEO of Duke Energy, argues, "to expand the world of possibilities" by driving all forms of innovation.

Source 6

"I didn't want to be the first generation telling my kids you can't have a life as good as I did," said K. R. Sridhar, the Indian-American fuel cell inventor and founder of Bloom Energy.

Now you can't click on the names or titles Friedman mentions to call up full-text articles confirming the material here the way you might in an online STEM field research article. But note that Friedman always provides a name, publication, or respectable authority to explain or represent ideas. Smoothly and convincingly, he reinforces his credibility, his ethos, at the same time that he delivers heaps of facts and opinions. This kind of skill shouldn't be taken lightly. You will need it in your own professional life whenever you want to reach wide audiences. So, every once in a while, notice when writers or journalists do their jobs well. Informal documentation tells a story, too.

YOUR TURN

15. You can probably think of at least one or two factual errors or mistaken beliefs that many people hold. (If you can't, search "popular misconceptions" online.) Select one such misconception and find at least three or four *credible* sources you could cite in a paper intended to falsify the belief. You need not write the paper; instead take the time to rank the sources you have located from most credible to less so. Also indicate which, if any, of the sources might be convincing to an academic audience.

16. Locate a scholarly article in an academic field, preferably one connected to subjects you are studying or to an area you might pursue in school. You can find print journals in a library or access them online via the information databases most libraries support. (You'll need to sign in to gain access to full-text professional journals there.) Examine the features offered to help readers manage a selected article's contents and sources: *abstract, bibliographic notes, explanatory notes, works cited/references pages* or *bibliography, charts, graphs,* and so on. If the article you find is specifically designed for online use (not just a PDF of a printed page), explore how the item enhances your access to information: For example, what happens when you click on its various options? Share what you've learned with a group of peers.

17. Find a scholarly article that employs traditional in-text notes or bottom-of-the-page footnotes to identify its sources. Select a page or two from the article and then rewrite the material to move all the key bibliographic information in the scholarly notes right into the text itself. For readability, you may have to eliminate many details, such as publishers' names, cities of publication, volume numbers, and so on. Model the revised pages from the article on what Thomas L. Friedman does with sources in *Hot, Flat, and Crowded* (see p. 72). What is gained or lost by the changes you have made?

18. Choose a piece of writing by a public intellectual or respected expert—perhaps an op-ed item in a newspaper or a short opinion piece in a familiar general interest or news magazine. (Ask librarians or instructors for suggestions; you can typically find such pieces online.) Then underline or highlight all the places in the text where the writer provides evidence for specific claims he or she makes. Does the writer provide names of other writers, titles of works, news reports, academic studies, government sources? Which sources could you trust immediately? Which would require research on your part to affirm their worth?

6

'Tis the good reader that makes the
good book.

—Ralph Waldo Emerson

Critical Reading

Five chapters in and you've set readings or syllabi in context,
gotten chummy with authors and publishers, figured out who
stands with you in their intended audiences, and examined the
way writers manage their sources. With the checklist punched,
you're not just ready for takeoff—you're already in flight. Prep
work of the sort described in the previous chapters—and
sometimes it takes only minutes—is what savvy readers do all
the time to make their encounters with new materials rich and
productive. They don't read Khaled Hosseini or Jane Austen
and expect vampires: They know what's coming.

So you've gained a sense of what an assigned reading is
about. Now comes the main event: settling in to read whole
books and articles, encountering them in all their marbled thick-
ness, wrestling with their contents and ideas, giving them the
attention they require. Time to see exactly what's on your plate.

Leave Tracks on a Text

Let's make this easy. In reading a book or article, you really
need to do just two things: understand the text and respond
to it. The processes can be almost simultaneous, but you'll be
better prepared later to discuss and write about texts if you can
keep some separation between what's in a text and your reactions to it. What I recommend is that you *get physical with your
readings*: mark them up, annotate them, and gloss them. (Just
to get this out of the way, don't ever mark up books, journals,
or magazines you don't own or have borrowed from libraries. If
you must use such material, work with photocopies.)

Separate
"content" notes
from "critical"
ones—but
respond in both
ways.

Highlight the key content elements in books and articles as you move through them. Look for solid stuff that provokes a response of *oh, I see*:

Note these key content elements in every text you read.

- thesis statements and claims
- supporting reasons and rationales
- essential supporting evidence
- objections and rebuttals
- memorable passages
- sentences you might quote

In literary works, mark turning points, stunning incidents, key passages, and so on. Don't try to keep tabs on these items in your head: You need a tactile connection to a reading made by a pen, highlighter, or electronic note. These physical motions inscribe ideas into your consciousness. Really. Pausing to make comments also slows down your reading (a good thing) so you can think about what a text actually says or stirs up.

You'll also want to return to highlighted passages to figure out the design or pattern of a work: Does the thesis of the report really connect to its supporting reasons or its underlying assumptions? Is the evidence offered in an editorial enough to make the argument plausible? Do the physical descriptions of places within a novel undercut the main actions? (For more on patterns, see Chapter 7, pp. 85–92.)

Exactly how to mark up a text is your business. There are now too many ways of reading and too many platforms and devices for responding to make simple recommendations. The important thing is to enter an academic text with some method for leaving tracks. Instructors once warned students against overusing those yellow or pink highlighter pens: What's the point of marking almost every paragraph for special attention? Such a warning applies equally to any technological equivalents. Your responses to readings should be selective: Zero in on just the details you might need later to prepare a summary or paraphrase or write a paper (see Chapter 10).

Highlight material to use in summaries or paraphrases.

Now what about those critical and evaluative reactions you'll have to any text? The principle is the same: If you don't record them, you'll forget them. But, obviously, you must separate opinionated remarks from factual notes. So decide on a tool to use exclusively for this purpose: marginal comments in red, comment boxes online, and so on. (My go-to method has long been sticky notes; the books I teach from look like they're being devoured by multicolored moths.) Evaluative comments are your starting blocks for response papers and class discussions. You want to get to this data quickly.

To be certain you don't later mistake personal comments for observations *from* the source, try using first person or maybe consistently pose questions as you respond. Use personal annotations, too, to draw connections to other source materials you have read. The key to critical commentary is honesty; annotations should record precisely what's on your mind.

I don't see the connection. What did I miss?

Evidence here looks partisan to me.

I think this is a rejection of Keynesian economics.

Is the author sexist—or just from an older era?

I expected a rebuttal. Where is it?

A hasty generalization here.

Compare with Clay Shirky's arguments?

Who is Nikola Tesla?

Why doesn't Hamlet just kill Claudius?

Examples of personal comments: Identify them clearly.

Don't be embarrassed if you have doubts about works you assume have status because they've been assigned in class. Most instructors want you to pose questions, even — and maybe especially — about so-called canonical texts (see Chapter 1). Chances are you're not alone in your suspicions, but even when you are, it might be because you bring a fresh perspective to a reading.

Ask frank questions.

Or not. It's embarrassing, but sometimes you dislike a text just because it reveals how much more an author knows about a subject than you do. Hostile comments then simply expose the gaps in your disciplinary knowledge. If that's the case, fill them in. Don't blame the author.

Read against the Grain: Logical Fallacies

As you see, it makes sense to read with an open mind, giving reputable writers and their ideas a fair hearing as you move through their texts, marking highlights and responding to them. But it is smart, too, especially in school, to *read against the grain*. Reading against the grain does not mean finding fault with

Scrutinize everything.

everything, but rather pushing yourself to entertain alternative points of view and letting little slip by without scrutiny. Honest, fair-minded writers have nothing to hide. But even the best may occasionally slip into logical fallacies that you should take note of in your reading. *Fallacies* are argumentative strategies that appear to be sensible, but which are flawed in some clear-cut way. Such rhetorical moves corrupt solid reasoning—they are the verbal equivalent of sleight of hand. Following are some familiar fallacies you should look out for whenever you read.

Watch for common logical fallacies.

- **Appeals to false or untrustworthy authority.** Be sure that any experts or authorities cited on a topic have genuine credentials in the field or that the knowledge they have has a bearing on the topic. Similarly, note any places where writers themselves claim or imply expertise that they may not actually have.

- **Ad hominem attacks.** Be suspicious of authors who advance their arguments by attacking the personal integrity of opponents when character isn't an issue. It's easy to resort to name-calling (*socialist, racist*) or character assassination, but it usually signals that a writer's case is weak.

- **Dogmatism.** Writers fall back on dogmatism whenever they want to give the impression, usually false, that there is but one plausible position on an issue or that they have all the right answers. Expect some form of dogmatism when writers begin sentences with "How can anyone argue that . . . ?" or "No serious person could disagree . . . "

- **Either/or choices.** A shortcut to winning arguments, which even Socrates abused, is to reduce complex situations to simplistic choices: good/bad, right/wrong, liberty/tyranny, smart/dumb, and so on. If you find writers inclined to use some version of the either/or strategy, call them out. Capable readers see right through this tactic and demolish it simply by pointing to alternatives that haven't been considered.

- **Straw-man arguments.** It's easy to knock down proposals that no one has actually made or to distort reasonable claims beyond all recognition. For good reason, such easily debunked but common maneuvers are described as straw-man arguments. You'll recognize them whenever politicians take brave stands against evil people who apparently intend to dismantle the military, shut the door to all immigrants, seize our guns, or turn every river into a cesspool.

- **Scare tactics.** Arguments that make their appeals by preying on the fears of audiences are automatically suspect. Targets may be as vague as "unforeseen consequences" or as specific as particular organizations or groups of people who pose various threats. While such fears may be legitimate, make sure a writer provides evidence for the danger and doesn't overstate it.

- **Sentimental or emotional appeals.** Maybe it's fine for the Humane Society to decorate its pleas for cash with pictures of sad puppies, but you can see how the tactic might be abused. Be wary of writers who use language that pushes emotional buttons or try to reduce complex social issues to one-dimensional human-interest stories.

- **Hasty or sweeping generalizations.** Drawing conclusions from too little evidence or too few examples is a hasty generalization: *Global warming must be a fraud because we sure froze last winter.* Making a claim apply too broadly is a sweeping generalization: *All Texans love pickups.* Competent writers avoid the temptation to draw conclusions that fit their preconceived notions—or pander to those of an intended audience. But the temptation is powerful, so you might find examples, even in college reading assignments.

- **Faulty causality.** Just because two events or phenomena occur close together in time doesn't mean that one caused the other. Many pundits and politicians do routinely exploit this weakness, particularly in situations involving economics, science, health, crime, and culture. Causal relationships are almost always complicated, and you will get credit for questioning potential errors in the reading you do.

Be Smart: Read beyond Your Range

Really want to learn something? Then, on your own volition, read *above* your current level of knowledge. That's the point of most college assignments: to push you one step closer to some goal or career. It may be fun to connect mainly with friends online who share your interests, but you'll often be gabbing with people who don't know much more than you do. Instead, spend time with academic material you can't just blow through. You'll know you're there when you find yourself looking up names, adding words to your vocabulary, and feeling humbled at what you still need to learn about a subject. That's when thinking occurs and ideas bloom.

Let's imagine, very plausibly, that you're asked to read "What Is a Liberal Education?" by Donald Kagan, Sterling Professor of Classics and History at Yale. Following is just the first paragraph of the 1999 essay, which runs for about ten densely printed pages. Give it a quick look:

> What is a liberal education and what is it for? In our time, in spite of the arguments over core curricula, canons, and multiculturalism, the real encounter is avoided and the questions ignored. From Cicero's *artes liberales* to the *trivium* and *quadrivium* of the medieval schoolmen, to the *studia humanitatis* of the Renaissance humanists, to Cardinal Newman's *Idea of a University*, to the attempts at common curricula in the first half of this century, to the chaotic cafeteria that passes for a curriculum in most American universities today, the concept has suffered from vagueness, confusion, and contradiction. From the beginning the champions of a liberal education have thought that it seeks at least four kinds of goals.

What do you take from the paragraph? Probably that "liberal education" is a confusing concept and that Professor Kagan intends to examine the four goals he mentions in that final sentence.

But now, as an experiment, look up all the items in the paragraph (names, words, and phrases) you couldn't handle on a quiz if you were asked to define or explain them. Take your time—let's say thirty minutes. Naturally, I assume you've got access to a computer, laptop, tablet, or smartphone. Life is different if you have to do this exercise at a library, and I'm not being disrespectful. There's a point to this.

What did you gloss? I'd guess your items include some of the following:

core curricula	canons
multiculturalism	Cicero
artes liberales	*trivium*
quadrivium	medieval schoolmen
studia humanitatis	Renaissance humanists
Cardinal Newman	*Idea of a University*

It's an exhausting process, even for just half an hour! And you'd probably hate to keep it up for the remaining twenty-three paragraphs of the article, most of them much longer. And yet, if you took this exercise seriously, you already have a slightly deeper understanding of concepts that come up almost daily on campus: the College of Liberal Arts, courses in the humanities, the college "core" requirements, maybe even Renaissance man. And I'd wager that you'd find the remaining pages of "What Is a Liberal Education?" much easier going because—no surprise here—Kagan continues to mention not only the terms above, but the ideas they embody and how they work their way into the present. If you are a conscientious reader, you'll find lots of other items to annotate in the essay—*Book of the Courtier*, Poggio Bracciolini, Georgian England, King Canute—but you'll soon find yourself fitting them into a pattern that looks more and more interesting.

And did you catch the phrase "in our time" in Kagan's second sentence? What's Kagan talking about? "Our time" for the article is way back in the Clinton administration. Putting this essay in context (see Chapters 1 and 2), you might search Donald Kagan online, where you'd discover quite easily that he was, in fact, deeply involved with educational issues, college curricula, and controversies over literary canons and multiculturalism. And, as Jaques in Shakespeare's *As You Like It* observes, "thereby hangs a tale." There's more to this story—and just about every story—for you to read about and discover.

What's the lesson here? For all the nasty things said about technology making us dumber (search Nicholas Carr in that regard), the fact is that online resources greatly enhance your capabilities as a critical reader if you employ them as the vast database of connected knowledge they represent. Sophisticated readers might come to Kagan's paragraph already aware of the liberal arts tradition, nodding smugly at allusions to Cicero and Cardinal Newman. Bully for them.

With a little competent Web surfing, you can gain enough traction to take on a formidable text like Kagan's with confidence. Connecting the dots on your own, you'll find layers of meaning in a text rather than just catching its drift. And what you gain from going one-on-one with hard readings like "What Is a Liberal Education?" and hundreds like it you'll encounter in a typical college career is competence in new areas of knowledge that, in the long run, will make you a sophisticated, maybe even learned, reader yourself. How cool is that?

YOUR TURN

19. You'd think logical fallacies would be easy to spot and even easier to agree upon. But that's not always the case. Readers often disagree about the interpretation of fallacies. For instance, either/or choices (usually considered suspect) sometimes seem reasonable, especially during election campaigns. And what appears to you like an irrelevant personal attack on the character of an admirable public figure (and an example of the *ad hominem* fallacy) might seem justified as an assault on a crafty swindler to your neighbor. Browse some blogs such as Politico, Huffington Post, or The Daily Caller to find examples of statements or claims that might seem fallacious to some readers but not to others.

20. Pick a passage from a reading you find especially challenging and, following the method used for "What Is a Liberal Education?" on pages 80-81, pull out the items you would look up to make the material more accessible. Then look up those items, keeping track of the time. How long did it take you to do the annotation? What did you learn?

TWO

You, the Respondent

Some books are to be tasted, others to be swallowed, and some few
to be chewed and digested; that is, some books are to be read only in
parts; others to be read, but not curiously; and some few to be read
wholly, and with diligence and attention.

— FRANCIS BACON, "OF STUDIES" (1625)

In many respects, Part Two of *A Reader's Guide to College Writing* is
about figuring out which books and readings fit into which of Francis
Bacon's famous categories. The first several chapters in this section deal
with strategies for reading texts closely enough to identify their claims
and make sound judgments about them. While some of these lessons
are simple, others will push your limits, asking you to read more attentively than usual. But as you figure out how texts work, you'll be more at
ease joining the conversations that good readings kindle. Far too many
readers grow quiet when such opportunities arise because they don't
know how to get inside a book or article and ask salient questions. This
section gives you the tools to join class discussions ably, confidently, and
productively.

7

In the case of good books, the point is
not to see how many of them you can
get through, but rather how many can
get through to you.

— Mortimer J. Adler

Claims and Contents

We become critics and commentators—that is, speakers or writers engaging in public dialogue—whenever we encounter ideas that trigger a response. Most people respond to ideas best in conversation with others, whether at a public forum, on an editorial page, in a social network, or, most relevant here, in a classroom. To move from *reader* to *respondent,* you need to recognize the ways experienced writers cue their claims and keep readers invested in a subject, especially when the going gets tough. If you suspect that there are lots of such rhetorical maneuvers, many more than you could usefully remember, you'd be correct. But writers don't memorize moves; they just make them. Then they refine them. Then they try yet again until they're satisfied that their ideas and audiences have both been well served. And that's your job, too. It all starts with paying careful attention.

Look for a Thesis: Statement and Proof

From elementary school on, you've likely been taught to read nonfiction (maybe even some fiction) by first looking for a point, often summarized in a thesis statement—a single, declarative sentence, conveniently provided by a writer at the end of an introductory paragraph or section. That thesis, you were assured, identifies an already narrowed subject, ties it to an assertion, and hints at supporting evidence to come. You know the routine well, likely having advanced your own educational career by producing steadily more sophisticated versions of thesis statements for papers of your own:

My teacher is good because she is kind and smart.

Our middle school needs better computers because we need to know how to use them and because it leads to jobs.

A familiar model: A claim supported by evidence makes a thesis.

If Bowie High offered more AP classes, more students would get into better colleges and be able to place out of freshman courses once they get there.

Because local tax bases are contracting, local community colleges often can no longer offer practical, job-oriented degrees and certificates that would attract students and increase their lagging graduation rates.

There's nothing wrong with thesis statements. Their pedigree is ancient. Even Aristotle thought that arguments needed just two parts: statement and proof, claim and support. Add an introduction and a conclusion, and call it a wrap.

So look for a thesis in nonfiction writing, especially in reports and arguments. You'll find this move routinely in professional articles within scientific fields, where the strategy of offering claims and evidence delivered in language free of bias and personality mirrors the objectivity researchers strive for in their work. Here's an example from a report describing problems with animals cloned using a technique called somatic cell nuclear transfer (SCNT):

Topic sentence

Although some clones may develop into healthy animals, the low success rate of SCNT is linked to the fact that donor cells are often reprogrammed incorrectly. In fact, gene expression analyses and extensive phenotypic characterization of cloned animals suggest that most, if not all, clones suffer from at

Supporting evidence

least subtle abnormalities.[7] Several studies present research data implying that even apparently normal cloned animals may have subtle abnormalities in gene expression.[8] The most severe errors in reprogramming result in death, obvious malformations, or metabolic derangements. They are reflected in the low success rate of cloning, the prenatal difficulties observed in some newborn clones, and occasional examples of altered metabolic pathways in very young animals.[9]

7. Konrad Hochedlinger and Rudolf Jaenisch, "Nuclear transplantation: lessons from frogs and mice," *Current Opinion on Cell Biology* 14, no. 6 (2002): 741–748.

8. David Humpherys, et al., "Abnormal gene expression in cloned mice derived from embryonic stem cell and cumulus cell nuclei," *Proceedings of the National Academy of Sciences* 99, no. 20 (2002): 12889–12894; Ian Wilmut, "Are there any normal clones?" *Methods of Molecular Biology* 348 (2006): 307–318; David Humpherys, "Epigenetic instability in ES cells and cloned mice," *Science* 293, no. 5527 (2001): 95–97.

9. Center for Veterinary Medicine, *Animal Cloning: A Draft Risk Assessment*, 47.

—J. A. RIDDLE, "BRAVE NEW BEEF:
ANIMAL CLONING AND ITS IMPACTS"

The topic sentence is directly supported by a series of footnoted statements that point to specific supporting research. The presentation of information could not be more clear, dispassionate, or credible (and thereby, oddly, comforting). As a reader, you have all the stuff you need to assess this claim.

Plainspoken theses and topic sentences can be just as helpful and appealing in more blatantly argumentative prose. In fact, writers can rouse readers bored by evasive or bureaucratic chatter simply by saying precisely what's on their minds. Such statements have the virtue of clarity enhanced by confidence. The strategy works nicely, for instance, in a paragraph from Thomas L. Friedman's book *Hot, Flat, and Crowded*, its subtitle especially relevant here: *Why We Need a Green Revolution—and How It Can Renew America*. The first sentences are like neon arrows pointing to the claim (underlined):

> I cannot stress this point enough. If you take only one thing away from this book, please take this: We are not going to regulate our way out of the problems of the Energy-Climate Era. We can only innovate our way out, and the only way to do that is to mobilize the most effective and prolific system for transformational innovation and commercialization of new products ever created on the face of the earth—the U.S. marketplace. There is only one thing bigger than Mother Nature and that is Father Profit, and we have not even begun to enlist him in this struggle.

You wouldn't be wrong to think that the *entire* paragraph amounts to a thesis, a highly directive and emphatic one, doing its job of anticipating many of the arguments and strategies Friedman intends to offer in the book to rescue the planet from climate change. More important, as a reader, you now have a set point by which to judge that subsequent material.

Expect Variations: It Gets Complicated

Well, that seems surprisingly easy: statement and proof, claim and support, idea and evidence—a key to insightful reading. But the problem with reading mostly in terms of thesis statements and topic sentences is that, as mentioned in Chapter 4, when it comes to making points or winning arguments, experienced writers often steer clear of the anvil-simple essay structure taught in school. This fact becomes painfully obvious once you start reading a piece—or try your hand at paraphrasing it (see Chapter 10)—only to discover that your diligent search for a thesis turns up several plausible candidates. Or you realize that no single statement captures a writer's gist.

It happens all the time: You expect to find a well-behaved declarative sentence, and an author throws strings of questions at you or spreads a claim across whole paragraphs. Anticipate a commitment to a thesis in an opening paragraph and you find it lurking instead in the final pages, like the villain in a murder mystery. And those neatly aligned supporting reasons and/or evidence mustered to support the claim? They're scattered across the text too, leaving you to assemble the pieces, draw inferences, make connections, and figure things out on your own. Worse, the claims keep coming, and in various guises—as topic sentences, transitional sentences, concluding sentences, sometimes several within a single paragraph.

And yet somehow you, the reader, don't get lost. You aren't confused. And you certainly aren't bored.

What's going on here? Were teachers who championed orderly (often five-paragraph) essay structures in high school lying about how writing works? Not exactly. What you are discovering are strategies that competent authors (including you) routinely invent whenever they develop ideas. There are usually good reasons for their departures from conventional structures, motivated by specific rhetorical needs. Sometimes writers simply want ideas to take new turns, and so they modify them within paragraphs or sections, keeping readers alert and engaged. If a concept has multiple dimensions, writers may find ways to emphasize them all rather than to make just a single point. Or, when topics require subtlety and nuance, writers may even demand that readers follow all the twists and turns of their logic, as they share assumptions, definitions, and even some doubts. It's not always an easy excursion from *here* to *there*. If you're a smart reader, you settle in, fasten your seat belt, and learn to enjoy the whole trip — wrong turns, pit stops, and all.

> **Writers vary and invent structures in service to their ideas.**

How Writers Direct a Claim

Consider how even a structure as conventional as a paragraph with a lead-off topic sentence can be modified to keep readers focused on content. That's what happens to a relatively simple claim (chosen almost at random) from a book entitled *Traffic: Why We Drive the Way We Do* (notice how the subtitle provides valuable insight into its contents; see Chapter 1, pp. 9–10):

> The reason we have speedometers, and why you should pay attention to yours, is that drivers often do not have a clue about how fast they are actually traveling — even when they think they do. A study in New Zealand measured the speed of drivers as they passed children playing with a ball and waiting to cross the street. When questioned, drivers thought they were going at least 20 kilometers per hour (or about 12 miles per hour) more slowly than they really were (i.e., they thought they were going 18 to 25 miles per hour when they were really doing 31 to 37).
>
> —Tom Vanderbilt

> **Topic sentence offers a straightforward observation.**

Good sense so far about speedometers and driving, the second and third sentences predictably developing the opening one. But then the paragraph takes a slight turn:

> Sometimes it seems as if we need someone standing on the side of the road, actually reminding us how fast we are really going.

> **Claim changes direction.**

The initial focus on drivers and speed now seems less like a topic sentence than a lead-in to a slightly more focused idea, what author Tom Vanderbilt calls the "crucial feedback" that helps drivers to control their pace. Nine subsequent sentences (it's a long paragraph) develop this idea by providing various examples of feedback mechanisms—for instance, flashing "speed trailer" signs, painted dots on roadways, or wind and road noise. Feedback becomes a new focus in the paragraph, logically related to speedometers and speeding, but not quite the same thing. So even this relatively simple paragraph on a mundane topic throws readers a curve. Maybe its opening sentence should have been more predictive, mentioning that concept of feedback so we can see it coming. Here's a possible revision:

Claim includes all points—but is dull.

The reason we have speedometers is that drivers often do not have a clue about how fast they are actually traveling, and so they require all the feedback they can get to keep their speed under control.

Or maybe Vanderbilt simply did not want to pack quite so many ideas into a single lead sentence and then have the remainder of the paragraph do nothing more than disgorge evidence. So he gives us a mid-paragraph blip—a turn that further develops an idea to keep us interested. Writers do that.

The technique of shifting or expanding the content works because, in reports and arguments, claims provide the push that moves readers along; they direct the flow of evidence and supporting reasons. Their placement, even within a single paragraph, is a rhetorical choice, a decision about how to influence readers or pique their interest: Do you lay down all your cards at once, or show them one at a time? That's a strategy to observe as a reader and to mull over when you outline a case of your own.

How Writers Orchestrate a Claim

Now consider an even more elaborate strategy for making claims and developing content, this from a book on unrelenting problems in American schools by Diane Ravitch, a highly respected authority on education. Near the end of *The Death and Life of the Great American School System: How Testing and Choice Are Undermining Education,* she draws together insights she has gained from her research. Here's the opening volley of the section, with its topic sentence marked:

Topic sentence

Our schools will not improve if we continually reorganize their structure and management without regard for their essential purpose. Our educational problems are a function of our lack of educational vision, not a management problem that requires the enlistment of an army of business consultants. Certainly we should mobilize expert managerial talent to make sure that school facilities are well maintained, that teachers have adequate supplies, that noninstructional services function smoothly, and that schools are using their resources wisely. But organizational changes cannot by themselves create a sound education program or raise education to the heights of excellence we want.

You'll recognize the familiar *statement and proof* (*claim and support; idea and evidence*) move here again, though the proof part of the paragraph looks more like a series of ideas and principles developed earlier in the book, and these specific ideas have now been recruited to support a more inclusive claim. Ravitch moves on:

> Our schools will not improve if elected officials intrude into pedagogical territory and make decisions that properly should be made by professional educators. Congress and state legislatures should not tell teachers how to teach, any more than they should tell surgeons how to perform operations. Nor should the curriculum of the schools be the subject of a political negotiation among people who are neither knowledgeable about teaching nor well educated. Pedagogy—that is, how to teach—is rightly the professional domain of individual teachers. Curriculum—that is, what to teach—should be determined by professional educators and scholars, after due public deliberation, acting with authority vested in them by schools, districts, or states.

This topic sentence parallels the earlier one.

You see how easy it is to establish a pattern, one that continues in the opening sentences of the next three paragraphs:

> Our schools will not improve if we continue to focus only on reading and mathematics while ignoring the other studies that are essential elements of good education.

Another parallel topic sentence . . .

> Our schools will not improve if we value only what tests measure.

and another . . .

> Our schools will not improve if we rely exclusively on tests as the means of deciding the fate of students, teachers, principals, and schools.

and another

Enough? Not quite. *Nine* more paragraphs follow in this section, each using the same basic (or "parallel") structure for its claim, the distinctive topic sentences giving them an orchestrated sense of power and cohesiveness. As a reader, you can feel Ravitch driving her points home—not to furnish new information but to make readers (who presumably have reviewed all the preceding pages) feel the weight of the crisis and to rouse them to action. Obviously, there's no way to miss Ravitch's implication that American education is in a pickle.

Sprawled across several pages, the matching paragraphs morph into something grander than a thesis statement. And, as a critical reader, you can review the section and say, yes, Professor Ravitch's call for reform in education is eloquent and convincing.

Writers make rhetorical moves to influence readers. Or you might look at the strategy and wonder whether all the repetition and parallelism is too emotional for her subject. That would be a potential objection you might make to her claim. Either way, by reading carefully, you can learn something from Ravitch's rhetorical maneuver: *Writers control the flow of information by the way they state their claims*. In other words, claims can be influential not only in what they say *but in how they say it*.

How Writers Lay Out Complex Ideas

But claims aren't always so direct and accessible as Ravitch's. What might a writer do when an idea requires readers to follow *and* understand a complex logical chain of ideas? Repetition alone wouldn't carry the argument, but there are other options that require you to pay careful attention, or maybe even highlight or outline the reasoning. Take a look at the intricate argument that follows from Walter Benn Michaels's controversial book (the title says it all): *The Trouble with Diversity: How We Learned to Love Identity and Ignore Inequality*. In the work, Michaels argues that the passionate concern of the political left (socialists, progressives, liberals, Democrats, and so on) with racism, sexism, and other identity issues has distracted it from what he regards as a greater problem in America: a permanent and unequal distribution of wealth.

At one point in the argument, Michaels wants to demonstrate that an obsession with group identity leads some on the left to extend protections rightfully given to groups who suffer prejudice on the basis of unchangeable characteristics (race, gender) to groups with whom we simply have differences of opinion (atheists, believers). It is a distinction not easy to grasp. And so Michaels goes to great lengths to explain it via a set of sequenced claims and rhetorical questions (underlined):

> If, as one of the Pew polls suggests, 66 percent of Americans have an "unfavorable" view of atheists, not only is there nothing surprising about that, there's nothing wrong with it. If you are devout, why shouldn't you have an unfavorable view of someone who seems to you profoundly mistaken about what you regard as one of the most fundamental issues of human life?

Provocative claim

Rhetorical question

Clear enough: It makes sense for people of faith to disapprove of atheists. But it is a setup. Michaels continues:

> And the argument obviously works both ways. If you don't believe in God, how can you help but have an "unfavorable" view of all the deeply deluded people who do? That's why when Alan Wolfe [a prominent political scientist] says that just as Americans have become "more sensitive to the inequalities of race and gender," they should "extend the same sympathy to those who are different in the sincerity of their belief," he is missing the point.

Claim

Rhetorical question

Are you surprised that author Michaels rejects Alan Wolfe's tolerance of religious difference? You shouldn't be after he asserts that *the argument obviously works both ways*. The logic in the remainder of the paragraph then turns on a fundamental distinction Michaels makes between responses to people based on *prejudice* and those based on *disagreement*. The contrast sets up a series of balanced claims and parallel examples, the obvious ones underlined, that frame the argument:

> He [Wolfe] is mistaking an inappropriate response to people who seem to us different (prejudice) with an inappropriate one to people who seem to us wrong (disagreement). The sympathy we extend to those who have been victimized by prejudice requires us to stop being prejudiced against them; the sympathy we might extend to those who have different beliefs cannot possibly require us to stop thinking they're mistaken. So although it's no doubt true that we shouldn't hate anyone, treating Christians (or atheists) with contempt is not the same as treating black people with contempt; even if we hate Christians (or atheists), we hate them for what they believe,

Complex claim

Contrasting two claims explains their differences.

not for what they are. When, in the run-up to John Roberts's confirmation hearings for the Supreme Court, Senator Patrick Leahy declared that we should be as "religious-blind" as we are "color-blind" in considering the qualifications of nominees, he got this exactly wrong. We should be color-blind because color has nothing to do with beliefs. But we shouldn't be religion-blind because religion has everything to do with beliefs. In the public square, the crucial thing about Christians, Muslims, Jews, et cetera, is not whether (like blacks and Asians and women) they are entitled to respect but whether they can convince us that their beliefs are true.

Got that? Read the passage again if you didn't follow it the first time. (I didn't.)

As you'll discover, Michaels structures the language of his paragraph to track the chain of his thoughts and make his logic accessible by emphasizing several forceful comparisons and contrasts. He no doubt labored over the delicate section (after all, he writes *we hate them for what they believe*) to make his claim plausible and convincing. As a reader, you can't race through the argument either: Its twists and turns slow you down (perhaps deliberately) and demand your attention, even though the language of the argument itself doesn't throw impediments in your way—no technical terms or post-modern abstractions here.

But you can see, too, that such sentence-level gymnastics open up possibilities for a reader. You're in a position, naturally, to ask what happens when the distinction Michaels makes between *prejudice* and *disagreement* is extended to other groups: Who exactly is protected and who isn't? Or you might probe the core distinction he insists on: Are the boundaries of *prejudice* and *disagreement* as firm in practice as they are made to seem in this paragraph? Has Michaels perhaps even oversimplified the character of religious belief, making it seem like a purely intellectual choice, not a cultural inheritance as deep as race or gender? We're a long way from simple statements and predictable topic sentences here, but if the logic and language are not beyond your abilities to understand, then you are ready to appreciate the robust content.

The defect, then, in reading works expecting merely to extract conventional theses, topic sentences, or other predictable patterns you learned in school is not that you won't find them if you

Writers may expect you to read very slowly and very carefully.

try (you will, especially when preparing summaries and paraphrases). It's that *in your single-mindedness to find patterns*, you'll miss the really interesting and endlessly variable rhetorical maneuvers writers make as they try to keep you reading—the ways they roll out their content and claims, give them heft and traction, make them seem solid and important. This is the meat and potatoes of serious writing, stuff that can't be readily outlined or diagrammed. But it is exactly what you pick up by careful attention to challenging authors. It's why you're being asked to engage with such works and respond to them. So don't be discouraged by tough reading. By tracking writers this closely, you learn how ideas take shape, how arguments get made, and how and precisely where you might later take them apart.

YOUR TURN

21. Claims aren't limited to thesis statements. In fact, most reports and arguments develop as a series of assertions. Find a short article or argument (a newspaper editorial or opinion piece might be ideal) and underline every sentence that might be considered as a claim. Then see if you can distinguish between sentences assertive enough to seem like genuine thesis statements or topic sentences and others that provide the facts, illustrations, or discussion necessary to develop the more significant statements. How do writers signal what sentences you should pay attention to?

22. Identify a passage in a recently assigned reading that stands out for being notably and elaborately patterned like the Ravitch example in this chapter (pp. 90–91). Then analyze the selection line by line, doing your best to explain how it works rhetorically—that is, how it conveys its ideas memorably or effectively to you.

23. Find a passage in a recently assigned reading that you find as daunting as the selection in this chapter (pp. 93–94) from Walter Benn Michaels's *The Trouble with Diversity*. Copy a page or so from the piece by hand (preferably a section that stands on its own) and annotate it carefully, marking key claims, supporting evidence, and logical moves. When you are done, try to summarize what you have read in one or two sentences. (For help with summarizing, see Chapter 10, pp. 120–24.)

8

... a good piece of legislation is like a good sentence or a good piece of music. Everybody can recognize it.

— BARACK OBAMA

Explain and Imply

While a candidate for the U.S. Senate in 1994, Barack Obama explained to the *New Yorker*'s William Finnegan how legislation worked: "A good compromise, a good piece of legislation, is like a good sentence or a good piece of music. Everybody can recognize it. They say, 'Huh. It works. It makes sense.'" You may find that impressive reports, convincing arguments, and even memorable narratives evoke similar responses — an unvoiced "Okay" at seeing an idea thoughtfully presented or a case neatly argued. Expanding on what we started in Chapter 7, we'll consider now exactly how writers achieve these effects, focusing specifically on techniques for framing evidence and building "It works" moments. In the process, we'll figure out where you — in the role of critical reader and respondent — enter the discussion.

Examine Evidence: Support a Point

In Chapter 7, we mentioned that Aristotle described arguments as simple, two-part actions (p. 86): Offer a claim and follow it up with the facts. But we found that too easy. Whenever words are involved, the presentation of evidence gets complicated and requires rhetorical choices — think of lawyers in courtrooms presenting closing arguments. Writers have to mull over which data, offered in what order, and with what emphases will have

Consider how evidence has been selected and sequenced — to what effect?

the greatest impact. And you, the reader, then need to assess how that evidence has been arranged, stacked, or even skewed.

Sometimes a simple data dump seems in order: *This is so for this reason and this reason and especially for this reason.* That's the pattern you might find in the following lengthy paragraph from Diane Ravitch—who should be familiar to you by now as a critic of the American educational system. She wants readers to grasp how thoroughly problems with schools have been documented, and so she lists works that corroborate and amplify her own concerns:

The issue	We have known for many years that we need to improve our schools. We keep stumbling, however, because there is widespread disagreement about what should be improved, what we mean by improvement, and who should do it. A
Evidence	strong case for improvement was made by *A Nation at Risk*, which warned in 1983 that our students and our schools were
Evidence	not keeping up with their international peers. Since then, many reports and surveys have demonstrated that large numbers of young people leave school knowing little or nothing about history, literature, foreign languages, the arts, geography, civics,
Evidence	or science. The consequences of inadequate education have been recently documented in books such as Mark Bauerlein's *The Dumbest Generation*, Rick Shenkman's *Just How Stupid Are We?*, and Susan Jacoby's *The Age of American Unreason*. These
The problem, now well supported	authors describe in detail the alarming gaps in Americans' knowledge and understanding of political issues, scientific phenomena, historical events, literary allusions, and almost everything else one needs to know to make sense of the world. Without knowledge and understanding, one tends to become a passive spectator rather than an active participant in the key decisions of our time.

—*THE DEATH AND LIFE OF THE GREAT AMERICAN SCHOOL SYSTEM: HOW TESTING AND CHOICE ARE UNDERMINING EDUCATION*

You could zip through a paragraph like this thinking that an author is just going through the motions, giving curtain calls to all the stuff she's read and the good company she keeps. But, rhetorically, the weight of the evidence Ravitch ropes together falls upon the phrase "alarming gaps" late in the paragraph. Clearly, something needs to be done to solve the problems

Ravitch and her troupe of experts have documented repeatedly and at length. Accumulating evidence in this fashion is usually a smart move.

Sometimes writers don't even have to name sources to make a point. Notice how in the following paragraphs, the authors of *Reckles$ Endangerment,* Gretchen Morgenson and Joshua Rosner (whom you've also met before in Part One) make readers keenly aware that some unspecified critics foresaw problems with a government initiative to increase homeownership in the United States—a program they blame for the 2008 financial meltdown and subsequent recession. Just as important, the paragraph raises the specter of powerful, though also unnamed, private and public interests who silenced these Cassandras (Cassandra was a character from Greek mythology whose dire predictions were always ignored):

> And yet, there were those who questioned the merits of the homeownership drive and tried to alert regulators and policymakers to its unintended consequences.
>
> A handful of analysts and investors, for example, tried to warn of the rising tide of mortgage swindlers; they were met with a deafening silence. Consumer lawyers, seeing the poisonous nature of many home loans, tried to outlaw them. But they were beaten back by an army of lenders and their lobbyists. Some brave souls in academia argued that renting a home was, for many, better than ownership. They were refuted by government studies using manipulated figures or flawed analysis to conclude that homeownership was a desired goal for all.
>
> *—Reckles$ Endangerment*

Identifies major players but gives no names

Readers of course are eager, after this paragraph, to learn more about these analysts, consumer advocates, and academic brave souls and, even more so, about their powerful opponents. If the authors' entire argument were no more factual than these paragraphs, it would carry little weight, but the passage comes in the prologue to a 300-page book. It is the setup for more factual claims to come, the thirty-second trailer for a blockbuster.

But lists are easy. As a reader you may find yourself far more interested when writers make you reason your way to their conclusions rather than just sift through facts they've dropped on you. Believe it or not, Aristotle had this concept covered.

Fact-based, countable, and documentable evidence and testimony, he argued, could be faked or falsified, and presenting it took little skill—so it was an "inartistic" approach to persuasion. In his mind, a more artful rhetorician was one who offered well-reasoned positions to audiences based on sound ethical principles and clarified by memorable illustrations and examples. Tugging at a few heartstrings was okay, too. *Modern audiences may prefer hard evidence* (Aristotle never watched *CSI*), but you'll find that writers today continue to use these artistic techniques because they work.

Consider the following paragraph from Thomas L. Friedman explaining quite reasonably in *Hot, Flat, and Crowded* why it has been so tough to get people to face up to the consequences and costs of climate change caused by our predominantly carbon-based economy. He's pushing for a high carbon tax in the book and knows it's a hard sell, so he tries *an artistic appeal to values and sympathy*:

Emotional appeals to common values

> The big challenge we have today in energizing a real green revolution is that the people most affected by any climate change are not likely to be "us." The people who will be most affected by energy and natural resources supply and demand, petrodictatorship, climate change, energy poverty, and biodiversity loss don't get to vote—because they haven't been born yet. They are the next generation. Historically, political reform movements emerge when the have-nots, the people who are negatively affected or aggrieved by some policy or situation become numerous enough to bring their weight to bear in a democratic system. But this green issue, particularly climate change, "doesn't pit haves versus have nots," says Johns Hopkins University foreign policy expert Michael Mandelbaum. It pits "the present versus the future—today's generation versus its kids and unborn grandchildren. The problem is the future can't organize. Workers organize to get worker rights. Old people organize to get health care. But how can the future get organized? It can't lobby. It can't protest."

Emotional appeal supports responsible energy policies.

You likely find this generational appeal at least plausible, especially if you haven't heard it before: It makes good sense. Notice how deftly Friedman presents his version of the future, an unborn generation living in energy poverty under a "petrodictatorship" because of decisions people make (or fail to make) today. Who's going to act for them if we don't make some hard choices now? His reasoning isn't quite factual or evidential, and yet you may find it satisfying and potentially convincing.

Or consider the "artistic" tack Diane Ravitch takes to amplify her appeal for better educational policy with a memorable and persuasive example of the sort Aristotle would especially admire:

> The policies we are following today are unlikely to improve our schools. Indeed, much of what policymakers now demand will very likely make the schools less effective and may further degrade the intellectual capacity of our citizenry. The schools will surely be failures if students graduate knowing how to choose the right option from four bubbles on a multiple-choice test, but unprepared to lead fulfilling lives, to be responsible citizens, and to make good choices for themselves, their families, and our society.

Appeal to common values

> —THE DEATH AND LIFE OF THE GREAT
> AMERICAN SCHOOL SYSTEM: HOW TESTING AND
> CHOICE ARE UNDERMINING EDUCATION

If writing were a soccer match, the broadcaster would shout "Score!" Any American who has ever endured a timed, high-stakes, multiple-choice examination (and that's just about all of us) will identify with Ravitch's convincing illustration.

But shouldn't you be wary of emotional appeals like this one? Doubtless you've heard of unscrupulous speakers, writers, and especially advertisers scheming to make us act contrary to our best interests by appealing to baser instincts—how else to explain our national fondness for burgers layered with cheese and bacon, an unhealthy meal choice by any rational standards? But is it even possible for writers or speakers reasoning their way through serious issues *not* to touch on matters that raise concern, sympathy, or empathy in audiences? National security, for example, may be a highly technical concern, but it is grounded in fears that our way of life might be threatened; economic issues connect to feelings of power, security, well-being, and happiness; educational matters are inseparable from questions of equity or dreams about the future. I don't mean to privilege emotional arguments, but thoughtful writers—particularly those advocating strongly for a cause—do use them legitimately to give logic and good reasons a human face. And you should recognize when it is done as well to give proper support to a claim.

Emotional appeals humanize fact-filled arguments.

Here, for example, is Barbara Ehrenreich explaining to an audience of fairly privileged Americans why low-wage workers don't often buck the systems oppressing them or do more to pull themselves up by their bootstraps. The paragraph follows earlier ones demonstrating that blue-collar employees have few resources for improving their lot when compared to more affluent Americans. Without basic economic information or skills, they are discouraged by employers from organizing or exercising their rights and cannot easily locate other jobs:

> So if low-wage workers do not always behave in an economically rational way, that is, as free agents within a capitalist democracy, it is because they dwell in a place that is neither free nor in any way democratic. When you enter the low-wage workplace—and many of the medium-wage workplaces as well—you check your civil liberties at the door, leave America and all it supposedly stands for behind, and learn to zip your lips for the duration of the shift. The consequences of this routine surrender go beyond the issues of wages and poverty. We can hardly pride ourselves on being the world's preeminent democracy, after all, if large numbers of citizens spend half their waking hours in what amounts, in plain terms, to a dictatorship.
>
> —*Nickel and Dimed: On (Not) Getting By in America*

The basic terms of Ehrenreich's discussion are clear and reasonable: Low-wage workers don't improve their lot because, practically speaking, they are not free to make better economic choices. But the words and phrases she chooses have powerful emotional connotations: "check your civil liberties at the door," "zip your lips," "half their waking hours in . . . a dictatorship." And, certainly, you didn't miss Ehrenreich's pronoun shifts from second-person *you*, inviting privileged readers to imagine dwelling "in a place that is neither free nor in any way democratic," to first-person *we*, nudging them to take responsibility for the situation.

Notice how language choices frame emotional appeals.

Do arguments like this cross a line? Well, that's precisely what you need to decide: Does Ehrenreich's amplification of her point persuade you or does it lead you to think she's manipulating the situation? The provocative terms invite you to review her reasoning: Are workplaces for many Americans really "dictatorships"? You may have to reread preceding paragraphs (or entire chapters in her book) to determine how good the evidence is for a claim this powerful, emotional, and perhaps extreme.

Find Meaning: Read between the Lines

"It makes sense" moments occur when writers provide exactly the evidence or reasoning that audiences need at a given moment to understand a claim. Suddenly, everything is illuminated. Yet not every author wants readers to come to their work expecting to find assertions supported by data—as you discover when you encounter the ambiguous, metaphorical, even contrary language in some of your assigned reading, especially literary narratives. I don't have to tell you that novelists are usually more interested in creating provocative experiences than in proving claims. (For a review of narratives versus reports or arguments, see Chapter 4.) They offer possibilities, hint at meanings, but leave to you the pleasures of interpretation, the putting-together-of-parts that makes sense out of works that don't (usually) offer helpful prefaces, TOCs, notes, or bibliographies. And by sense, I *don't* mean logical, clear, rational, or step-by-step, syllogistic reasoning.

Literary texts often imply meanings rather than explain or state them.

Consider a paragraph as simple and provocative as the following one, which opens Chris Cleave's novel *Little Bee*. We are overhearing the thoughts of a sixteen-year-old Nigerian girl who has fled her native country and been held in a detention center in England, a self-described "born-again citizen of the developing world":

> Most days I wish I was a British pound coin instead of an African girl. Everyone would be pleased to see me coming. Maybe I would visit you for the weekend and then suddenly, because I am fickle like that, I would visit with the man from the corner shop instead—but you would not be sad because you would be eating a cinnamon bun, or drinking a cold Coca-Cola from the can, and you would never think of me again. We would be happy, like lovers who met on holiday and forgot each other's names.

The girl's wish is unsettling: Her odd desire to become a currency of exchange welcomed everywhere, useful, and yet almost invisible, provides a glimpse into the world she currently inhabits, though we don't yet know what that might be. She goes on, revealing a bit more:

> A pound coin can go wherever it thinks it will be safest. It can cross deserts and oceans and leave the sound of gunfire and the bitter smell of burning thatch behind.

The coin, we understand, has a power that the girl does not possess, and it is connected in her mind to some grim past—the quick mention of "burning thatch." Just a paragraph or two further on, her story comes more into focus; we get it that the narrator—the African girl—is confined by a relationship to British authority and power, embodied in that coin. She is dropping clues to explain her relationship to a new country and culture:

Metaphor develops the character.

> How I would love to be a British pound. A pound is free to travel to safety, and we are free to watch it go. This is the human triumph. This is called, *globalization*. A girl like me gets stopped at immigration, but a pound can leap the turnstiles, and dodge the tackles of those big men with their uniform caps, and jump straight into a waiting airport taxi. *Where to, sir?* Western Civilization, my good man, and make it snappy.

Themes, motifs, and ideas introduced at the beginning of a literary narrative like this one commonly expand over the course of the work and may not be resolved until its very end—if then. Your role as a reader is to note them, collect them, find patterns or contrasts, merge ideas and images with characters and action, and immerse yourself in the unfolding experience, allowing yourself to become part of the story and (don't forget) taking pleasure and knowledge from it.

Literary study can be the work of a professional lifetime, but you are native to literary experiences. They've been part of your world from childhood—remember those *stories* we talked about early in this book (Chapter 4)? You don't need to be an expert to respond to the African girl in *Little Bee*, but you better lend an ear to what this narrator (and any others you encounter) reports. You've got to watch how a tale moves forward—but don't expect a predictable sequence. You've got to become comfortable with ideas offered by indirection and suggestion, caught up in metaphor and, perhaps, tinged with irony, sarcasm, or even humor. Enjoy the experience and share it.

That's not to say you'll *always* be puzzled by narratives. Junior, the semi-autobiographical narrator of Sherman Alexie's *The Absolutely True Diary of a Part-Time Indian,* speaks pretty directly late in the book, explaining a problem endemic to the Spokane reservation where he still lives:

> After my grandmother died, I felt like crawling into the coffin with her. After my dad's best friend got shot in the face, I wondered if I was destined to get shot in the face, too.
>
> Considering how many young Spokanes have died in car wrecks, I'm pretty sure it's my destiny to die in a wreck, too.
>
> Jeez, I've been to so many funerals in my short life.
>
> I'm fourteen years old and I've been to forty-two funerals.
>
> That's really the biggest difference between Indians and white people.
>
> A few of my white classmates have been to a grandparent's funeral. And a few have lost an uncle or aunt. And one guy's brother died of leukemia when he was in the third grade.
>
> But there's nobody who has been to more than five funerals.
>
> All my white friends can count their deaths on one hand.
>
> I can count my fingers, toes, arms, legs, eyes, ears, nose, penis, butt cheeks, and nipples, and still not get close to my deaths.
>
> And you know what the worst part is? The unhappy part? About 90 percent of the deaths have been because of alcohol.
>
> Gordy gave me this book by a Russian dude named Tolstoy, who wrote: "Happy families are all alike; every unhappy family is unhappy in its own way." Well, I hate to argue with a Russian genius, but Tolstoy didn't know Indians. And he didn't know that all Indian families are unhappy for the same exact reason: the fricking booze.
>
> Yep, so let me pour a drink for Tolstoy and let him think hard about the true definition of unhappy families.

(margin note: Dramatic voice develops the story.)

At first, these paragraphs seem less artful than those from *Little Bee* with its self-conscious reflections on the British pound. And politically incorrect, too, maybe—all that negativity about Native American communities. But then Junior, the narrator, like the book's author, is a Spokane Indian with license to complain about "fricking booze," and he's just fourteen and so speaks like any slightly foulmouthed teen. Except we discover that he's read at least the opening page of Leo Tolstoy's *Anna Karenina,* a book given to him by a white-kid genius, whom the narrator makes a point to befriend earlier in the story. And

Junior's critique of the famous novelist makes us think twice about the Native American boy and his experiences. There's a lot going on in his mind and we want to figure out what. And it turns out that's also the reason the narrator writes (and draws cartoons): to figure *himself* out. And no five-paragraph essay will suffice to pluck out the heart of his mystery.

Narratives, especially those you'll likely read in academic settings, tend to be about processes of discovery. In this way, they may offer claims as readily and often as reports and arguments do. But their authors make such assertions as much to evoke responses from you as to advance any arguments of their own. Reading of this kind, full of suggestions and implications, is not limited, of course, just to narratives and fiction. Reports and arguments, too, can be open-ended and exploratory, especially when they deal with issues that evade easy resolution—think of religious wars, endemic poverty, the meaning of art. Evocative, open-ended writing in any genre is by design disconcerting, more thought-provoking than settling, more truth-like than truthful. Yet this refusal to offer easy answers is exactly what you should learn to prize. It's a cliché to suggest that you have to be "open to such experiences." But, sometimes, even clichés are true.

> **YOUR TURN**
>
> **24.** Find a recent editorial or newspaper op-ed on a political, social, or cultural issue of some concern to you, preferably a text you can print out or mark up. Go through the piece carefully to locate its key claims. Then spend time examining the evidence it offers to support its claims. Try to separate the factual evidence from evidence based more upon reasoning or emotional appeals. What types of evidence does it use? Does it show a preference for one type over the other? Can you offer a reason to explain the author's preference, perhaps based upon the subject matter of the piece?
>
> **25.** If you have a best-loved passage from a literary narrative of any kind (fiction or nonfiction) or perhaps a favorite short poem, write a paragraph to explain how you think it works to someone who has never read it. Use the analysis of the selection from *The Absolutely True Diary of a Part-Time Indian* on page 105 as a model.

9

Dispute, Concede, and Rebut

In *On Liberty* (1859), philosopher John Stuart Mill made a cogent recommendation to all who would engage in public discussion of "morals, religion, politics, social relations, and the business of life"—that is, just about anything except "natural philosophy," which today we call science. Mill exhorts readers to follow the practice of Cicero, the great Roman lawyer, politician, and rhetorician:

> The greatest orator, save one, of antiquity, has left it on record that he always studied his adversary's case with as great, if not with still greater, intensity than even his own. What Cicero practised as the means of forensic success, requires to be imitated by all who study any subject in order to arrive at the truth. He who knows only his own side of the case, knows little of that. His reasons may be good, and no one may have been able to refute them. But if he is equally unable to refute the reasons on the opposite side; if he does not so much as know what they are, he has no ground for preferring either opinion.

As you see, it's not enough just to know your position in an argument. You've got to understand the reasoning of people on every side of an issue well enough to anticipate and answer their plausible objections. Only then, according to Mill, can you even claim to have an opinion of your own. Naturally, knowing an argument in full—eggs to apples, as the Romans would say to describe a full-course meal—enables you to dispute accepted ideas strategically, concede points gracefully (if it makes sense to do that), and defend your own positions powerfully whenever that's necessary. In this chapter, we'll examine all these moves from the point of view of a critical reader watching how other writers manage the strategies artfully and, as composers direct, *con brio*.

This is going to be fun.

Dispute and Challenge: Build Interest

Cicero's ideal echoed by Mill—to know an adversary's positions as well as one's own—is strong stuff, but creative, too. As we've already noted, much of what you read in college will be written in response to what other writers and researchers have professed. Sometimes the work you are reading adds to or builds upon existing claims. But just as often, writers frame their ideas as straightforward challenges to conventional opinions: They repudiate unfounded beliefs or reject failed or ineffective policies.

Composing this way can be a rhetorical ploy, writers setting up big, easy targets to make themselves look like sharpshooters. When a victim is too obvious or familiar, it's described as a "straw man" and the attack is even labeled an argumentative fallacy (see Chapter 6, p. 78): Republicans going after fat-cat labor bosses again or Democrats demanding that the rich should pay their fair share. As a reader, you're better served when writers examine consequential and nuanced issues and offer fresh and coherent arguments, providing you with openings for analysis as well as models for your own work. And, heck, it's just more fun to read writers who challenge deeply rooted prejudices and/or take on villains with the means to strike back: *You might believe this claim, but the fact is _____.*

Enter Malcolm Gladwell, myth-slayer. His *Outliers* is a book-length defense of the claim—contrary to common belief—that "extraordinary achievement is less about talent than it is about opportunity." What? Stefani Germanotta and Wolfgang Amadeus Mozart didn't make it on their musical talent alone? Say it isn't so, Malcolm:

> "Lift up your heads," Robert Winthrop told the crowd many years ago at the unveiling of a statue of the great hero of American independence Benjamin Franklin, "and look at the image of a man who rose from nothing, who owed nothing to

Conventional
opinion

parentage or patronage, who enjoyed no advantages of early education which are not open—a hundredfold open—to yourselves, who performed the most menial services in the businesses in which his early life was employed, but who lived to stand before Kings, and died to leave a name which the world will never forget."

In *Outliers*, I want to convince you that these kinds of personal explanations of success don't work. People don't rise from nothing. We do owe something to parentage and patronage. The people who stand before kings may look like they did it all by themselves. But in fact they are invariably the beneficiaries of hidden advantages and extraordinary opportunities and cultural legacies that allow them to learn and work hard and make sense of the world in ways others cannot. It makes a difference where and when we grew up.

Challenge

Why, that's absurd, you think, and then read more to find how Gladwell can possibly support so un-American a claim. And so dissent becomes a way to draw readers in and to suggest alternative views that might change cultural assumptions and expectations. Gladwell wants us to see a bigger picture.

Writers can draw you in by provoking you.

The technique is used gleefully by economist Steven D. Levitt and writer Stephen J. Dubner, authors of the hugely popular *Freakonomics: A Rogue Economist Explores the Hidden Side of Everything*. Note the "rogue" in the title. Here's an example of their appealing repudiation of a "truism," part of a discussion of misconceptions about money in American elections:

And what about the other half of the election truism—that the amount of money spent on campaign finance is obscenely huge? In a typical election period that includes campaigns for the presidency, the Senate, and the House of Representatives, about $1 billion is spent per year—which sounds like a lot of money, unless you care to measure it against something seemingly less important than democratic elections.

Conventional opinion

Wait for it.

It is the same amount, for instance, that Americans spend every year on chewing gum.

Challenge

It seems effortless, doesn't it? And the section ends right there; the writers don't even need to draw the conclusion that spending on political campaigns in the United States is not exorbitant. Readers do it themselves.

Which is fair warning to you to probe a little deeper, in the manner of Levitt and Dubner themselves. They've given you a different way of looking at election spending. *But is it the relevant one?* You might perhaps ask, for example, whether the problem is not how much money is spent on elections but where it comes from. In that way, you've nicely reframed the argument and provided some dissent of your own—exactly what you would want to do at this point when reading and annotating an argument.

Ask if a writer is overlooking plausible alternatives.

Writers ask provocative questions all the time to frame arguments they want to make: *You've probably heard this claim, but consider the alternative.* Following is an example of this strategy from an essay by media expert and futurist Marc Prensky, a strong advocate for teaching methods that incorporate digital technologies. (He introduced the term "Digital Natives" to describe students who grew up with computers, the Web, and video games.) He uses teachers to set up a counterclaim:

Conventional claim

We hear teachers complain so often about the Digital Natives' attention spans that the phrase "the attention span of a gnat" has become a cliché. But is it really true?

"Sure they have short attention spans—for the old ways of learning," says a professor.[25] Their attention spans are *not* short for games, for example, or for anything else that interests them. As a result of their experiences Digital Natives crave *interactivity*—an immediate response to their each and every action. Traditional schooling provides very little of this compared to the rest of their world (one study showed that students in a class get to ask a question *every ten hours*).[26] So it generally isn't that Digital Natives *can't* pay attention, it's that they choose not to.

New idea challenges the old one.

—"Do They Really Think Differently?"

Prensky cites two sources (not reproduced here) to backstop his key assertions: "Their attention spans are *not* short for games" and "Digital Natives crave *interactivity*." In this way he clearly implies that maybe it's teachers, not students, who need to change. Naturally, there's room here to squeeze in objections, especially if you are not impressed by students' infatuation with the bells and whistles of games. But Prensky at least sounds plausible.

It should be obvious by now that taking on "opponents"—understood here as ideas or people worthy of serious attention—

is a common and worthy rhetorical move. In earlier chapters, we've seen Barbara Ehrenreich and Annette Lareau challenge assumptions about the poor, Jonathan Safran Foer and Eric Schlosser raise questions about the food we eat, and Luis Alberto Urrea undermine myths about immigration policies.

Couldn't you do the same thing in your academic reading? Sure, and the first step is to grow accustomed to reading and responding to authors (and speakers) regularly and cogently—which itself is a very good argument for engaging with the social, cultural, and political issues raised by the Ehrenreichs, Schlossers, and Urreas of the world. You don't have to agree with their claims or their dissents to appreciate how well they have expressed them.

> Know how authors frame their challenges to conventional opinions.

Concede and Correct: Build Trust

At some point, writers accept the fact that rethinking and correction are part of the game: A topic that initially seemed simple or self-evident to them becomes more nuanced as they dig into it. Or earlier work is challenged by new research and they see good sense in what critics now have to offer. When that's the case, conscientious authors simply admit problems in their positions or missteps in their arguments. And, though concession is rarely a pleasant task, it can give authors opportunities to enhance their ethos and even turn weaknesses into strengths.

Consider Diane Ravitch, a professor at New York University and respected critic of the American educational system whom we've met in previous chapters, admitting that she has changed her views about the merits of school choice and high-stakes testing, two controversial educational reforms she once championed. Here is how she explains her flip-flop:

> What should we think of someone who never admits error, never entertains doubt but adheres unflinchingly to the same ideas all his life, regardless of new evidence? Doubt and skepticism are signs of rationality. When we are too certain of our opinions, we run the risk of ignoring any evidence that conflicts with our views. It is doubt that shows we are still thinking, still willing to reexamine hardened beliefs when confronted with new facts and new evidence. . . .

> Defense set up with a provocative question

Rationale for the concession

I wanted to believe that choice and accountability would produce great results. But over time I was persuaded by accumulating evidence that the latest reforms were not likely to live up to their promise. The more I saw, the more I lost the faith.

—*The Death and Life of the Great American School System: How Testing and Choice Are Undermining Education*

This is called making a virtue of necessity: Ravitch shows how an admission of error can enable a writer to seem like a model of reason and common sense. Another shrewd move here is to open the paragraph with the first-person plural "we" ("What should *we* think") before shifting to first-person singular ("*I* wanted to believe"); in this small way, Ravitch asks readers to share her concession. And aren't you more likely to trust her after reading this paragraph?

Concessions can subtly affirm challenged positions.

It's even possible to use a concession to affirm a position. Nicholas Carr is well known for the "Yes!" answer he gave to a question he posed in the *Atlantic*, "Is Google Making Us Stupid?" Fearing that online reading is restructuring our minds (and citing research to support those claims), Carr nonetheless concedes that critics in the past worried needlessly over literacy innovations we now take for granted—the book, the printing press, pens, typewriters. He spends two full paragraphs describing a few of them:

Concession

Maybe I'm just a worrywart. Just as there's a tendency to glorify technological progress, there's a countertendency to expect the worst of every new tool or machine. In Plato's *Phaedrus*, Socrates bemoaned the development of writing. He feared that, as people came to rely on the written word as a substitute for the knowledge they used to carry inside their heads, they would, in the words of one of the dialogue's characters, "cease to exercise their memory and become forgetful." And because they would be able to "receive a quantity of information without proper instruction," they would "be thought very knowledgeable when they are for the most part quite ignorant." They would be "filled with the conceit of wisdom instead of real wisdom."

Strategic affirmation

Socrates wasn't wrong—the new technology did often have the effects he feared—but he was shortsighted. He couldn't foresee the many ways that writing and reading would serve to spread information, spur fresh ideas, and expand human knowledge (if not wisdom).

The arrival of Gutenberg's printing press, in the 15th century, set off another round of teeth gnashing. The Italian humanist Hieronimo Squarciafico worried that the easy availability of books would lead to intellectual laziness, making men "less studious" and weakening their minds. Others argued that cheaply printed books and broadsheets would undermine religious authority, demean the work of scholars and scribes, and spread sedition and debauchery. As New York University professor Clay Shirky notes, "Most of the arguments made against the printing press were correct, even prescient." But, again, the doomsayers were unable to imagine the myriad blessings that the printed word would deliver.

> —"Is Google Making Us Stupid?"

Concession

Affirmation

What lesson could you draw from these lengthy paragraphs? When your argument has a flaw or weakness, acknowledge it for two reasons: (1) such an admission is intellectually honest, and (2) well-read readers in your audience will likely raise these factual objections on their own. So beat them to it with the timely concession and enhance your credibility.

Concessions suggest intellectual honesty.

But there's much more going on—and this is the fun part. Notice that Carr has put himself in the company of distinguished Greek philosopher Socrates and a lesser-known Italian humanist. Not a bad crowd. In explaining the objections these men had to new technologies in their eras, Carr admits that Socrates underestimated the value of the written word and that critics of Gutenberg couldn't imagine the "blessings" of the printing press. But each paragraph insists that these same skeptics got *part* of the story right: Socrates was shortsighted, not wrong, about the effects of reading, and the advent of printing did have exactly the effects some critics warned of. So Carr's concessions pull their punches—as does even the good-natured descriptor he applies to himself: *worrywart*. No ego there. He puts readers at ease, even those who think he's wrong.

Rebut and Reply: Build Authority

With Carr, we've already made the transition from concession to rebuttal, so here we'll just look at a few more examples to help illustrate the principle. You will discover in most of your academic reading that pointing out problems or reservations with someone else's position isn't the shouting match that debates on cable news shows lead you to expect. In effective refutations (including any you offer yourself), critics stay on target, present opposing ideas fairly and completely, and offer facts or good reasons to undermine them, in whole or in part. Rebuttals need not be antiseptic in tone, however; some of the best parts of a reading catch authors with their hackles up. Admittedly, rebuttals are a danger zone for many people. It's easy to get carried away, to raise one's voice in discussions (see Chapter 11) or to call someone the equivalent of a butthead in prose. Yet you'll discover that acknowledging positions counter to your own and then smartly rebutting them are essential rhetorical skills. You'll thrive—especially in discussions—once you learn how to be a gracious winner.

Effective rebuttals are fair.

Rebuttals take many forms, the easiest being purely factual explanations, easily handled in a few sentences. Here's Mark Robert Rank, author of *One Nation, Underprivileged,* doing a more compact version of the kind of concession/rebuttal we just examined with Carr:

Concession

This is not to say that economic movement is nonexistent [in the United States]. Individuals do move up and down the economic ladder across adulthood (Duncan, 1988; McMurrer and Sawhill, 1998; Rank and Hirschl, 2001c). However, when such movement does happen, people often do not move far from their economic origins. In fact, contrary to popular myth, the United States tends to have somewhat less intergenerational mobility than a number of other developed countries (Kangas, 2000). The empirical evidence clearly points to the fact that children from lower-class backgrounds face a much greater risk of economic vulnerability in their adult lives than do children from wealthier families.

Factual rebuttal

The pattern here is simple, but one you will encounter routinely: *It may be true that . . . However . . .* The paragraph can be so concise because Rank ties his argument to published research, even providing three citations to support the position he intends to undercut. And don't miss the phrases Rank inserts to enforce his position, a predictable "however," a timely "in fact," and an emphatic "empirical evidence clearly points." As mathematicians say, Q.E.D.

Not infrequently, authors frame rebuttals as the answer to questions they imagine people who object to their position might have. It's a technique used by orators as well, especially politicians on the stump. The move gives writers and speakers control since they ask the question. You'll recognize the maneuver the moment you see it, here deployed by Diane Ravitch in *The Death and Life of the Great American School System* in a section dismissing failed approaches to reform education:

Answer questions with a rebuttal.

> <u>Why not let well enough alone, and let the textbook publishers decide what all children should learn?</u> To anyone who might be satisfied with this response, <u>I say: sit down and read a textbook on any subject.</u> Read the boring, abbreviated pap in the history textbook that reduces stirring events, colorful personalities, and riveting controversies to a dull page or a few leaden paragraphs. Read the literature textbooks with their heavy overlay of pedagogical jargon and their meager representation of any significant literature. Note that nearly half the content of these bulky, expensive books consists of glitzy graphics or blank space. Challenge yourself to read what your children are forced to endure, and then ask why we expect that textbooks—written and negotiated line by line to placate politically active interest groups in Texas and California—are up to the task of supplying a first-rate curriculum.[9]

Objection

Rebuttal

This is a refutation with more blood in it. Though no data is cited and the single source referenced at the end is to Ravitch's own book, *The Language Police*, readers likely feel the author's confidence (even anger?) in the command she gives readers: "sit down and read a textbook." You could question the shaded language here: "boring, abbreviated pap"; "dull page"; "leaden paragraphs"; "bulky"; "glitzy." But Ravitch is counting on readers to nod in agreement with her explanation, remembering their own textbooks or having seen their children's.

It's true that some instructors discourage students from using questions of this kind in their own work to introduce paragraphs. That's because it's all too easy to pose queries that close down issues rather than explore them. For example, Ravitch could have asked her question bluntly and stupidly, such as: *And what's the deal with textbooks? Does anyone read them anyway?* In contrast, her powerfully argued paragraph explodes with details. Her initial query doesn't stifle ideas; it opens them up and seems to refute any hard-and-fast prohibition of questions at the beginning of paragraphs, doesn't it? (To learn more about paragraphs, see Chapter 14.)

For a final example, we return to Marc Prensky, who you recall believes that education should be revamped to better serve "Digital Natives"—that is, students who have grown up with technology. Unfortunately, the younger generation remains under the tutelage of "Digital Immigrants," instructors not born into this brave new world. Their assumptions about education need to change:

> We need to invent Digital Native methodologies for all subjects, at all levels, using our students to guide us. The process has already begun—I know college professors inventing games for teaching subjects ranging from math to engineering to the Spanish Inquisition. We need to find ways of publicizing and spreading their successes.
>
> **Objection** A frequent objection I hear from Digital Immigrant educators is "this approach is great for *facts,* but it wouldn't **Rebuttal** work for my 'subject.'" Nonsense. This is just rationalization and lack of imagination. In my talks I now include "thought experiments" where I invite professors and teachers to suggest a subject or topic, and I attempt—on the spot—to invent a game or other Digital Native method for learning. *Classical* philosophy? Create a game in which the philosophers debate and the learners have to pick out what each would say. *The Holocaust?* Create a simulation where students role-play the meeting at Wannsee [where Nazi officials planned the extermination of the Jews], as opposed to the films like *Schindler's List.* It's just dumb (and lazy) of educators—not to mention ineffective—to presume that (despite their traditions) the Digital Immigrant way is the *only* way to teach, and that the Digital Natives' "language" is not as capable as their own of encompassing any and every idea.
>
> —"Digital Natives, Digital Immigrants"

I conclude the chapter with this counterargument because, unlike the others, it has the feel of informal discussion: It's easy to imagine Prensky addressing these remarks to a live and probably sympathetic audience. Consider his direct and colloquial language: "Nonsense. This is just rationalization. . . . It's just dumb (and lazy) of educators." Does the tone of the remarks hint that Prensky is confident about his position, or maybe just arrogant? Would his "thought experiment" satisfy teachers skeptical about teaching through interactive games? Or might some question the feasibility of his approach? What does Prensky achieve, if anything, by describing "Digital Immigrants" as lazy and dumb? Does it motivate them to rise to his challenge or spur them to walk away?

I'll leave such questions to you.

YOUR TURN

26. Given time and the necessary research resources, what conventional belief or cultural assumption might you challenge in a paper—the way Malcolm Gladwell questions our culture's admiration for people who make it on their own (see pp. 108–109)? Where would you start with such a project? Where might you go with it? Summarize your idea in one or two paragraphs.

27. Describe a time when you needed to make the kind of admission that Diane Ravitch does in this chapter, repudiating positions she had taken on American education. If you can't remember such an occasion, look through a recent paper you have written and decide where you might effectively concede a point, if you were to revise it now.

28. Nicholas Carr's essay "Is Google Making Us Stupid?" as well as another related essay entitled "Does the Internet Make You Dumber?" is (not surprisingly) available on the Web. Find one of them, read it through, and then prepare a thoughtful response to the way Carr frames his arguments. You might analyze a few paragraphs from Carr the way the selection from Walter Benn Michaels's *The Trouble with Diversity* is analyzed in Chapter 7, almost line by line (see pp. 92–94).

29. Find a reading in one of your current courses that provides examples of concession or rebuttal used as a rhetorical strategy. Then identify the moves the writer makes, paragraph by paragraph, to make the concession or offer the refutation. Does the strategy work? Does it win you over?

10

Summarize, Annotate, and Paraphrase

Speaking at the 1988 Republican National Convention, President Ronald Reagan, in a slip of the tongue, declared, "Facts are stupid things." He intended to quote his predecessor John Adams, who had called them "stubborn" in 1770 when, still a colonial lawyer in Massachusetts, he defended British soldiers accused of shooting colonists at the Boston Massacre. What Adams said, fully, was "Facts are stubborn things; and whatever may be our wishes, our inclinations, or the dictates of our passions, they cannot alter the state of the facts and evidence." Yet, in an odd way, Reagan got it right, too. Facts may be facts, but they don't mean much until we understand and interpret them correctly, free of biases and emotions. Reagan also inadvertently described a problem many students have today and many teachers bemoan: Students often don't read carefully enough even to know what the facts are.

As a result, many instructors now expect students to either summarize or paraphrase what they've read, especially when preparing research projects or responding to common reading assignments. Such tasks can seem purely mechanical—in a word, *busywork*—but they serve a purpose if they press you to figure out what authors actually wrote as opposed to what you think or wished they'd said. Reading new material is tough, especially when articles or books are technical, use lots of sources (see Chapter 5), and quote from them freely. You've got to identify the claims authors actually make and separate them from all the other voices you hear in a text, especially any that present contrary or alternative opinions. How bad is it when you get an entire reading backwards because you mistake a counterargument for an author's thesis! But it happens embarrassingly often.

Teachers are hard-nosed, too, about keeping *your* opinions out of summaries and paraphrases. That's because reporting exactly what others say or write, without shading or sarcasm, has become an endangered species in an era of instantaneous, off-the-cuff ripostes to everything. So instructors insist on just the facts in summaries or paraphrases, and not your spin on the material. You may find practicing open-mindedness surprisingly hard work, but the exercise prepares you for making astute comments in class or in writing.

Let me acknowledge, however, that *summary* and *paraphrase* are not exactly technical terms, defined with scientific precision. In your academic life, you'll find the words used interchangeably, for example, to describe any process of taking notes from sources, and that's fine. Here, however, I separate summaries from paraphrases based on the way they are typically used in research. I treat summaries first because that's what you'll usually do when reviewing a source for a paper—take a quick look at it before deciding whether you'll need more detailed notes, which is what a paraphrase is all about.

Summarize a Reading

The key question in preparing any summary is *What is the main point of the book or article?* As we've seen in Part One, authors of books sometimes volunteer that information in their front matter. And articles practically force-feed you an answer if they come with an abstract. You need go no further than a summary when it's obvious that a particular source is *not* relevant to your research project. But even so, you need a record that you've seen the material—which is what a summary provides.

To summarize a reading assignment, you must of course *do the reading*—which, you may recall, was the first piece of advice offered in this book (see p. xxxi). So let's examine a sample text carefully, identify its separate claims, and decide what are its major insights, key points, and thesis. Our piece is an editorial from *USA Today*, on a topic you might be familiar with; admittedly, the text is much shorter than what you'll typically read in school, but brevity makes it useful for demonstration. To make the job easier, the editorial has been annotated to highlight its claims, facts, and evidence.

SANITY 101

Parents of adolescents usually strive for an aura of calm and reason. But just two words can trigger irrational behavior in parent and child alike: "college admissions."   **Claim**

It's not an unreasonable response, actually, given the list of exasperating questions facing parents seeking to maximize their children's prospects: Do I tutor my child to boost college admissions test scores? Do I rely on the school admissions counselor or hire a private adviser? Do I hire a professional editor to shape my child's college essay?   **Facts / evidence**

The price tags behind those decisions drive up the angst. A   **Claim** testing tutor "guaranteeing" a 200-point score boost on the SAT admissions test will charge roughly $2,400. Hiring a private college counselor can cost from $1,300 to $10,000. And hiring an   **Facts / evidence** essay editor can cost between $60 and $1,800. Wealthy suburbs are particularly lucrative for the college prep industry. Less affluent families are left with even greater reason to fret: Their children face an unfair disadvantage.

Now, private employers are stepping in to help out.   **Claim**

In a front-page article on Tuesday, *USA Today*'s education reporter Mary Beth Marklein revealed a range of counseling packages that companies are offering parents of college   **Facts / evidence** applicants, from brown-bag discussion lunches to Web-based programs that manage the entire admissions process.

It's thoughtful of the employers, but it shouldn't be necessary.

Thanks to overanxious parents, aggressive college admissions officials and hustling college prep entrepreneurs, the admissions system has spun out of control. And the colleges   **Claim** have done little to restore sanity.

Take just one example, the "early decision" process in which seniors apply to a college by November 1 and promise to   **Facts / evidence** attend if admitted.

Early decision induces students to cram demanding courses into their junior year so they will appear on the application record. That makes an already stressful year for students and parents even more so. Plus, students must commit to a college long before they are ready. The real advantages of early decision go to colleges, which gain more control over their student mix and rise in national rankings by raising their acceptance rates.

Claim

Parents and students can combat the stress factor by keeping a few key facts in mind. While it's true that the very top colleges are ruthlessly selective—both Harvard and Yale accept slightly less than 10 percent of applicants—most colleges are barely selective. Of the 1,400 four-year colleges in the United

Facts / evidence

States, only about 100 are very selective, and they aren't right for every student. Among the other 1,300, an acceptance rate of about 85 percent is more the norm.

And the best part of all: Many of those 1,300 colleges are more interested in educating your child than burnishing their rankings on lists of the "top" institutions. So the next time you hear the words "college admissions," don't instantly open your wallet. First, take a deep breath.

—Editorial, *USA Today*

What are some candidates for the thesis or major point of "Sanity 101"? Could it be the concluding sentence of the brief first paragraph: "two words can trigger irrational behavior in parent and child alike: 'college admissions'"? The statement is true enough, but likely just a starting block, an observation to hook readers into the piece. Read on. How about "Now, private employers are stepping in to help out [with college admissions prep]"? Again, this is a factual statement that needs to be supported by some evidence (which the next paragraph supplies), but it's still not the reason *USA Today* gave editorial space to the issue of college admissions.

Okay, but how about "the admissions system has spun out of control. And the colleges have done little to restore sanity"? That's better. We're closer to a rationale for the editorial—and an explanation for the anxiety spotlighted in its opening paragraph. Then we get this interesting move two short paragraphs later, indicating a shift from problems to solution: "Parents and students can combat the stress factor by keeping a few key facts in mind," followed by facts suggesting that getting into college isn't all that tough. Can we bring all these ideas together: anxiety over college admissions, out-of-control admissions procedures, the realities of getting into school? How about the following?

> In "Sanity 101," the editors of *USA Today* (January 19, 2006) criticize current college admission practices, which, they argue, make students and parents alike fear that getting into an appropriate school is harder than it really is.

Notice three things about this summary: (1) it is purely descriptive— no opinion or commentary, (2) it borrows no language at all from the editorial, and (3) it is written in third person, without an *I* or *you* in sight. Were you developing a paper, you could use the language in the summary without fear of plagiarism, provided that you credit *USA Today* properly for its editorial ideas. Now, wasn't that easy?

A summary offers no opinions.

Not exactly: There's plenty of mental labor in any summary faithful to a text, no matter how brief. You have to think about the reading and then tinker with the parts to see how (and whether) they mesh. Naturally the job is tougher when a source is longer, makes several points, moves in various directions, or includes concessions and rebuttals. (See Chapters 7–9 for a more intimate survey of how texts work.)

A summary works only if you can return to it weeks later and get an accurate sense of what a source like "Sanity 101" is about—especially if you've already forgotten you've read it. And that's also the reason for always incorporating basic publication information into a summary, so you can quickly relocate the source if you have to.

Include publication info so you can find sources later.

How can a summary go wrong? Let me count the ways. Or take a look at this alternative attempt to synopsize "Sanity 101":

> According to the editorial I read, most students get into the colleges they want. But admission into most colleges is so tough that many parents blow a fortune on tutors and counselors so that their kids can win early admission. But the newspaper's advice to parents is don't instantly open your wallet. First, take a deep breath.

Inaccurate summary

Note, first, that the piece omits the title of the editorial, who published it, and when, making it useless for research. Then, following an inappropriate first-person intrusion (*I*), the summary presents a claim the editorial doesn't actually make: "most students get into the colleges they want." Then it contradicts itself immediately ("admission into most colleges is so tough that . . .") while simultaneously misrepresenting what the editorial does actually say—that admission into most schools is *not* highly selective. Finally, the last ten words of this recap are lifted word for word from the editorial and distinctive enough to post a red flag for plagiarism. The summary is a disaster.

Now I'm going to contradict *myself* a bit. The body of a summary must always describe the original piece factually and do so without commentary or bias. But there are often good reasons to attach *separate* evaluative or interpretive comments to summaries. Such remarks can capture ideas useful later during discussions or research. You could, for instance, attach a line to a summary noting how the source material might help you defend a specific point in a discussion or paper. You might even be *required* to attach evaluative comments to summaries of the sources you use in some research projects: Such a list is called an "annotated bibliography," which we'll discuss shortly.

Evaluative comments are appropriate as long as you don't slant the summarized material itself or blur the distinction between the source's words and ideas and your own. The following are two acceptable summaries of "Sanity 101," with comments attached and underlined:

Summaries can include your ideas— *separately*.

Identifies the source and outlines the two main issues

Notes an extra source to be examined

In "Sanity 101," *USA Today* (January 19, 2006) describes the efforts of college applicants and parents to deal with the progressively more competitive admissions policies of elite institutions. The editorial claims that most schools, however, are far less selective. The article includes a reference to another *USA Today* piece by Mary Beth Marklein on the support some companies offer employees to assist them with college admissions issues.

Source noted in MLA form, ready for use

Student comment notes a limitation

Source: "Sanity 101." Editorial. *USA Today* 19 Jan. 2006: 10A. Print. In an editorial (January 19, 2006) entitled "Sanity 101," *USA Today* counsels parents against worrying too much about hypercompetitive current college admission practices. In reality only a small percentage of schools are highly selective about admissions. The editorial doesn't provide the schools' side of the issue.

Annotate a Bibliography

Instructors sometimes ask you to attach an annotated bibliography to the final version of a lengthy project, enabling them to determine at a glance how well you've done your research. Others may ask for an annotated bibliography earlier in the writing process — sometimes even as part of a topic proposal — to be sure you're on track, poring over good materials, and getting the most from them. In an annotated bibliography, you summarize all the sources you use (or expect to use) in a paper or research project and then add the type of commentary your instructor wants for each item. You might be asked to appraise its quality, authority, thoroughness, length, relevance, usefulness, age (e.g., up-to-date/dated), reputation in field (if known), and so on. The list is usually alphabetical, with the items following guidelines for the documentation system preferred in your field, for example, MLA, APA, CSI, or *Chicago*. (Documentation systems are listed in Appendix A.)

If an instructor wants you to explain what role sources have played in a project, draw attention to articles or book chapters that have provided creative ideas, authoritative coverage, up-to-date research, diverse perspectives, or helpful bibliographies. Remarks should be professional and academic: You aren't writing movie reviews. The following three items are from an annotated bibliography offered as part of a topic proposal on the cultural impact of the iPod:

Stephenson, Seth. "You and Your Shadow." *Slate.com* 2 Mar. 2004. Web. 3 Mar. 2007. This article from *Slate.com*'s "Ad Report Card" series argues that the original iPod ads featuring silhouetted dancers may alienate viewers by suggesting that the product is cooler than the people who buy it. Stephenson explains why some people may resent the advertisements. The piece may be useful for explaining early reactions to the iPod as a cultural phenomenon.

> *Bibliographical entries follow MLA style.*

Sullivan, Andrew. "Society Is Dead: We Have Retreated into the iWorld." *Sunday Times* 20 Feb. 2005. Web. 27 Feb. 2007. In this opinion piece, Sullivan examines how people in cities use iPods to isolate themselves from their surroundings. The author makes a highly personal, but plausible case for turning off the

> *Objective summary of the work is included.*

machines. The column demonstrates how quickly the iPod has changed society and culture.

Walker, Rob. "The Guts of a New Machine." *New York Times Magazine* 30 Nov. 2003. *OneFile*. Web. 1 Mar. 2007. This lengthy report describes in detail how Apple developed the concept and technology of the iPod. <u>Walker not only provides a detailed early look at the product, but also shows how badly Apple's competitors underestimated its market strength.</u> May help to explain Apple's later dominance in smartphones as well.

Items comment on a text or assess its value. This item does both.

As you can see from the annotations, all three items in this brief alphabetical list follow the same efficient structure: publication details about the work already correct enough to use in a paper; a clear and objective summary of the contents of the reading; an assessment of the item on its own merits and as a potential source in a project.

Paraphrase a Selection

Paraphrases provide much more complete synopses of the works you read than do summaries. In effect, they are the notes you take to remember precisely what you've covered, perhaps for a class discussion or upcoming test, or to provide material for a research paper or thesis. Like a summary, a paraphrase explains what an article or a book chapter is about, but it offers more details (namely, it includes key supporting points). You may decide to paraphrase materials selectively, giving attention just to those portions of a source you need to understand best or expect to quote from extensively. Other sections of a book, for example, might simply be summarized.

As with a summary, you identify the thesis or major claims of any material you paraphrase, but you also give attention to the way its ideas or concepts are organized and how (and in what order) evidence or information is presented. Be sure your paraphrase mimics the structure of the source. For example, your paraphrase will be sequential when a work tells a chronological story (as in a narrative), be organized by topics and subtopics when you're dealing with reported information, or be structured to reflect the chain of arguments in editorials or persuasive articles.

Paraphrases follow the structure and tone of the original text.

A paraphrase should be succinct, mirroring, to some extent, the tone and style of the source. In effect, you are preparing a prose outline of the material (or a fuller abstract), complete and readable in itself. Of course you should adapt your paraphrases to specific needs. Preparing for a discussion, for example, you might focus on finding quotations to bring up at an appropriate time.

Thanks to photocopies and downloaded files, you rarely have to copy crucial data manually into notes—and you probably shouldn't. (Opportunities for error skyrocket whenever you transcribe information by hand.) Be certain, though, that your paraphrase sets down supporting reasons for all major claims, as well as key facts and evidence. Key evidence is whatever proves a point or seals the deal in an argument. Keep track of page numbers for all important data so you can cite the material in your paper without having to return to the original source.

As with summaries, keep paraphrased notes in your own words (always avoiding first- and second-person references: no *I* and *you*). If you copy the actual language of sources as you paraphrase them, you risk plagiarism. Deliberately or not, you could transfer big chunks of someone else's writing into your project. But if you've paraphrased by the rules, setting any borrowed words between quotation marks, it's fine to import those notes directly into your project—giving the original writers due credit for their ideas, of course. Think of it this way: When you write competent paraphrases, you've already started composing your own paper. There's no lost motion.

The following is a competent paraphrase of "Sanity 101," an article which appears earlier in this chapter. You may want to compare it to the briefer summaries of the same piece on pages 123–24:

> In an editorial entitled "Sanity 101" (January 19, 2006), the editors of *USA Today* worry that many fearful parents are resorting to costly measures to help assure their child's college admission, some hiring private counselors and tutors that poorer families can't afford. Companies now even offer college admission assistance as part of employees' job packages. Colleges themselves are to blame for the hysteria, in part because of "early admission" practices that benefit them more than students. But parents and students should consider the facts. Only a handful of colleges are truly selective; most have acceptance rates near 85 percent. In addition, most schools care more about students than about their own rankings.

What makes for a bad paraphrase? Obviously, you should not rearrange the information in the original source, give it the slant you prefer, or interrupt the factual report with your opinions on a subject. If you do comment in your notes, make your views stand out as commentary separate from the paraphrased material. That way, you won't misread your paraphrased notes months later and give readers a wrong impression about an article or book. The following is a paraphrase of "Sanity 101" that gets almost everything *wrong*:

Omits title	Parents of teens usually try to be reasonable, the editors of *USA Today* complained on January 19, 2006. But the words "college admission" can make both child and parent irrational. The response is not unreasonable, given all the irritating questions facing parents seeking to improve their children's prospects. But the fact is that just a few colleges are highly selective. Most of the four-year schools in the country have acceptance rates of 85 percent. So high school students and parents should just chill and not blow their wallets on extra expenses. Rely on the school admissions counselor; don't hire a private adviser or professional editor to shape your child's college essay. A testing tutor might charge $2,400; a private college counselor can cost from $1,300 to $10,000. This is unfair to poorer families too, especially when companies start offering special admissions services to their employees. As always, I think the colleges are to blame, with their pushy "early admissions" programs, which make them look good in rankings but just screw their students.
Language too close to original	
Ignores structure of editorial	
Inappropriate style	
Lifts language from source	
Personal opinions and inappropriate tone	

As you see, the paraphrase borrows language much too freely from "Sanity 101," and makes a jumble of its structure and content. The paraphrase shifts tone oddly, too; it's more colloquial than the editorial and even turns raw and inappropriately personal ("*I think*") at the end. Almost nothing works.

YOUR TURN

30. Practice writing summaries by pairing up with a classmate and finding (probably online) a newspaper or blog page with a variety of short, opinion-oriented articles. For instance, check out the "Opinion" page in the *New York Times* or the home page of Arts & Letters Daily or the Huffington

Post. Agree on two or three pieces that both of you will summarize separately. Then write the paired summaries, being careful to identify the items, describe them accurately, and separate your recaps from any comments you make about the material you have read. When done, compare your summaries. Discuss their accuracy and make sure that neither of you has copied language from the original articles.

31. Practice writing paraphrases by pairing up with a classmate and choosing a fairly substantial online essay to paraphrase. Look for something challenging, not a two-paragraph blog posting. Write your paraphrases of the agreed-upon essay separately, just as if you intended to cite the piece later in a discussion, research paper, or argument yourself. When both of you are done, compare your paraphrases. What did you identify as the main point(s) or thesis of the piece? What kind of structure did the article follow: narrative, report, or argument? What evidence or details from the article did you include in your paraphrases? How did your paraphrases compare in length? Discuss the differences. How might you account for them?

11

Discuss

College instructors probably enjoy spirited classroom discussions more than you do. Watch for it on their faces—they live for such moments, if they give a darn about teaching. Why? Because honest talk about big ideas embodies the whole point of education and learning—and has at least since Socrates conducted his eponymous dialogues in the fifth century BCE. There's just something rousing and yet civilized about discussions in what Jane Austen's heroine in *Persuasion* describes as "the company of clever, well-informed people."

So we've spent ten chapters shoring up the "clever, well-informed" part to get you ready for this moment because, too often, classroom deliberations go something like this:

> INSTRUCTOR: In what ways, if any, did reading Jonathan Safran Foer's *Eating Animals* change your views about factory farming?
>
> SILENCE.
>
> INSTRUCTOR: Does anyone want to explain what we mean by factory farming?
>
> STUDENT: It's sorta like when animals are raised for food in factories.
>
> INSTRUCTOR: Uh-huh. And how do you feel about that?
>
> SILENCE.
>
> INSTRUCTOR: Uh-huh. And did anyone here read *Eating Animals*?
>
> *PROFOUND* SILENCE.

Okay, the imaginary instructor's questions are awful, but we've all endured these moments. Truth be told, even successful classroom dialogues rarely move more than seven or eight people, maybe a dozen, to speak—even in larger classes. But those students enjoy an experience that many of their class-mates come to envy, especially any who *have* read the course materials but are just reluctant to jump in.

Why the hesitation to join classroom discussions? Some-times it's shyness, not an easy state to overcome. But more often, students doubt their ability to add fresh ideas to the deliberations in motion. They fear saying something irrelevant, naïve, or, worst of all, dumb. Maybe they anticipate rebuttals from smart-aleck classmates or a sometimes-acerbic teacher. Or they're unsure even how to enter the conversation or get a word in edgewise, especially when the participants involved are glib and persuasive. So they resign themselves to the role of spectator, figuring that silence has fewer risks than participa-tion. But it also has fewer rewards.

So here's a chapter all about strategies for taking part suc-cessfully in classroom discussion.

Write a Response Paper in Your Head

What might prepare you better to discuss a text in class—that is, in addition to reading for all the elements we've already dis-cussed in Part One, including context, authorship, audiences, genres, and so on? Simple answer: Approach the book or article with a mission. Lots of instructors prime the pump themselves by requiring students to write short "response" or "position" papers whenever they assign important readings, just as I did when I asked my own students to wrestle with Stanley Fish's essay "Rhetoric" (see Chapter 3, p. 33). In a response paper, you react in some focused way to a text, explaining what about it impressed, surprised, confused, or maybe even angered you. So, with an important book or article in hand, prepare for a dis-cussion by reading the text as if you're composing such a paper in your head, whether one is assigned or not. The stratagem will prime you for talking.

Understand, of course, that not every kind of reading requires such active and critical inquiry. Some stuff you just have to learn, especially in those STEM fields we discussed in Chapter 5. No one's going to ask for a response paper to a chapter on thermo-dynamics or fractals. But they might in fields where course readings make debatable, disputable, and vexed claims. For obvious reasons, texts chosen for common reading programs tend to be thought provoking or controversial, too. Some of these books even come with study questions attached, like these:

- Cultural markers can be defined as the behaviors, speech patterns, ways of seeing the world, ethics, and principles that identify a person as belonging to a particular culture. When Rowdy and Junior play one-on-one at the end of the book—and they don't keep score—how is their friendship solidified by their deep knowing of who they are and what they come from?

  —On Sherman Alexie's *The Absolutely True Diary of a Part-Time Indian*

- Were your perceptions of blue-collar Americans transformed or reinforced by *Nickel and Dimed*? Have your notions of poverty and prosperity changed since reading the book? What about your own treatment of waiters, maids, and salespeople?

  —On Barbara Ehrenreich's *Nickel and Dimed: On (Not) Getting By in America*

- *The Devil's Highway* is the story of the U.S.–Mexico border, but it is also about many other invisible borders. Aside from the physical border itself, what other borders separate the people in this story?

  —On Luis Alberto Urrea's *The Devil's Highway: A True Story*

Any of these prompts could set off a discussion.

As you read a text, assemble that response paper in your head by trying to figure out what makes the work persuasive, memorable, or powerful. Mark exemplary paragraphs. Linger over passages where you sense problems, inconsistencies, or oddities— anything that strikes you as "problematic" (a word you'll encounter often in school). The point isn't to define a reading as good or bad, right or wrong, effective or ineffective—at least not yet. It's to give you sites for drilling even deeper into its meaning. It's the lack of such reference points in a text that keeps many people silent in discussions: *I just don't know what to say.*

Note what works and what doesn't work in a reading.

Read a work in terms of its contexts—cultural, social, and political—asking questions constantly. Does it mesh smoothly with worries we have, say, about education or energy or ethics, or is the piece interesting because it seems out of sync with the times—maybe a forecast of things to come? Think about the author. Is he or she a part of the story or merely a conduit of information? Someone crusading for a cause, exploiting a trend, or initiating one? Good credentials or merely hoofing it? What's distinctive, if anything, about the audience of the piece? Are you impressed by what the text contains—its wealth of evidence and quality of reasoning? Or do some sections disappoint you, maybe because the author keeps saying the same thing over and over? Look for smooth and rough spots, for patterns and connections, and try to frame a few hypotheses to test as you read.

If you have done prep work for a text and then actually read it, you're going to notice its salient points. Composing that position paper in your head will then generate the questions, opinions, and doubts that you can bring up in a discussion. If you still remain silent in class despite all this spadework, time and again someone more vocal will get credit for splendid observations you've been sitting on, maybe for days. And you'll regret the missed opportunity. Don't let that happen.

Agree or Disagree

So what exactly do salient points look like? To begin with, you'll find lots of places where you either agree or disagree with a reading and will discover many options for expressing that

Frame your own opinions with ideas from the text.

opinion (see Chapters 7–9). Consider all the different ways that a single quotation, here from Thomas L. Friedman in *Hot, Flat, and Crowded*, might be introduced into a discussion or framed in a paper. The words in bold type constitute that frame, which consists of the words and phrases you use to contextualize borrowed words or ideas (for more on frames, see Chapter 16):

> **Given the threat of global warning, I think** that Thomas L. Friedman **is exactly right** to **insist** that "to push through a green revolution, we will need a president who isn't afraid to do whatever it takes to lead it."

> **It's hard to disagree with Pulitzer Prize–winning author** Thomas L. Friedman when he **observes** that . . .

I can understand why Thomas L. Friedman **might argue** that . . .

Given his fondness for the efficiency of the Chinese political system, I get *very* **nervous when** Thomas L. Friedman **speculates** that . . .

With claims like these, you've already stoked a discussion. Though each sentence heads off in a different direction, what they have in common is a demand for amplification—that is, more sentences to explain or defend that statement just made. Notice that the frames around the quotation aren't simple either: Every gesture sends a signal, whether it's the difference between "insist," "observe," and "speculate" or the inflection in voice (telegraphed via italics in print) at *very* in the final frame.

Identify Strengths and Weaknesses of a Text

Strengths and weakness are always worth mentioning during the discussion of a text. But it's important to separate your judgments about technical elements of a report, argument, or narrative from your reactions to ideas or points of view. You can admire the *strategies* that writers use without endorsing their opinions. Following are sentences that make such technical comments, polished up as they might appear in an actual position paper. But remarks of this kind could be offered just as easily in the informal language of classroom debates.

In *The Immortal Life of Henrietta Lacks*, I was surprised how well author Rebecca Skloot makes readers appreciate the life of an ordinary woman doomed by cancer whose donated cells changed modern medicine.

Praise for a writer's connection to readers

Because Barbara Ehrenreich actually lives among blue-collar workers and experiences how they survive in low-wage jobs, her report of their experiences in *Nickel and Dimed* reaches politically influential audiences that more objective academic studies of poverty cannot.

Explanation of how an author's method broadens her appeal

I respect what Barry B. LePatner tries to do in *Too Big to Fall: America's Failing Infrastructure and the Way Forward*, but I get lost in his endless description of reports, legislation, and government policies. His is a book more for technocrats than for general readers.

Objection to the level of detail in a report

Each of these opinions could be challenged—maybe especially the claim about *Nickel and Dimed*—so in a discussion you'd expect to defend them. But that would be the whole point, wouldn't it? You've discovered something worth saying and arguing.

See Similarities and Differences

Looking for similarities and differences is a natural move while reading texts, especially when you need to evaluate or rank them. Just by suggesting such relationships, you'll inevitably turn up matters worthy of discussion.

> Reading *The Devil's Highway*, Luis Alberto Urrea's account of immigrants struggling and dying in the Arizona desert to find a new life in the United States, I wonder why so many Americans disparage Mexicans like these while they celebrate earlier Western pioneers or newcomers who crossed the seas to get here.

> Malcolm Gladwell uses the same technique in *Outliers* that I also found in his best seller *The Tipping Point*: taking one good idea and then illustrating it with dozens of examples. It gets tedious after a while.

> Though based on facts, Dave Eggers's *Zeitoun*, the story of a man and his family caught up in the natural and man-made horrors of Hurricane Katrina, works because it uses the techniques of fiction to make readers experience a fully documented, real-life event.

In discussions or position papers, never shy away from connecting readings you encounter in one class with articles and books (or ideas) you meet in another. Most teachers welcome such comparisons because they throw fresh light on a subject and, in many cases, demonstrate how much expertise students actually have.

Point Out Complications

Portions of what you read may make you feel uneasy and conflicted, and naturally those sections become ground zero for discussion. You may be disturbed by the treatment given to a topic (too much, too little, or too slanted), the evidence presented (too scant, too old, or too confusing), the language used (too formal, too technical, or too sarcastic), or even what a piece does to your cherished opinions and beliefs. So analyze these tensions or put those misgivings into notes you can use in class for discussion or in a possible paper. Here, for example, is one response to a highly argumentative book, Mark Helprin's *Digital Barbarism*:

> I've read some Lawrence Lessig and consider myself to be, like him, an advocate for "free culture," especially music and software, but I find myself unable to answer critic Mark Helprin's basic argument in *Digital Barbarism* against open sources and free use: "One pays for access to the internet. One pays for hardware and (presumably) for software. One pays for telephones and PDAs. One pays for advertising on the internet. . . . None of these things is free. To facilitate the fluidity of information, why must 'content' be free?" He's got me there.

Response #1: Surprised to agree with Helprin

What a splendid point to raise in a discussion! You can imagine classmates working together to figure out where exactly Helprin's analogy between paying for Web access, hardware, software, and so on and paying for content breaks down—if it does. Here's another response to a statement by Helprin:

> I'm tempted to side with Mark Helprin, author of *Digital Barbarism*, when he resists our overreliance on machine technology: "to read a book, all you need is a book. If you want to take notes or write your own book all you need is a pencil or a pen and some paper. The rest will make you neither a better reader nor a better writer." But I know how easy writing is on a computer and how much I rely on the campus library's online digital resources. How exactly would scratching out my ideas on paper and trudging to the library late at night to photocopy articles improve my writing? What am I missing?

Response #2: Inclined to support Helprin, but can't

I'd wager that someone who agrees with Helprin would happily reply to that last rhetorical question. And so a discussion moves forward.

Express Any Doubts

Naturally, you should be prepared in discussion to bring up any confusing or troubling issues you notice in a book or article, places where you find an author's claims to be inaccurate, questionable, or seriously at odds with your own experiences. You may have different views of McDonald's and Wendy's than those expressed by Eric Schlosser in *Fast Food Nation*, or know Wal-Mart employees happier working there than Barbara Ehrenreich was as she did her research for *Nickel and Dimed*. Maybe you have an engineering background and hence find

In discussion, point out a text's confusing or troubling issues.

yourself skeptical about some of the utopian accomplishments Thomas L. Friedman spends almost fifteen pages listing in *Hot, Flat, and Crowded* as he describes America just twenty years into what he calls the Energy-Climate Era:

> After the meeting, you returned home and docked your car back in the garage, around 4:00 p.m. As you were mowing the lawn with your all-electric mower, your kids came back on their hybrid electric school bus, just another big energy storage unit that actually makes money for the school district by storing and selling clean electrons the way you do.

The notion of school buses earning profits as energy storage units may strike you as technically unfeasible (or wishful thinking) and so it makes you wonder just how realistic Friedman's green view of the future really is. That's surely a perspective to share in a discussion, given your expertise.

Is it possible to be *too* skeptical about readings assigned in class? A recent controversy suggests otherwise. Just a few years ago, among the most popular books on the list of campus readings was *Three Cups of Tea* (2006) by Greg Mortenson and David Oliver Relin. It tells how mountain-climber Mortenson, after failing in an attempt to climb K2 in Pakistan, gets himself lost in the neighboring Karakoram region. Aided by a porter, he stumbles his way into the uncharted village of Korphe, "a sort of Shangri-La," where generous but impoverished people do all they can to help him recover from his experiences. Impressed by their selflessness, Mortenson resolves to build a school in Korphe, the first of many that he will establish over the next decade in a region hurt by America's war in Afghanistan. As you might guess, it's an inspiring story.

Except it may not be entirely truthful, at least according to Jon Krakauer, author of *Three Cups of Deceit*, an e-book released in April 2011, a day after *60 Minutes* aired a story critical of Mortenson on CBS. Writes Krakauer:

Points out issues

> The first eight chapters of *Three Cups of Tea* are an intricately wrought work of fiction presented as fact. And by no means was this an isolated act of deceit. It turns out that Mortenson's books and public statements are permeated with falsehoods. The image of Mortenson that has been created for public consumption is an artifact born of fantasy, audacity, and an apparently insatiable hunger for esteem.

Holy gullibility, Batman! Krakauer's charges get even worse because money is involved, Mortenson overseeing a huge nonprofit group intended to improve education, especially for girls, in Central Asia. But that's not the end of the story: Allies rise to defend Mortenson and the authenticity of his accomplishments, despite whatever hyperbole might appear in his narrative. The controversy resembles that which surrounds the accuracy of another book once widely assigned in college courses, *I, Rigoberta Menchú*, the autobiography of 1992 Nobel Peace Prize–winner Rigoberta Menchú Tum. Critics claimed that portions of her life story were not based in fact, a charge the author rebutted by claiming that she had "a right to my own memories."

Does she? And does Mortenson? An interesting discussion awaits, given the serious questions raised. Naturally, you won't have the time to do the detailed background checking and research that raised doubts about these two well-regarded authors and their work. But what matters is to cultivate a healthy skepticism toward whatever claims you encounter in your reading, including those introduced in course work. There's no better place for inquiry than a classroom.

Get Involved

One last way to enter a discussion: Bring yourself into it. I've hinted at this tactic in previous sections, but here I mean actually shaping your response to texts by reviewing them in terms of categories you encounter so often on campus these days: gender, race, economic class, sexual orientation, religion, veteran status, and so on. How do these considerations play out in the works you read, and especially as they affect you? Recall Chapter 3 on your background as a reader (see pp. 31–33). Indeed, membership in even narrower categories can influence your reading, too; you may find yourself monitoring what authors have to say, good or bad, about southerners, Libertarians, frat boys, fanboys, fashionistas, foodies, techies, or any of a thousand other groups with whom you could identify.

Disciplined reactions of this kind bring texture and honesty to discussions of "difference" that otherwise have ways of dissolving into piety and silence in mixed company. Or the presentation of an unexpected point of view may suddenly

Consider how *difference* shapes your response to texts.

upend a discussion or frame it in a fresh way. Most people welcome such occasions.

So bringing your experiences of diversity into a discussion is often essential and almost always fascinating—just so long as you don't become wearisomely predictable or unable to see matters from any other point of view. Recognize, too, that the instant you claim a camp, you push others into categories of their own: *speaking as a Millennial, as a working woman, as a gay Latino, as one of the minority who actually pays income taxes.* And yet because we talk about issues of identity with such interest and vigor, points in a text that raise them are always salient in discussions and papers.

Learn the Right Moves

If you read online and pay attention to the *comments* sections that now routinely follow articles in everything from sports blogs to serious online newspapers, you may be spooked by what you find. *Mean-spirited, vicious, unfair, vile, extreme,* and *bigoted* are terms that come to my mind to describe such discussions, and I'm talking about what I find in the *Chronicle of Higher Education.* If teachers and scholars sometimes descend to the level of back-alley goons when responding to ideas from their *colleagues,* what's a student to do in a classroom situation?

Well, audiences have always been prickly and demanding. But why such gross misbehavior in the very environments that early Web advocates imagined as ideal forums for democratic debate? I'd suggest *spontaneity* and *anonymity:* Allow people to post opinions on impulse under the cover of darkness and you're closer to creating mobs than audiences. So don't draw hasty parallels between the rat-tat-tat-tat tirades you find online and the moderated responses to serious writing that occur in classrooms. There aren't many. (Still, do occasionally browse online comment sessions just to learn what *not* to do in academic situations.)

Effective Strategies in Discussions

Let's talk, then, about the intersection of good strategies and good manners in class discussions and other public places. You engage in such conversations in the classroom primarily to test your knowledge and to learn from clever, well-informed peers—and not just to please instructors. But teachers do notice students who distinguish themselves as capable respondents in a classroom—knowledgeable about their subjects, articulate in their claims, confident in their demeanor, and gracious in their treatment of opponents and colleagues.

Sounds too much like Fidditch's Finishing School and Dance Academy, you say? Sorry, but I promised an "insider's guide" and here's a shocker: Most professionals, and that includes both teachers and prospective employers, still admire well-prepared people who can handle themselves in public with skill and grace. If it's any comfort, standards have slipped so much that it doesn't take much to stand out in a discussion, and, fortunately, all the good moves can be learned. You don't have to be a natural.

Competent public comments will set you apart.

So imagine that your instructor opens a discussion by posing a question, usually a fairly generic one, about a book or article: *What did you learn from* The End of Men: And the Rise of Women*? Be among the first responders. You'll help break the ice and have a clear field for introducing ideas in the text that interest you. Sure, there's risk in raising your voice early, but it's lower than sitting there silently for thirty minutes. One tip: Make it a point to slip your name into the conversation ("I'm Jennica") and to keep track of the names of other speakers, even asking for them when you respond to their comments.

If you are not among the first speakers, look for entry points reflecting the kinds of strategies discussed earlier in the chapter, jumping in when the conversation lags, maybe with a question:

> "Am I the only one to notice that . . . ?"
>
> "Most of you seem to agree that _____, but how do you explain _____?"
>
> "Prensky says everyone here at the table is a 'Digital Native' because we grew up with computers. But do you all feel that way? I don't, at least not always, because . . ."

Look for opportunities to enter a discussion.

Once you're in the game and others have spoken, become a connector in the group, someone who occasionally summarizes the direction of the discussion and then pushes it forward. Here's where giving attention to names pays off:

> "So Jennica agrees with Michael Pollan that we should rethink our eating habits and Erik believes people are ready to make big sacrifices so that animals can be treated better. But what about . . . ?"

Learn to respond to specific colleagues thoughtfully and sincerely, looking them in the eye:

Use people's names, including your own.

"I agree with you, Jon, when you say _____, and furthermore . . ."

"I agree with your first two points, but I have an objection to the third . . ."

"I see your point, Andrea, but what do you think about . . . ?"

As the discussion rolls along, consider inviting people who've been silent to speak if you have enough confidence to do that and know individual classmates well enough to ease them into the discussion, not put them on the spot. Maybe you've talked about the book or article briefly with your neighbor before class and were struck by an idea he might introduce:

"Marc, you mentioned that you had a job at a real estate agency this past summer. Is the housing market really as bad as Morgenson says it is?"

Don't overdo the orchestration, however; you aren't a master of ceremonies. Fortunately, once you show good grace, you'll see other colleagues pick up the moves (especially your attention to names), and the discussion will flow productively without seeming forced or fussy: just capable people talking to each other like adults.

What to Avoid in Discussions

Good manners don't mean avoiding substantive issues or frank opinions. Say what's on your mind, maybe drawing from the text you've annotated or notes you prepared in front of you. Cite short passages that make important points and quote them aloud (for colleagues who didn't bring the book to class), but don't read anything at length. Focus your remarks on claims as much as possible and follow up with evidence or examples. You know you have a problem if classmates shrug off your three-minute monologue with, "So what's your point?"

Don't let controversial remarks rile you.

When someone makes a controversial statement, don't let it upset you or push you into an unforced error. But neither should you let the claim go unanswered, especially when it is offensive or prejudiced in some inappropriate way. You won't be able to sleep that night if you stay silent, hoping someone else in the class or maybe the instructor takes up the challenge. One simple move might be to restate the position to the classmate, modifying it to make it more palatable or to give the speaker a way to back down or modify the remark:

"I think I hear you saying _____. Is that right?"

"Can we look at the issue this way instead . . . ?"

I have seen students use the following move, with mixed but generally good results:

"Can you see how saying _____ might upset some people?"

Avoid being maneuvered into an *ad hominem* attack on the character of the speaker (see Chapter 6) or a reckless rebuttal (see Chapter 9). You damage your own ethos and lose credibility in such moments. When you can't find a substantive reply to a strong position on the spot, a timely "I need to think about that" can defuse the situation or at least give you a graceful exit.

Be careful not to let discussions turn into dialogues between just two or three people. There are moments when an interchange between charismatic students engaged by a topic can be exhilarating, a pleasure to experience because ideas, not personalities, are on a tear. But these moments should be brief and exceptional, or the discussion will fall apart or become a spectator sport. If you are one of the enthusiastic speakers, pull back and invite others to express their thoughts. If you're on the outside, but with something to say, interrupt graciously in a way that signals to the speakers they've debated too long: "Can I break into this discussion?" "Excuse me, but I'd like to suggest . . ." You aren't being rude; in fact, you're doing them a favor. **Avoid hogging the discussion.**

Fortunately, most classroom discussions—at least in my forty years' experience—aren't hard-nosed, angry, or out-of-control affairs. And do remember that an instructor bears chief responsibility for keeping matters civil. No student should be asked to carry all the weight.

But neither should you cede the conversation to the teacher. Students instinctually direct most of the comments they make in class discussions to the instructor, even when responding to what a classmate has said. Try not to do that. Discussions come to life—I'm not making this up—when ideas move from Geoffrey to Dhruva to Jacob to Ritika to Tempestt to Kerry to Christian and, maybe, then to Mr. Ruszkiewicz, and **Talk to peers more than to the instructor.**

back to Dhruva. So talk *with* your colleagues, not *at* them. Use their names and follow up on their remarks; don't wait to hear from the teacher. Believe me, instructors will intervene if you all go seriously off track, have too much fun, or endanger Western civilization with your misinterpretation of *The Republic*. Discussions of common or canonical texts especially are about hearing what *many* have to say about consequential ideas. Without give-and-take from everyone, the session might as well be a lecture.

Which leads me to raise a last, delicate issue in this section. Remember that a discussion is not about *you*. Your opinions matter, but if you have a tendency to ramble on or dominate every conversation, find a way to restrain yourself. Classmates and instructors are often too polite to interrupt well-meaning students who turn every comment they make into an endless personal narrative about not only themselves but their families, friends, and ancestors. You know who I'm talking about. Statement and proof was enough for Aristotle; it should suffice for you, too.

It's not all about you.

YOUR TURN

32. Many blogs encourage readers to comment on their postings. You can use such sites to practice your skill at responding to what you read. On a news or cultural blog you scan regularly, locate a fairly lengthy and serious article to which some readers have already offered substantive responses, more than a line or two. After reading the article, think about what you might post in response. Then review the actual postings, considering questions such as these:

- How does your brief response compare with what others have said?
- What strategies have they used that you admire?
- How did the best responders establish their credibility?
- Which responders did you take less seriously and why?

Chances are you'll be disappointed in much of the online commentary. People may respond from prejudiced positions, focus on irrelevant points, or just take crude potshots at the original author. But from such respondents, you may learn what not to do in a serious academic paper.

33. If you can recall a great discussion that occurred recently in a class or other forum, write a paragraph describing it and, as best you can, explaining why it went so well. Did the subject drive the session or was it the behavior of the participants that made it memorable? Maybe a bit of both?

34. Be honest—do you hog the stage or are you a wallflower? Or something in between? How have your contributions gone so far in college? Make a list or a diagram of your habits in class discussion. Spend a few minutes jotting down your reflections. Then, write freely for another ten minutes on what you might do to improve your success in class discussions. From this exercise, extract a list of the top three things you will do—or avoid doing—from now on, to be a skillful contributor. Practice these skills for at least two weeks.

THREE

You, the Writer

Histories make men wise; poets witty; the mathematics subtile; natural philosophy deep; moral grave; logic and rhetoric able to contend.
— Francis Bacon, "Of Studies" (1625)

If anything's predictable in college, it's that assigned readings and the discussions they spark usually lead up to writing assignments. The chapters in this section should help you deal with the peculiar demands of academic writing. You might even foresee that familiar topics such as thesis statements, audiences, paragraph structure, reliable sources, and handling quotations will rear their heads yet again. You would be right.

What will be fresh, however, is reviewing this material in light of what you've newly learned about scholarly and professional writers, audiences, genres, and sourcing. For chapter after chapter you've looked closely at the work of other authors — watched them offer and defend their ideas. Now it is time to step out and make claims of your own.

12

Everything should be as simple as possible, but no simpler.

— ALBERT EINSTEIN

Compose

I'm talking with Andrew about the first paper he's submitted in an upper-division course, an essay thick with ideas but as glutinous as sludge and about as appealing. The student I know from class—bright, articulate, and excited by the subject matter—has to be in the paper somewhere. But I can't find him, not in a thicket of complex clauses and abstract phrases that reads like a parody of academic writing. Straining to sound serious and learned, Andrew has lost his voice. It's a common problem, especially among *good* students.

So, line by line, we review the first few paragraphs of the essay and I ask one question over and over: "What's your *real* subject in this sentence?" At first, Andrew resists my bullying, insisting that his complex clauses, with all their amplifications and modifiers, can't be pared down without sacrificing the nuances he wants to explore. But I keep demanding that he point to someone or something that can actually perform an action within each sentence and move it along. Slowly, he sees what I have in mind and offers plausible subjects that unfurl in just a word or short phrase. And then we find action verbs—honest-to-goodness expressions like "disagrees" or "explains" or "misconstrues," not lame variants of "to be" or "to have"—that connect logically to these now clear-cut and sometimes even living-and-breathing subjects. Once key actor/action relationships have been ironed out, Andrew notices how smoothly the remaining elements of the sentences slide into place. We work over clause after clause this way until the revisions come readily, unforced and obvious, and ideas in Andrew's paper bloom

Clear sentences frame clear ideas.

into clarity. More important, they now sound as if they belong to him.

I do a mental fist pump. Andrew is even happier than I am—though he's upset to realize that, with the best of intentions, he's been muddying his prose for years just to sound intellectual. He never again writes a bad sentence for me. More important, he's learned how to make his academic writing "as simple as possible, but no simpler," to borrow a line usually attributed to Albert Einstein.

You might think I'm offering the tactic I gave to Andrew as the key to all effective college prose: Build concise sentences around specific subjects and strong action verbs. Honestly, it's pretty good advice and exactly the fix that Andrew needed at that time. But truth is, there are no magic bullets for slaying the wildly varying problems people face when composing. Writing has too many slippery surfaces to make life easy. College guides that try to treat every element of the writing process—from finding effective topics to placing commas correctly—are the all-American, double bacon cheeseburgers of the textbook world, topping off at more than a thousand pages. I know; I wrote one. The details they cover *do* matter: It *is* important to know how to set up comparison/contrast essays, how to get subjects and verbs to agree, how to document books with three authors or none at all in MLA style, and so on. Yet such technicalities are for looking up, not for explaining how to behave as a writer.

There are no magic formulas for college writing (but see Chapter 18).

Let me offer an analogy. More years ago than I care to admit, I spent a day at a mountain biking workshop for novices. We learned lots of details: what to check before every ride, how to lubricate derailleur and chain, how to fix a flat. But the most practical tip for riding seemed rather crude, even though it addressed a worry that plagues most new bikers—how to navigate rock-strewn, narrow, single-track trails or, even worse, cross streams on trail bridges barely wider than planks. The advice? Simple and sweet: Don't look down at the rocks, the ruts, the narrow boards, or even try to aim your wheel; just keep your eyes focused on where you want to go. The wheel will follow your gaze. And it works. Suddenly I could manage single track capably, if not perfectly.

In this section, I'm going to offer advice about writing that's as simple as possible, but no simpler—the sort that's easy to remember and works *most* of the time. There are lots of resources to consult—many of them online—when you need specific and technical advice, for example, about writing a chemistry lab report, capitalizing proper nouns and adjectives, or figuring out exactly how to label charts and tables in APA style. (A writing handbook is usually a good investment, too.) Here, I'll be happy just to get you rolling smartly down the trail.

Manage Assignments

Obvious but essential advice is to read writing assignments carefully. I wouldn't raise the point if problems in this area didn't come up a lot. Sure, instructors sometimes propose vague or grotesquely complicated tasks that leave everyone confused (including themselves when they have to deal with the stupefying papers). But more often, writing assignments are carefully designed—and revised semester after semester—to achieve specific goals. If your instructor is on the ball, you'll get an assignment sheet worth studying. Don't hurry through. Instead, mark it up, underlining key points. Basic instructions should be obvious: genre expected (i.e., report, argument, personal essay, position paper), project length (five hundred words; eight to ten pages, double-spaced), due dates, and so on. Note especially if a teacher wants a topic proposal, annotated bibliography, or first draft. Such items are increasingly common, and *d'oh!* is no excuse for missing them or turning them in late.

Highlight key assignment information to avoid careless mistakes.

Much tougher is figuring out how to come to grips with an assignment. When asked for a **report**, think about the kinds of data you need to examine and the types of report you might prepare. Will your report merely answer a factual question about an assigned reading and deliver basic information? Or are you expected to do additional study or compare different points of view, as you might when responding to a controversial common reading assignment? Or should the report deliver new information based on your own recent research?

Determine your approach.

Consider, too, updating or enlarging an idea introduced in a reading, lecture, or discussion session. If oil prices are spiking or workers are protesting in Greece, make that a focal point of your general response to a book on international financial crises; if your course covers globalism, consider how a world community made smaller by Twitter feeds complicates the responses of governments to political turmoil. Make the report current and relevant.

Asked to write an **argument**, draw on your knowledge, experiences, and inclinations, as well as your reactions to specific readings. Given an option, choose subjects about which you genuinely care—not issues the media or someone else defines as controversial. You'll do a more credible job defending your defiant choice not to wear a helmet when cycling than explaining, one more time, why the environment should concern us all. And if environmental matters do roil you, stake your claim on a well-defined ecological problem—perhaps from within your community—that you might actually influence by the power of your rhetoric.

Choose a topic that's relevant to you.

If you really are stumped, the Yahoo! Directory's list of "Issues and Causes"—with topics from abortion to zoos—offers problems enough to keep both congressional Democrat Debbie Wasserman Schultz and conservative commentator Ann Coulter busy to the end of the century. To find it, search "Yahoo" and "Society and Culture" or "Issues and Causes" on the Web.

Asked to write a **personal narrative**, you face intriguing choices. Perhaps in response to a reading such as Leslie Marmon Silko's *Ceremony* (fiction) or Tracy Kidder's *Strength in What Remains* (nonfiction), you may be encouraged to describe an event that has defined or changed who you are. Or perhaps an instructor wants a story that explores your experiences with reading and writing—sometimes called a *literacy narrative*—or one that examines the communities to which you belong. When no narrative ideas present themselves, try scrolling through old photographs on your computer or paging through a yearbook. Talk, too, with others about their choices of topics or share ideas on a class Web site or Facebook. Trading ideas might trigger a memory worth retelling.

Find an original angle.

Initially, you may be tempted to write about life-changing events so dramatic that they can seem clichéd: deaths, graduations, car wrecks, winning hits, or first love. For such topics to work, you have to make them fresh for readers who've likely undergone similar experiences—or seen the movie. If you find a new angle on such stereotypical events, then take the risk. Alternatively, narrate just a slice of life rather than the whole side of beef—your toast at a friend's wedding rather than the three-hour reception or a single encounter on a road trip instead of the full cross-country slog. Most big adventures contain within them dozens of more manageable tales.

Whatever the assignment or genre required, look for published examples of comparable writing. Sometimes an instructor will point to or even distribute successful responses to an assignment. When the paper is based upon a specific reading assignment, you could do worse than study its features and imitate them creatively and respectfully, what artists fondly describe as an *homage*.

Figure Out Audiences

By now, you appreciate how complicated audiences can be and how thoughtfully you need to work them (recall Chapters 3 and 11). In college, you usually write first for an instructor and then for your peers—who often have a chance to read and even maybe edit your drafts. But you will have other relationships with readers, based on the genres you compose and the purposes you have for writing.

In preparing a **report** or **argument**, for example, you typically aim to satisfy knowledgeable people who expect reasonable claims supported by solid evidence presented in accessible language. But if a potential audience includes a wider range of readers, from experts to amateurs, you need to reach them all. Perhaps you can use headings to ease novices through your report while simultaneously signaling to more knowledgeable readers what sections they might skip. Or maybe you take care to define quickly and unobtrusively all technical terms the first time you use them. Audience-sensitive moves like these make sense.

However, often it's not only the content that you must tailor for potential audience members, but their perceptions of you. They'll read you differently, according to the expertise you bring to a piece. What are some options? Let's suppose you are an expert—like the authors of many of the books and articles you'll encounter in courses. You could find yourself in this stance when, after spending months researching a class project or senior thesis, you are asked to present material you know almost well enough to teach. It's a flattering situation, one that allows a writer to use language and references geared to very knowledgeable readers, as Eric Ormsby does in this opening paragraph of a paper he wrote for an upper-division course on the history of rhetoric:

What to do when you're an expert on a subject

Plato, the Greek philosopher whose writings have played a fundamental role in the development of Western thought, rarely looked kindly on rhetoric. Several of his dialogues, particularly *Gorgias*, express a profoundly negative view of this practice and frame rhetoric as a destructive force in human society, an obstruction between us and true knowledge. To borrow a term Stanley Fish himself takes from Richard Lanham, Plato was a supremely "serious man." In light of this hostility, *Phaedrus*, one of Plato's later dialogues, is an exceptionally intriguing work. Not only does Plato tacitly acknowledge the possibility of a benign rhetorical art, itself a significant departure from his previous writings, but in a sense, he fully embraces the art of persuasion himself, though perhaps unwittingly.

Ormsby's confident analysis of Plato's dialogues, the authors and texts he cites, and the vocabulary he wields all signal that he has earned an expert's relationship to readers.

Smart people in this role, however, make two common mistakes in presenting information or arguments. Either they assume their audience is as well informed as they are, and so omit the very details and helpful transitions that many readers need, or they underestimate the intelligence of the members of their audience and bore them with trivial and unnecessary exposition. Readers want you to be a confident guide but also one who knows when—and when not—to define a term, provide a graph, or supply some context.

Now let's suppose a situation more typical for you in school: You're the novice dealing constantly with new subjects and concepts and having to come up to speed quickly. For example, you need to write ten pages on "childhood language acquisition" for a psychology course even though at the outset your expertise amounts to only two journal articles and a book chapter on the subject. In situations like this, you not only have to find a credible way to treat the subject; you also have to convince an expert reader—your instructor—that you're acquiring the credentials to address it at all. And you know what that involves: lots more reading of good sources, lots of note taking, and conscientious attention to detail. Your style, too, needs to mirror what's expected from writers in the field—all the more reason to study the strategies that successful writers employ to present and defend ideas (see Parts One and Two). Here's

What to do when you're a novice on a subject

Katherine Thayer's response on such an occasion, offering a well-informed judgment (based on research) as to whether the classic, but much-criticized, writing manual *The Elements of Style* is sound enough to use in writing centers. Her voice in the research essay is clear, informed, and appropriately moderate:

> If nothing else, *The Elements of Style* makes novice writers begin to think about concerns of style and usage that they may not previously have considered. It offers a straightforward, reassuring set of general guidelines about composition, and it acknowledges that more experienced writers may wish to break these guidelines under certain circumstances. Its view of writing, though not all-inclusive, is appropriate to an academic setting. Therefore, writing centers should offer the so-called "little book" a place on their shelves among other handbooks. *The Elements of Style* should not—and was never meant to—stand as a student's only reference. However, its usefulness as a starting point for beginners and as a reminder for more experienced writers deserves appreciation and respect.

Now imagine a third option: that you are the peer of those in your primary audience and you are addressing them. The situation comes up in school or professional life whenever you're asked to offer a presentation, oral or written. You have to be informative, but in a way that signals your identification with peers. Here's Matt Portillo in that role—on Facebook—explaining to his friends how he has learned to catch a bus in Guatemala while in that country on a service project. The language of his "report" is casual and familiar, but also artful and informative:

What to do when you're addressing peers

> So, you're in Guatemala City and you need to get somewhere in a hurry. No car? No taxi? No jet pack? No problem.
>   Unlike in the States, here you don't have to be at a bus stop to be picked up by a bus. In fact, there are no bus stops along most streets anyway. Stand on the sidewalk (if there's a sidewalk) and look down the street; you'll wait no more than two minutes before a bus comes. When it does, wave or whistle at the guy hanging out of the doorway. The bus will stop for you. As it grinds to a halt, get ready to move quick. Everyone at the "bus stop" boards, and the bus is in motion once again as the final boarding passenger's foot is leaving the ground.
>   Back to that guy who was hanging out the door—he's the driver's partner. Each bus is run by two men working

together: one driver, one attendant. The attendant is there to collect fares and corral people on and off the bus quickly. Waiting around while people take their sweet time boarding and getting off the bus? Ain't nobody got time for that.

For academic projects directed to peers, you no doubt realize that an instructor will be reviewing and likely evaluating the content—including your topic, organization, and sources. But that superior may also be checking how well you adapt that peer-oriented material to the interests and capabilities of your colleagues. As a result, every move you make has to satisfy two audiences.

Audience considerations may be markedly different, too, when an assignment involves writing a **narrative**. Fact is that people like to read other people's stories, so audiences for narratives are large, diverse, and usually receptive. (Consider Matt Portillo's bus story.) Most of your readers probably prefer a narrative to make a point or reveal personal insights. Typically, too, they hope to be moved by the piece, learn something from it, or perhaps be amused by it.

Capitalize on those expectations and use stories to introduce ideas that readers might be less willing to entertain if presented formally in a report or argument. Earlier in this book we've seen that strategy employed by writers in narratives as different as Dave Eggers's *Zeitoun* and Rebecca Skloot's *The Immortal Life of Henrietta Lacks*. Likely you can think of other examples.

Sometimes, though, audiences already exist for particular subjects or points of view. For instance, people within well-defined social, political, ethnic, or religious groups are often eager to read and share life experiences. Women and members of minority groups have used such narratives to document the adversities they face or to affirm their solidarity (recall our discussion of difference in Chapter 3, pp. 31–33). Similarly, members of religious groups recall what it was like to grow up Jewish or Catholic or Baptist—and their readers appreciate when a story hits a familiar note. The best of these personal narratives, naturally, attract readers from outside the target audience, too. So you might consider how your own experiences narrated effectively might resonate with readers who share—or are interested in—your cultural perspectives. Novelist Gloria Naylor puts it nicely:

Specific audiences have specific expectations.

Joyce wrote about the Irish, Philip Roth about the Jews, Maxine Hong Kingston about Chinese-Americans. You write where you are. It's the only thing you have to give. And if you are fortunate enough, there is a spark that will somehow ignite a work so that it touches almost anyone who reads it, although it is about a very specific people at a very specific time.

—"THE LOVE OF BOOKS"

You might even decide that the target of a personal narrative is you—so you compose a song of yourself to discover what made you who you are. Even then, be a demanding audience. Find a way to see yourself from some distance or a new perspective. Imagine, for example, how your story might read ten or twenty years from now. Will your attitudes seem then as odd as your hairstyle?

Overcome Writer's Block

Didn't see this topic coming, at least not so early? It's here for good reason. Making the first moves can be one of the toughest parts of composing—easily on par with understanding an assignment and imagining potential readers. Getting writing done is hard not because the process is painful, but because it's so vulnerable to ridiculous excuses and beguiling distractions. Who hasn't opened a video game or washed a car rather than compose a paragraph?

Like baseball, writing is a game without time limits. When a paper isn't going well, you can stretch into fruitless twelfth and thirteenth innings with no end in sight. And if you do finish, readers may not like what you have done—even when you know the work is solid, based on honest reading, observation, and research. Writing comes with no necessary connection between labor put in and satisfactory pages churned out. No wonder writers get blocked. So what to do when you'd rather crack walnuts with your teeth than write a position paper on *Escape from Camp 14* or *Caleb's Crossing*?

First, break the assignment into parts. Getting started is especially hard for writers when a project, taken as a whole, seems overwhelming. Even a one-page position paper can ruin a weekend, and a term paper—with its multiple drafts, abstract, notes, bibliography, tables, and graphs—stretches beyond the pale.

But what if, instead of stewing over how much time the whole project will absorb, you divide it into manageable stages? That position paper might be broken down into two, maybe three, less daunting steps: doing the assigned reading, brainstorming the paper, and writing the page required. The same procedure makes a research paper less intimidating: You have more elements to organize, but you also have more time to deal with them.

Make the project doable.

Be sure, however, to set feasible goals. Unless you're very disciplined, writing projects sop up all the time available for them. Worse, you may expend more energy fretting than working. To gain control, set levelheaded goals for completing a project and stick to them. Don't dedicate a whole Saturday to preparing an abstract of a reading or finishing a book review; instead, commit yourself to the full and uninterrupted two hours the task will actually take when you sit down and concentrate. If you have trouble estimating how much time a project may require, consider that it is better to establish a goal than to face an open-ended commitment. That's one good reason both teachers and publishers set deadlines.

For really big projects that extend over weeks or even months, create a calendar or timeline and abide by it. First break the task into parts and estimate how much time each stage of the project might take, drawing on past experiences with similar assignments to construct a plan. Believe me, you'll feel better once you've got one. Don't create a calendar so elaborate that failure is built in. Figure that some stages, especially research or drafting, may take more time than you originally expect. But stick to the plan, even if it means starting the draft of a paper with some research unfinished. Or cut the drafting process short to allow time for adequate revision.

Stick to a schedule for big projects.

To meet your goals, put yourself in an environment that encourages composing and minimizes temptations and distractions. Schedule a specific time for writing and give it priority over all other activities, from paying your bills to feeding the dog. (On second thought, feed that dog to stop the barking.) Log off your Facebook and e-mail accounts, turn off your cell phone, shuffle from Beyoncé to Bill Frisell on your iPod, start writing, and don't stop for an hour.

Do the parts you like first. Movies aren't filmed in sequence and papers don't have to be written that way either. Compose those sections of a project that feel ready to go or interest you most. You can work on the transitions later to make the paper feel seamless, the way editors cut disparate scenes into coherent films. The psychology here is simple: Once you have completed portions of a project, you'll be more inclined to continue working on it. The project suddenly seems manageable.

Write the parts you like first.

When you're *really* blocked, try a zero draft—that is, a version of the paper composed in one sitting, virtually nonstop. Of course, you'll need to have done the required reading and research. You might even have a thesis and outline in hand. But you lack the confidence to turn this prep work into coherent sentences. Repress these inhibitions by writing relentlessly, without pausing to reread and review your stuff. If need be, keep at it for several hours. If it helps, imagine you're writing a timed essay exam. The zero draft you produce won't be elegant (though you might surprise yourself), and some spots might be rough indeed. But keep pushing until you've completed a full text, introduction to conclusion. Then put this version aside, delaying any revision for a few hours or, better yet, a few days if you have that luxury. When you return to the project, instead of facing an empty tablet or screen, you have full pages of prose to work with. What a difference.

One more tip. Since people respond remarkably well to incentives, promise yourself some prize correlated to the writing task you face. Finishing a position paper is probably worth a personal-size pizza. A term paper might earn you dinner and a movie. A dissertation is worth a used Honda Civic.

Reward yourself.

> **YOUR TURN**
>
> **35.** Managing a project by breaking it into parts can also reveal something about your work habits. In a detailed paragraph, describe the stages you typically go through whenever you compose a familiar assignment, let's say a response paper, an annotated bibliography, a review of any kind, or a short research paper. Be honest about the process: Do you plan ahead or does most of the work get done just hours before the paper is due? Do you see a need to tweak your habits? Why or why not?

36. Describe some of the audiences you've addressed in speaking or writing during your time in school or, maybe, in community service projects. What role do you prefer: expert, novice, or peer? Why?

37. Have a good writer's block story to share? Describe what you've done to avoid composing a paper—especially any activities far more arduous than putting words down on a page. Or maybe you have figured out a fail safe method for overcoming writer's block? Or you've endured a roommate's endless excuses for not completing a writing assignment? Tell the story in a paragraph or two, which you will start writing *now*.

13

Get a bicycle. You won't regret it, if you live.

—Samuel Clemens

Make a Point

Writing to make a point is like riding a bicycle: Once you learn to do it, you forget how hard it is—or that you ever needed training wheels. Training wheels for writers are called *thesis statements*, unloved but useful academic contrivances designed to help novices figure out what's on their minds. Serious writers don't talk much about thesis sentences in their work, but we've seen in Part Two (particularly in Chapter 7) that they spin them out readily enough, especially in the introductions and prefaces to their books. Maybe you remember Eric Schlosser from Chapter 1 describing his intentions in *Fast Food Nation?*

> I've written this book out of a belief that people should know what lies behind the shiny, happy surface of every fast food transaction.

Thesis in one sentence

Or here, from Chapter 4, is an example in which Barry B. LePatner spends a full paragraph explaining his argument (because experienced writers know you can do that):

> The risks of continuing to ignore our ill-maintained national infrastructure are almost unimaginable. We can no longer fail to devote massive amounts of money to repair our aging roads and bridges. We must begin to set a national policy that goes beyond the myopic vision of state and local politicians who prefer to use federal transportation funds on pork-barrel projects. We will need to reorganize our priorities for years to come, or risk the lives and well-being of our fellow citizens.
>
> —*Too Big to Fall: America's Failing Infrastructure and the Way Forward*

Thesis in a paragraph

What likely gives thesis statements their bad rap is an association with by-the-numbers school writing assignments: *You must present a fully developed thesis at the end of the introductory paragraph of your essay, followed by a minimum of three paragraphs of development and a concluding paragraph.* Yep, the thesis is a key element of the familiar five-paragraph essay, in fact, the hinge upon which the entire enterprise swings. No wonder serious writers (in school and out) associate thesis statements with canned, uninventive, and predictable writing—or, worse yet, standardized exams. Or maybe they just resent teachers insisting that claims in papers always be followed by a trio of supporting elements, as if all truths in life had exactly three parts.

And yet the training wheels that thesis statements represent *do* keep many novice writers on track through difficult school assignments, helping them gain the know-how for more daring projects. You see, many college papers fail simply because writers won't focus. They wander around potential subjects, follow whims, throw out scattered ideas, even make contradictory assertions, hoping perhaps that all the effort counts for something. Some writers even plead that their thinking is too complex, subtle, nuanced, or shaded to be imprisoned within a single sentence—usually shorthand for admitting that they haven't yet done all the work a project requires. For them, the thesis requirement is a timely head slap.

Thesis statements keep writers on track.

The point of this chapter, again a simple one, is to champion the virtues of making clear points in academic writing. If it takes a conventional thesis statement to do that, fine. You'll grow out of it.

Find a Thesis

Need a definition of *thesis*? Try this one. It is a statement in which a writer *affirms or defends the specific idea that will focus or organize a paper.* Typically, a thesis appears in an opening paragraph or section, but it may also emerge as the paper unfolds. In some cases, it may not be stated in classic form until the very conclusion. A thesis is often just one sentence, but the point of a paper can be complex enough to need more room. You'll find a thesis stated or strongly implied in most reports and arguments and even many narratives.

State your thesis in a complete, declarative sentence.

What's the surest way to shape a thesis? Here your high school teachers were right: Don't settle for a phrase; force yourself to write a complete sentence. Phrases can single out topic areas, even intriguing ones, but they don't make assertions or claims that excite readers or require support. Sentences do. None of the following phrases comes close to providing direction for a paper.

Reasons for global warming

Economist Steven D. Levitt's controversial theory about declining crime rates

Problems with college rankings

What's required is a significant claim or assertion. *Significant* here means that the notion provokes discussion or further inquiry. In other words, give readers a rationale for spending time with your writing.

Global warming won't stop until industrial nations either lower their standards of living or admit the need for more nuclear power.

College rankings published annually by *U.S. News & World Report* do more harm than good.

Economist Steven D. Levitt theorizes that crime has dropped in the United States because abortion was made legal, but he ignores other important explanatory causes.

In most cases, you're better off framing a thesis as a declarative sentence rather than a question. Questions certainly focus attention, as Diane Ravitch's did in Chapter 9 (p. 115), but they usually don't take enough of a stand. So while you can introduce a topic with a question, don't rely on it to carry the full weight of your thinking. In fact, a humdrum question acting as a thesis can encourage simplistic responses. There's always the danger, too, that in offering your thesis as a question, you invite strong reactions from readers—and not the ones you want.

Why don't we do something about global warming?

— "Hey, man, I like warm winters."

— "Fixing global warming costs too darn much!"

— "You know where you can stick your carbon taxes."

— "Global warming? What global warming?"

You simply gain more control when you introduce your claim as an assertion. But there's an exception to this guideline: Provocative questions do work well in personal and narrative writing.

So you have a claim. Is that enough? Not even close. You couldn't formulate that initial thesis without doing lots of reading, but expect much more. That additional research will cause your thesis to grow more complicated. That's natural. Fortunately, as a thesis develops, the topic usually narrows because of the issues and conditions you specify. So you find yourself with less work to do, thanks to qualifying words and phrases such as *some, most, a few, often, under certain conditions, occasionally, when necessary,* and so on. Compare the original thesis statement here with a more fully developed version, with the qualifying expressions underlined:

Your thesis will mature as you draft.

ORIGINAL

The college rankings published annually by *U.S. News & World Report* do more harm than good.

DEVELOPED

The statistically unreliable college ratings published by *U.S. News & World Report* usually do more harm than good to students because critics claim that they lead admissions officers to award scholarships on the basis of merit rather than need.

Avoid the tendency to develop any topic simply by breaking it into loosely related parts (usually, unadventurously, three). Thesis statements that follow this pattern read like shopping lists if the connections between the supporting ideas are weak—and they often are. But putting those ideas into clearer relationships often makes for a more compelling thesis.

THESIS AS A LIST

Crime in the United States has declined because more people are in prison, the population is growing older, and DNA testing has made it harder to get away with murder.

THESIS WITH IDEAS CONNECTED

It is far more likely that crime in the United States has declined because more people are in prison than because the population is growing older or DNA testing has made it harder to get away with murder.

Where does a thesis belong in a paper? Usually in an introductory section or, if the paper is short, a paragraph. This traditional guideline makes sense in position/response papers, most academic projects, and term papers because instructors usually want to know up front what the point of a paper is, especially in reports and some arguments. Here's the thesis (underlined) of Andrew Kleinfeld and Judith Kleinfeld's essay "Go Ahead, Call Us Cowboys," at the end of an opening paragraph that offers a context for their claim:

> Everywhere, Americans are called *cowboys*. On foreign tongues, the reference to America's Western rural laborers is an insult. Cowboys, we are told, plundered the earth, arrogantly rode roughshod over neighbors, and were addicted to mindless violence. So some of us hang our heads in shame. We shouldn't. <u>The cowboy is in fact our Homeric hero, an archetype that sticks because there's truth in it.</u>

Thesis stated early in a project

Still, it is not unusual, especially in some arguments, for a paper to build up toward a major point—and so the thesis statement may not appear until the final paragraph or sentence. Such a strategy is worth trying when a claim might not be convincing or rhetorically effective if stated baldly at the opening of the piece. Bret Stephens uses this strategy in an essay entitled "Just Like Stalingrad" to debunk frequent comparisons made between former president George W. Bush and either Hitler or Stalin. Stephens's real concern turns out to be not these exaggerated comparisons but rather what happens to language when it is abused by sloppy writers. The final two paragraphs of his essay summarize this case and, arguably, lead up to a thesis in the very last sentence of the essay—more rhetorically convincing there because it comes as something of a surprise:

> Care for language is more than a concern for purity. When one describes President Bush as a fascist, what words remain for real fascists? When one describes Fallujah as Stalingrad-like, how can we express, in the words that remain to the language, what Stalingrad was like?
>
> George Orwell wrote that the English language "becomes ugly and inaccurate because our thoughts are foolish, but the slovenliness of our language makes it easier for us to have foolish thoughts." In taking care with language, we take care of ourselves.

Thesis stated late in a project

> — *WALL STREET JOURNAL*

Finally, write a thesis to fit your audience and purpose (recall Chapter 3). Almost everything you compose will have a purpose and a point (see the following table), but not every piece will have a formal thesis.

TYPE OF ASSIGNMENT	THESIS OR POINT
Narratives	Thesis is usually implied, not stated.
Reports	Thesis usually previews material or explains its purpose.
Arguments	Thesis makes an explicit and arguable claim.
Evaluations	Thesis makes an explicit claim of value based on criteria of evaluation.
Causal analyses	Thesis asserts or denies an explanatory or causal relationship, based on an analysis of evidence.
Proposals	Thesis offers a proposal for action.
Literary analyses	Thesis explains the point of the analysis.
Rhetorical analyses	Thesis explains the point of the analysis.
Essay examinations	Thesis previews the entire answer, like a mini-outline.
Position papers	Thesis makes specific assertion about reading or issue raised in class.
Annotated bibliographies	Each item may include a statement that describes or evaluates a source.
Synthesis papers	Thesis summarizes and paraphrases different sources on a specific topic.
Lab reports	Thesis describes purpose of experiment.
Oral reports	Introduction or preview slide describes purpose.

Fit your thesis to your audience and purpose.

YOUR TURN

38. Many writers have a tough time expressing their topic in a complete sentence. They'll offer a tentative word or phrase or sentence fragment instead of making the commitment that a full sentence demands, especially one with subordinators and qualifiers that begin to tie ideas together. So give writing a thesis a try. (You may want to review Chapter 7 on *claims*.) Take a topic from a current class reading assignment and turn it into a full-bore sentence that tells readers what your claim is and how you intend to support it. If you don't have a current assignment, pick a general subject you are knowledgeable about, narrow that topic, and write your proposed thesis statement.

14

Structure

Since we've already said so much in the previous chapter about the five-paragraph pattern of organization prevalent in school writing, let's take a look at what it has to offer. You might be surprised to discover that longer and more sophisticated essays *can* be built on its principles:

Introduction narrowing to a claim or thesis statement

- **Initial reason and supporting evidence (stronger)**
  - **—Objections/Counterarguments/Rebuttals**
- **Additional reason(s) and supporting evidence (strong)**
  - **—Objections/Counterarguments/Rebuttals**
- **Final reason and supporting evidence (strongest)**

Conclusion(s) broadening to implications

Typical five-paragraph essay pattern

A pattern like this is comforting and utterly defensible, particularly if the supporting reasons and evidence for the thesis are closely related and logically connected, not just haphazard. The structure also has rhetorical dimensions. A savvy introductory section (one paragraph or more) gets readers invested in a subject. A strong conclusion puts a bow on the package by reinforcing the claims made and, perhaps, suggesting what a reader (or other writers) might take away from the piece. In between, the supporting materials are strategically positioned: All the material should be good stuff of course, but it helps to lead with compelling evidence and to conclude with the strongest and most memorable details, with weaker stuff shunted to the middle of the essay. The structure even opens space for recognizing and dealing with objections, but—thinking rhetorically again—not after the final round of evidence. Why? Because you don't want readers to walk away from a piece thinking about contrary positions. So the conventional essay pattern is sensible, rhetorical, and entirely workable. You shouldn't be ashamed to use it if you can cloak its five-paragraph-essay bones.

The problem is, as discussed in Chapters 7 and 8, that you won't read many effective arguments, either in or out of school, that actually follow this cautious template. The structure isn't defective, just too predictable to describe the way ideas and arguments really move when writers get excited by them. Some controversies need lots of context to get rolling, some require detours to resolve other issues first, and a great many articles work well when writers simply lay out the facts and allow readers to draw their own conclusions—or be nudged toward them.

Organize a Paper

So you won't write a horrible paper if you use the traditional template because all the parts will be in place. Thesis? Check. At least three supporting reasons? Check. Counterarguments? Check. But you may sound exactly like what you are: a writer going through the motions instead of engaging with ideas. Here's how to get your ideas to breathe in an argument—while still hitting the marks.

Explain why readers should care.

Open by explaining what's at stake. Why is the issue you are addressing consequential? Why does a particular reading or author matter? Why should readers listen to you? When writing arguments, for instance, you usually introduce some controversy, so explain why—as recent college graduate Scott Keyes does in an essay he published in the *Chronicle of Higher Education* entitled "Stop Asking Me My Major." In fact, he spends five paragraphs to explain his point; that's the equivalent of a full high school essay *just to launch his subject*:

> One of my best friends from high school, Andrew, changed majors during his first semester at college. He and I had been fascinated by politics for years, sharing every news story we could find and participating in the Internet activism that was exploding into a new political force. Even though he was still passionate about politics, that was no longer enough. "I have to

get practical," he messaged me one day, "think about getting a job after graduation. I mean, it's like my mom keeps asking me: What can you do with a degree in political science anyway?"

A brief narrative raises the essay's issue.

I heard the same question from my friend Jesse when students across campus were agonizing about which major was right for them. He wasn't quite sure what he wanted to study, but every time a field sparked his interest, his father would pepper him with questions about what jobs were available for people in that discipline. Before long, Jesse's dad had convinced him that the only way he could get a job and be successful after college was to major in pre-med.

A second incident amplifies the issue.

My friends' experiences were not atypical.

Choosing a major is one of the most difficult things students face in college. There are two main factors that most students consider when making this decision. First is their desire to study what interests them. Second is the fear that a particular major will render them penniless after graduation and result in that dreaded postcollege possibility: moving back in with their parents.

The conflict is explained.

All too often, the concern about a major's practical prospects are pushed upon students by well-intentioned parents. If our goal is to cultivate students who are happy and successful, both in college as well as in the job market, I have this piece of advice for parents: Stop asking, "What can you do with a degree in (fill in the blank)?" You're doing your children no favors by asking them to focus on the job prospects of different academic disciplines, rather than studying what interests them.

Point of the paper is finally stated.

Do you, like Keyes, hope to raise a weighty problem in a paper, perhaps one mentioned (or ignored) in a course reading? Then describe your concern and make readers share it. Do you want to correct a false notion or bad reporting? Tell readers what setting the record straight will accomplish. Appalled by the apathy of voters, the dangers of global warming, the infringements of free speech on campus? Explain why readers should give a hoot. Take a few sentences or paragraphs to set up the situation. Quote a nasty politician, tell an eye-popping story, or paraphrase a gripping passage from an assigned book or article. Get readers invested in what's to follow.

Get readers hooked on your topic.

Then, to borrow a line from novelist and essayist Virginia Woolf, "Arrange whatever pieces come your way." Writing a report, you may find the conventional academic structure works perfectly, one point neatly following another. Arguments can unroll in the same patterned way, with unmistakable claims followed by reams of supporting evidence. But they can also work like crime dramas, in which the evidence in a case builds toward a compelling and occasionally surprising conclusion—your thesis perhaps.

Consider the ethanol issue, which has the federal government lavishly subsidizing the use of corn for fuel. You could argue straight up that this policy causes more problems than it solves—including the nasty matter of food scarcity in poorer nations. Or you could open by asking whether ethanol really is the responsible environmental solution some claim it to be and then offer evidence that contradicts media hype and political self-interest. In both cases, audiences get the same claim and reasons. But the first approach might work better for readers already interested in environmental issues, while the second might grab those who aren't. This is your call, one appropriately driven more by rhetorical considerations than by preexisting structural patterns.

Serve your subject *and* your readers.

Similarly, you should address objections and counter-points (see Chapter 9) when rhetorically necessary in an essay, not when an outline predicts you should. *Necessary* is when your readers start thinking to themselves, "Yeah, but what about . . . ?" Such doubts likely surface approximately where your own do—and, admit it, you have some misgivings about materials you present in reports and arguments. So take them on then.

On the plus side, dealing with opposing arguments can be like caffeine for your prose, sharpening your attention and reflexes. Here's Lee Siegel, for example, demolishing the notion that Web 2.0 interactivity has been a liberating and democratic technology. Just the opposite, he claims:

Offers strong counter-arguments

> What I've been describing is the surreal world of Web 2.0,
> where the rhetoric of democracy, freedom, and access is often
> a fig leaf for antidemocratic and coercive rhetoric; where
> commercial ambitions dress up in the sheep's clothing of
> humanistic values; and where, ironically, technology has
> turned back the clock from disinterested enjoyment of high
> and popular art to a primitive culture of crude, grasping

self-interest. And yet these drastic transformations are difficult to perceive and make sense of. The Internet is a parallel universe that rarely intersects with other spheres of life outside its defensive parameters.

—*Against the Machine: Being Human in the Age of the Electronic Mob*

The traditional pattern does get one tactic right: Hold your best material for the end, especially when you are composing arguments. It's not a bad strategy for many kinds of (nonscientific) reports and position papers too, especially any that might be presented orally. Of course, you want to make compelling points throughout a paper. But you do need that high note early on to get readers interested and then another choral moment as you finish to send them out the door humming. If you must summarize material at the end of a paper, don't let a dull recap of your main points squander an important opportunity to influence readers. End with a rhetorical flourish.

End with a powerful rhetorical move.

Think in Paragraphs

Paragraphs are a practical invention, created to make long continuous blocks of writing easier to read by dividing them up. Because they give you a physical way to shape ideas and transmit them to readers, paragraphs are a powerful tool for presenting ideas. Following are some pragmatic ways to manage them.

First, make sure paragraphs lead somewhere. Typically in college reports and arguments, you'll use a straightforward topic sentence to introduce a claim or make a point that the rest of your paragraph amplifies or develops. Look at how many ways Ian Frazier, for example, riffs on his topic idea in the following paragraph from *On the Rez*:

> The Cherokee are among the three or four best-known American Indian tribes. "Cherokee" is especially popular as a brand name, appearing on products from cars and airplanes to hospital scrubs and soda pop. If a person claims to have a little Indian blood, chances are the tribe mentioned will be the Cherokee; Bill Clinton claims he is one-eighth Cherokee. In both Oklahoma and North Carolina, the Cherokee are involved in many business ventures, including gambling, tourism,

Topic sentence offers a claim.

Multiple examples illustrate the claim.

manufacturing, and ranching. In Oklahoma, the tribe issues its own VISA card. The Cherokee are sometimes called the largest American tribe. Of those who identify themselves as American Indian on the census form, more say they are Cherokee than say they belong to any other tribe.

After the topic sentence, Frazier's paragraph is almost a list.

But topic sentence *plus* development is not a paragraph rule set in stone. Quite often, the final sentence in a paragraph drives home the point. Or a paragraph simply moves a narrative forward, event by event. You may even weave a notion throughout the fabric of an entire paragraph, inviting readers to see an idea from several points of view.

Whatever your strategy, all paragraphs have to do *something* that readers interpret as purposeful and connected to what comes before and after: identify an idea, offer a new argument, provide support for a claim already made, contradict a point, even bring discussion to an end. You name it; paragraphs do it.

How lengthy should paragraphs be? Instructors who insist that these units run a minimum number of sentences (say six to ten) are usually just tired of students who won't back up claims with adequate details and evidence. No writers count sentences as they build paragraphs. Instead, they develop a sense for paragraph length, matching the swell of their ideas to the reading habits of their intended readers.

Paragraph length should best suit the subject.

Consider the following paragraph, which describes the last moments of the final Apollo moon mission in December 1972. The paragraph might be reduced to a single sentence: *All that remained of the 363-foot Apollo 17 launch vehicle was a 9-foot capsule recovered in the ocean.* But what would be lost? The pleasure of the full paragraph resides in the details the writer musters to support the final sentence, which contains his point:

> A powerful Sikorsky Sea King helicopter, already hovering nearby as they [the *Apollo 17* crew] hit the water, retrieved the astronauts and brought them to the carrier, where the spacecraft was recovered shortly later. The recovery crew saw not a gleaming instrument of exotic perfection, but a blasted, torn, and ragged survivor, its titanic strength utterly exhausted, a husk now a shell. The capsule they hauled out of the ocean was all that remained of the *Apollo 17* Saturn V. The journey had spent, incinerated, smashed, or blistered into atoms every

Strong, contrasting details build to the paragraph's claim.

other part of the colossal, 363-foot white rocket, leaving only this burnt and brutalized 9-foot capsule. A great shining army had set out over the horizon, and a lone squadron had returned, savaged beyond recognition, collapsing into the arms of its rescuers, dead. Such was the price of reaching for another world.   Topic sentence

—David West Reynolds, *Apollo:*
The Epic Journey to the Moon

Given what paragraphs do, it would be surprising if they didn't sometimes borrow the structures used by full essays: thesis and support, division, classification, comparison/contrast. (Again, you likely remember these patterns from middle and high school; if not, check any writing handbook.) But, truthfully, it's ideas that drive the shape of paragraphs, not patterns of organization. Few writers, if any at all, pause to consider whether their next paragraph should follow a narrative or cause-and-effect plan. They just write it, making sure it has a point and pleases readers.

Some workaday considerations about paragraphs: They were invented to make texts more readable, so compose them with that goal in mind. Be sure that paragraph breaks coincide with shifts or divisions within your writing itself, so readers understand when your thoughts head in a new direction. Consider, too, the value of a short paragraph for emphasizing an idea (like a conclusion or turn in the argument) or giving readers a break after a few lengthy passages.

Learn to appreciate what excellent transitional devices paragraphs are, especially when writers can use them as meta-discourse (see Chapter 3) to explain what they intend to do. Here is Thomas L. Friedman, for example, in *Hot, Flat, and Crowded* moving from a section describing America's failure to meet "the challenges of the Energy-Climate Era" into one explaining that dereliction:

> What is our problem? If the right things to do—most notably raising the gasoline tax and putting a fixed, durable, long-term price on carbon—are so obvious to the people who know the most about the energy business, why can't we put them in place?

You could write a paragraph like this to set the scene in a narrative or to preview the content of a report. Or you might write very brief paragraphs—sometimes just a sentence or two long—to mark turns in your thinking or offer strong judgments. You've likely even seen paragraphs that consist of nothing more than an indignant "Nonsense!" or a sarcastic "Nuts!" or "Go figure." There's always a risk in penning a paragraph with so much attitude, but it's an option when the occasion calls for it.

Use Transitions

Ah, transitions! What exactly makes words, sentences, and ideas glide from paragraph to paragraph as fluidly as Olympic swimmer Michael Phelps through water? Transitional words and phrases, many writers would reply—thinking of devices such as *and, but, however, neither . . . nor, first . . . second . . . third,* and so on. Transitional words certainly make a paper move, and, fortunately, there's nothing complicated about them. You'll recognize every word in any list of transitions. But be aware that they have different functions and uses, with subtle differences even between words as close in meaning as *but* and *yet*.

Transitional words help move ideas.

Common Transitions				
CONNECTION OR CONSEQUENCE	CONTRAST	CORRELATION	SEQUENCE OR TIME	INDICATION
and	but	if . . . then	first . . . second	this
or	yet	either . . . or	and then	that
so	however	from . . . to	initially	there
therefore	nevertheless		subsequently	for instance
moreover	nonetheless		before	for example
consequently	on the contrary		after	in this case
hence	despite		until	
	still		next	
	although		in conclusion	

Of course, transitional words and phrases are only part of the story when it comes to connecting ideas.

Almost any successful piece of writing is held together by more devices than most writers can consciously juggle. A few of the ties—such as connections between pronouns, their referents, and synonyms for nouns—are almost invisible and seem to take care of themselves. Yet clarity in a piece suffers if the relationships between nouns and pronouns aren't clear. Note how effortlessly Adam Nicolson moves between *George Abbot, he*, and *man* in the following paragraph from *God's Secretaries* (2003), which describes one of the men responsible for the King James translation of the Bible:

> George Abbot was perhaps the ugliest of them all, a morose, intemperate man, whose portraits exude a sullen rage. Even in death, he was portrayed on his tomb in Holy Trinity, Guilford, as a man of immense weight, with a heavy, wrinkled brow and coldly open, staring eyes. He looks like a bruiser, a man of such conviction and seriousness that anyone would think twice about crossing him. What was it that made George Abbot so angry?

Nouns and pronouns connect people to ideas and actions.

Fortunately, readers usually don't mind encountering a pronoun over and over (*he* in this example)—except maybe *I*—so long as the repetition keeps a passage connected.

Synonyms for important nouns have almost the same subtle effect. Simply by repeating a noun from sentence to sentence, you make obvious and logical connections within a paper—whether you are naming an object, an idea, or a person. To avoid monotony, vary any terms you have to use frequently. But don't introduce archaic or inappropriate synonyms that only distract readers. Note the sensible variants on the word *trailer* in the following paragraph:

> Hype and hysteria have always been a part of movie advertising, but the frenzy of film trailers today follows a visual style first introduced by music videos in the 1980s. The quick cut is everything, accompanied by a deafening soundtrack. Next time you go to a film, study the three or four previews that precede the main feature. How are these teasers constructed? What are their common features? What emotions or reactions do they raise in you? What might trailers say about the expectations of audiences today?

Synonyms provide connection and variety.

Consider, too, the role that various sequences and directions play in moving readers through papers and articles. Such expressions can simply mark off stages or sequences—*first, second, third; if . . . then; on the one hand . . . on the other*. More complicated or specialized directions have a similar value as signposts: *early in the project, as the study progressed, in the final stages*. Over the course of a paragraph or an entire work, transitional phrases like these give structure to your work while bits of meta-discourse and chatter keep you in touch with readers. There are probably more such signals than can be listed:

as you can see	doubtless
to be sure	of course
certainly	naturally
it might be said, [argued, objected]	

Sentence structures, too, can connect ideas within paragraphs. For example, readers will assume that ideas in sentences with parallel or repetitive structures are related. In the following example, notice how rhythmically Ian Frazier repeats the phrase *I don't want to* to organize a paragraph about his "wannabe" relationship with Native American culture:

I kind of resent the term "wannabe"—what's wrong with wanting to be something anyway—but in my case there's some truth to it. I don't want to participate in traditional Indian religious ceremonies, dance in a sun dance or pray in a sweat lodge or go on a vision quest with the help of a medicine man. The power of these ceremonies has an appeal, but I'm content with what little religion I already have. I think Indians dress better than anyone, but I don't want to imitate more than a detail or two; I prefer my clothes humdrum and inconspicuous, and a cowboy hat just doesn't work for me. I don't want to collect Indian art, though pots and beadwork and blankets made by Indians remain the most beautiful art objects in the American West, in my opinion. I don't want to be adopted into a tribe, be wrapped in a star quilt and given a new name, honor though that would be. I don't want to stand in the dimness under the shelter at the powwow grounds in the group around the circle of men beating the drums and singing ancient songs and lose myself in that moment when all the breaths and all the heartbeats become one. What I want is just as "Indian," just as traditional, but harder to pin down.

—ON THE REZ

Repetition and parallelism can establish connections between ideas.

Compare this item with the less deliberately patterned paragraph from Frazier on pages 171–72 to appreciate how a structural device can sharpen a reader's response.

For many kinds of academic work, it's also perfectly fine to use physical devices to mark transitions. Writing has fewer visual markers than, let's say, the movies to manage quick cuts, dissolves, and fade-ins, but they are important. Titles and headings in lab reports, for instance, let your reader know precisely when you are moving from "Methods" to "Results" to "Discussion." In books, you encounter chapter breaks as well as divisions within chapters, sometimes marked by asterisks or perhaps just a blank space. Seeing these signals, readers expect the narration to change in some way.

Visual markers can highlight transitions, especially in longer texts.

To locate weak transitions, listen to yourself while you read something you wrote. Mark every point in the draft where you pause, stumble, or find yourself adding a transitional word or phrase not in the original text. Fix even the smallest problem because tiny slips in coherence have a way of escalating. Look for words or phrases that make difficult passages simpler, clearer, or more readable. (See Chapter 18 for more about clarity and economy.)

Make Introductions

An introduction has to grab and hold a reader's attention, but that's not all. It also must introduce a topic, a writer, and a purpose. Like the music over a film's opening credits, an introduction tells readers what to expect. Any doubts about where the following opening paragraph is heading?

Introductions create first impressions.

> At a liquidation sale, every day is Black Friday. Customers hover outside the store before it opens like vultures waiting for a dying animal to become a fresh carcass.
>
> —MICHAEL NANCE, "EVERYTHING MUST GO"

Of course, you will want to write introductions that fit your projects. To get a short paper rolling, one or more paragraphs may provide all the push you need. But in a senior thesis or report, a separate introductory section or chapter may set the stage for your project.

What should these materials accomplish?

First of all, check whether you need to follow any templates that spell out how to enter a subject. Writing a story for a newspaper, you typically begin by providing essential facts, identifying *who, what, where,* and *when.* You'll also follow conventions with technical materials (lab reports, research articles, scholarly essays). You can't ignore these details without raising eyebrows.

To get such introductions right, study models of these genres and then copy their structures.

When you're not constrained by a template, you have many options for an opening, the most straightforward being simply to announce your project. This blunt approach is common in academic papers where it makes sense to identify a subject and preview your plan for developing it. Quite often, the introductory material leads directly into a thesis statement or a hypothesis, as in the following student paper:

General topic or theme is identified.

In her novel *Wuthering Heights* (1847), Emily Brontë presents the story of the families of Wuthering Heights and Thrushcross Grange through the seemingly impartial perspective of Nelly Dean, a servant who grows up with the families. Upon closer inspection, however, it becomes apparent that Nelly acts as much more than a bystander in the tragic events taking place around her. In her status as an outsider with influence over the families, Nelly strikingly resembles the Byronic hero Heathcliff and competes with him for power. Although the author depicts Heathcliff as the more overt gothic hero, Brontë allows the reader to infer from Nelly's story her true character and role in the family.

Thesis states what the paper will prove.

The author draws a parallel between Nelly Dean and Heathcliff in their relationships to the Earnshaw family, in their similar roles as tortured heroes, and in their competition for power within their adoptive families.

— Manasi Deshpande, "Servant and Stranger: Nelly and Heathcliff in *Wuthering Heights*"

Many reports and arguments open more slowly, using an introductory section to cue up the material to follow so that readers appreciate why an issue deserves attention. You might, for example, present an anecdote, describe a trend, or point to some phenomenon readers may not have noticed. Then you can thrash out its significance or implications.

Opening paragraphs can also deliver necessary background information. The trick is always to decide what exactly readers need to know about a subject. Provide too little background information on a subject and readers may find the project confusing. Supply too much context and you lose fans quickly. And yet, even when readers know a subject well, be sure to answer basic questions about the project—once again, *who, what, where*, and *when* and maybe even a little *how* and *why*. Name names in your introduction, offer accurate titles, furnish dates, and explain what your subject is. Imagine readers from just slightly outside your target audience who might not instantly recall, for instance, that Shakespeare wrote a play entitled *Henry V* or that Edwin "Buzz" Aldrin was the *second* person to walk on the surface of the moon. Don't leave readers puzzled, especially in academic papers. But you can intrigue them.

Intrigue readers, but don't puzzle them.

Give them a reason to enter your text. Invite them with a compelling incident or provocative story, with a recitation of surprising or intriguing facts, with a dramatic question, with a memorable description or quotation. Naturally, any opening has to be in sync with the material that follows—not outrageously emotional if the argument is sober, not lighthearted and comic if the paper has a serious theme.

Your introduction, after all, sets a tone and sends readers all sorts of signals, some of them almost subliminal. Typically, readers use an introduction to determine whether they belong to the audience of the piece. A paper that opens with highly technical language says "specialists only," while a more personal or colloquial style welcomes a broader audience. Readers are also making judgments about you in those opening lines, so you can't afford errors of fact or even grammar and usage there. Such slips-ups cloud the reading of all that follows.

One last bit of advice: Don't write an introduction until you're ready. The opening of a project can be notoriously difficult to frame because it does so much work. If you are blocked at the beginning of a project, plunge directly into the body of the paper and see what happens. You can even write the opening section last after you know precisely where the paper goes. No one will know.

Introductions can be written later.

Draw Conclusions

Writing introductions carries all the trepidations of asking for a first date. So conclusions should be much easier, right? By the time you need a conclusion, you've established a relationship with readers, provided necessary background, laid down arguments, and discussed important issues. All that remains is the verbal equivalent of a good-night kiss . . . Okay, maybe conclusions aren't that simple.

Like introductions, conclusions serve different purposes and audiences. An e-mail to a professor may need no more of a sign-off than a signature. A response paper may end best with a paragraph that briefly explores the implications of a reading. A senior thesis, however, could require a whole chapter to wrap things up. In reports and arguments, you typically use the concluding section to recap what you've covered and tie major points together. The following is the no-nonsense conclusion of a college report on a childhood developmental disorder, cri du chat syndrome (CDCS). Note that this summary paragraph also leads where many other scientific and scholarly articles do: to a call for additional research.

Major point

Major point

Conclusion ties together main points.

Though research on CDCS remains far from abundant, existing studies prescribe early and ongoing intervention by a team of specialists, including speech-language pathologists, physical and occupational therapists, various medical and educational professionals, and parents. Such intervention has been shown to allow individuals with CDCS to live happy, long, and full lives. The research, however, indicates that the syndrome affects all aspects of a child's development and should therefore be taken quite seriously. Most children require numerous medical interventions, including surgery (especially to correct heart defects), feeding tubes, body braces, and repeated treatment of infections. Currently, the best attempts are being made to help young children with CDCS reach developmental milestones earlier, communicate effectively, and function as independently as possible. However, as the authors of the aforementioned studies suggest, much more research is needed to clarify the causes of varying degrees of disability, to identify effective and innovative treatments/interventions (especially in the area of education), and to individualize intervention plans.

—MARISSA DAHLSTROM,
"DEVELOPMENTAL DISORDERS:
CRI DU CHAT SYNDROME"

In some writing, including many arguments, you may not want to disclose your key point until the very end, following a convincing presentation of claims and evidence. This sort of project *does* unfold a bit like a mystery, keeping readers on edge, eager to discover your point. You don't open with a thesis, nor do you tip your hand completely until the conclusion.

On many occasions you will want to finish dramatically and memorably, especially in arguments and personal narratives that seek to influence readers and change opinions. Since final paragraphs are what readers remember, it makes sense that they be powerfully written. Here's the conclusion of a lengthy personal essay by Shane McNamee on gay marriage that leads up to a poignant political appeal:

> Forget for the moment the rainbow flags and pink triangles. Gay pride is not about being homosexual; it's about the integrity and courage it takes to be honest with yourself and your loved ones. It's about spending life with whomever you want and not worrying what the government or the neighbors think. Let's protect that truth, not some rigid view of sexual orientation or marriage. Keep gay marriage out of your church if you like, but if you value monogamy as I do, give me an alternative that doesn't involve dishonesty or a life of loneliness. Many upstanding gay citizens yearn for recognition of their loving, committed relationships. Unless you enjoy being lied to and are ready to send your gay friends and family on a Trail of Queers to Massachusetts or Canada—where gay marriage is legal—then consider letting them live as they wish.
>
> —"Protecting What Really Matters"

Repetition focuses readers on the point.

Appeals directly to readers (you)

Appeals through images and language

Choose Titles

Titles may not strike you as an important element of writing, but they can be. A proper title lets readers know what a book, article, essay, or just about any publication is about and, later, makes it easier to find in an electronic archive or library collection. Coming up with a title can even help you structure a piece: A title that is too broad early in a project is a sure sign that you have yet to find a workable topic. If all you have is "Sea Battles in World War II" or "Children in America," you need to do more research. If no title comes to mind at all, you're still just hunting for ideas.

Titles help to focus documents.

For academic papers, titles need to be descriptive. Consider these items culled at random from one issue of the *Stanford Undergraduate Research Journal* (Spring 2008). Scientific papers aimed at knowledgeable specialists have highly technical titles; titles in the social sciences and humanities are less intimidating, but just as focused on providing information about their subjects.

> "Molecular and Morphological Characterization of Two Species of Sea Cucumber, *Parastichopus parvimensis* and *Parastichopus californicus*, in Monterey, CA"
>
> —CHRISTINE O'CONNELL, ALISON J. HAUPT, AND STEPHEN R. PALUMBI

> "Justifiers of the British Opium Trade: Arguments by Parliament, Traders, and the Times Leading Up to the Opium War"
>
> —CHRISTINE SU

> "The Incongruence of the Schopenhauerian Ending in Wagner's *Götterdämmerung*"
>
> —JAMES LOCUS

For academic or professional papers, a thoughtful title makes sense standing on its own and out of context. It should also include keywords by which it might be searched for in a database or online. For example, an essay entitled "Smile!" wouldn't offer many clues about its content or purpose; far more useful is the title of a real journal article by Christina Kotchemidova, "From Good Cheer to 'Drive-By Smiling': A Social History of Cheerfulness." When Professor Kotchemidova's paper winds up in someone's bibliography or in an online database, readers know what its subject is.

If you must be clever or allusive, follow the cute title with a colon and an explanatory subtitle:

> "'Out, Damn'd Spot!': Images of Conscience and Remorse in Shakespeare's *Macbeth*"
> "Out, Damn'd Spot: Housebreaking Your Puppy"

Avoid whimsical or sexually suggestive titles. At this point you may not worry about your publications, but documents have a life of their own once uploaded to the Web or listed on a résumé. A bad title, like a silly screen name or e-mail address, will haunt you, especially when you approach the job market.

39. Find a passage about a dozen paragraphs long in a recent reading and analyze the structures of its paragraphs to see how much variation you find. Begin by highlighting a topic sentence or major point in each paragraph, if you can find one. Then try to determine how that main point is developed. Following are some possibilities: topic/support; claim/evidence; cause/effect; problem/solution; definition; sequence of events. How much structural variety do you find in the paragraphs? Do you find paragraphs whose structure you can't describe? Is that a problem?

40. What transitional signals, signposts, or transitions do you appreciate most when you're reading? Do you scan the chapter titles of a book before you read it or the headings in an article? Do you find pull quotes in magazines—highlighted sentences framed in boxes—helpful? Do any structural or textual features turn you off or distract you—especially when reading online? Use specific examples to illustrate your preferences.

41. As this chapter suggests, there's more to transitions than just the familiar transitional words or phrases listed on page 174. If you want a paper to cohere, you need a variety of connectors. As an exercise, take a paper you have written recently and highlight all the types of transitions listed in this chapter that you can find in your work: transitional words and phrases, parallel sentence structures, deliberate repetitions, connections between nouns and pronouns, or synonyms and varied terms. Which of the transitions would you say you created deliberately and which probably came without much thought? Does the paper seem to cohere, or would readers benefit from a few more signposts?

42. Examine the opening paragraphs or sections in several chapters of *A Reader's Guide to College Writing*. What strategies do you notice? How do the chapter openers differ? Do you find any of the chapters more successful than others? Why?

43. What exactly do conclusions accomplish? To find out, review a selection of published pieces from a variety of genres—

for example, sports column, editorial, research article, movie review, blog entry—and then examine what happens if you remove the final paragraph in each piece. Is anything lost? Pay attention not only to the content of these conclusions, but also to their rhetoric and language. How do they make you think and feel as you leave the articles?

44. In the library or online, compare the titles of articles in the table of contents of a popular magazine with those in a scholarly journal that covers a roughly equivalent subject. (For example, you might pair the widely read magazine *Smithsonian* with an academic journal on American history or culture.) In what specific ways do titles in the periodicals differ? What do the titles reveal about the intended audiences of the articles?

15

The truth is incontrovertible.
— WINSTON CHURCHILL

Evidence

On May 17, 1916, Winston Churchill declared that "the truth is incontrovertible." He was addressing Great Britain's House of Commons during an argument over support for the nation's fledgling "Aeroplane Service," and no doubt his claim struck home. The former First Lord of the Admiralty had just offered his listeners specific evidence that British aircraft had been successful in thwarting German Zeppelin attacks on Britain. Challenging anyone who doubted his account, Churchill amplified his assertion: "Panic may resent it, ignorance may deride it, malice may distort it, but there it is." Today, we admire the words and include them in books of quotations, but what probably mattered more in 1916 were the facts and logic that preceded the stirring rhetoric, offered within the context of a lively debate on military policy. Churchill pointed out, for example, that "after twenty-two months of war no object of any military or naval importance . . . has yet been struck by any Zeppelin bomb."

Not much has changed about the rhetorical power of evidence: It still counts with readers, from the data you assemble to support claims, to the authorities you cite or quote in the process of reporting, analyzing, and disputing them. So where you find your materials and how you use them will make or break many college projects. It's that simple.

Evidence is everything.

Find Sources

This is basic stuff. When doing an academic paper that requires facts, data, and reputable research or opinion, look to three resources in this order: local and school libraries, informational databases and indexes, and the Internet. Libraries remain your first resource because they have been set up specifically to steer you toward materials appropriate for academic projects. Informational databases and indexes are usually available to you only through libraries and their Web sites, so they are a natural follow-up. And the Internet places third on this list, an undeniably useful resource, but still a rugged frontier when it comes to reliable information, particularly for a novice.

At the library you'll find books, journals, and newspapers and other materials, both print and electronic, in a collection expertly overseen by librarians and information specialists, who are, by the way, the most valuable resources in the building. They are specifically trained to help you find what you need. (Get to know them.)

Librarians: your secret weapon

Library Catalogs and Resources

Of course, the key to navigating a library is its catalog. All but the smallest or most specialized libraries now organize their collections electronically (rather than with printed cards), but there's still a learning curve. The temptation will be to plunge in and start searching. After all, you *can* locate most items by author, title, subject, keywords, and even call number. But spend a few minutes reading the available help screens to discover the features and protocols of the catalog. Most searches tell you immediately if the library has a book or journal you need, where it is on the shelves or in data collections, and whether it is available.

Learn *how to use* the catalog first.

Don't ignore, either, the advanced features of a catalog (such as searches by language, by date, by type of content); these options help you find just the items you need or can use. And since you will often use a library not to find specific materials, but to find and develop topics, pay attention to the keywords or search terms the catalog uses to index the subject you're exploring. Why? Because you can use index terms for sources you find to look for other similar materials—an important way of generating leads on a subject.

In the age of Wikipedia, an all-too-convenient resource many instructors regard with suspicion, it's easy to forget that libraries still offer truly authoritative source materials in their reference rooms or online reference collections—the sort of tools you need when you want in-depth information on an author, topic, or event. Such standard works include encyclopedias, almanacs, historical records, maps, and so on. Quite often, for instance, you'll need reliable biographical facts about important people—dates of birth, countries of origin, schools attended, career paths, and so on. For people currently in the news, you might find enough data from a Web search or a Wikipedia entry. But to get accurate facts on historical figures, consult library tools such as the *Oxford Dictionary of National Biography* (focusing on the United Kingdom) or the *Dictionary of American Biography*. The British work is available in an up-to-date online version. Libraries also have many more specialized biographical tools, both in print and online. Ask about them.

If you want information from old newspapers, you'll need ingenuity. Libraries don't store newspapers, so local and a few national papers will be available only on microfilm or microfiche, probably housed in a library basement next to aging microform readers. Just as discouraging, very few older newspapers are indexed. So, unless you know the approximate date of an event, you may have a tough time finding a specific story in the microfilmed copies of newspapers. Fortunately, both the *New York Times* and *Wall Street Journal* are indexed and available in some format in most major libraries. You'll also find older magazines in microfilm. These may be indexed (up to 1982) in print bibliographies such as the *Readers' Guide to Periodical Literature*. Ask a librarian for assistance.

When your own library doesn't have resources you need, ask the people at the checkout or reference desks about interlibrary loan. If cooperating libraries have the books or materials you want, you can borrow them at minimal cost. But plan ahead. The loan process takes time.

Information Databases and Indexes

Professional databases and indexes—our second category of research materials—are also found at libraries, among their electronic resources. These tools give you access to professional journals, magazines, and newspaper archives, in either summary or full-text form. Your library or school purchases licenses to make these valuable, often password-protected, resources available—services such as *EBSCOhost, InfoTrac,* and *Lexis-Nexis*. And, once again, librarians can teach you how to navigate such complex databases efficiently.

Many academic research projects, for instance, begin with a search of multidisciplinary databases such as *LexisNexis*

Academic, Academic OneFile, or *Academic Search Premier.* These über-indexes cover a wide range of materials, including newspapers, reputable magazines, and many academic periodicals. Most libraries subscribe to one or more of these information services, which you can search much like library catalogs, using basic and advanced search features.

For even more in-depth research, you need to learn to use databases within your specific field or major, tools such as *Ei* in engineering or the *MLA International Bibliography* in language and literature studies. There are, in fact, hundreds of such databases, far too many to list here, and some of them may be too specialized or technical for projects early in a college career. Librarians or instructors can direct you to the ones you can handle and, when necessary, explain how to use them. Such databases are sometimes *less* accessible than they seem on first glance.

An excellent but often ignored Web option for jump-starting academic projects is to use research sites designed by libraries or universities for students working in specific fields. Check to see whether your school has developed such materials. Or simply search the phrase "library research guides" on the Web. These sites typically gather resources both from within and outside of specific schools or institutions, and they may also suggest topic ideas for writing. Use these guides carefully, since they

Research Guides and Databases

INSTITUTION	SUBJECT GUIDES AT
Columbia University Library	www.columbia.edu/cu/lweb/eresources
New York Public Library	www.nypl.org/collections/nypl-recommendations/research-guides
University of Chicago	http://guides.lib.uchicago.edu/home
University of Virginia	www.lib.virginia.edu/resguide.html
Electronic Books	www.lib.utexas.edu/books/etext.html
Infomine	http://infomine.ucr.edu
The Internet Public Library	www.ipl.org
Library of Congress Research and Reference Services	www.loc.gov/rr

may contain links to materials that libraries and schools cannot vouch for entirely. Some of the university-based materials may also be restricted to students at particular schools. But, even then, the guides may help you to identify authors or databases to explore through your own institution. The chart on page 188 may help you find databases for your subject, field, or major.

The Internet

Finally, as you well know, you can find information simply by exploring the Web from the comfort of your laptop or tablet, using search engines such as Google and Bing to locate data and generate ideas. The Web taps into just about every subject imaginable (and some beyond that), but the quality and reliability of online sites vary tremendously. The territory may seem familiar because you spend so much time online, but don't overestimate your ability to find what you need. Browsing the Web daily to check sports scores and favorite blogs is completely different than using the Web for academic work.

Find trustworthy sources on the Web.

Research suggests that many students begin their projects by simply typing obvious terms into Web browsers, ignoring the advanced capabilities of search engines. As a result, they don't scour the environment as thoroughly as they might or they succumb to the algorithms of the Web browsers themselves, which generally select items more for popularity and commerce than for reliability. To take more control of searches, follow the links on search engine screens you now mostly ignore and learn to use the tools available right in front of you: *Advanced Search*; *Search Help*; *Help*; *Fix a Problem*; *Tips & Tricks*; *Useful Features*; *More*. You'll be amazed what you discover.

Use browsers' *advanced* search tools.

Exercise care with all Web sources. Be certain you know who is responsible for the material you are reading (for instance, a government agency, a congressional office, a news service, a corporation), who is posting it, who is the author of the material or sponsor of the Web site, what the date of publication is, and so on. A site's information is often skewed by those who pay its bills or run it; it can also be outdated, if no one regularly updates the resource.

Keep current with Web developments, too. Web companies such as Google are making more books and journal articles both searchable and available through their sites. Although

Google Scholar
is an academic
research tool.

these and other projects to broaden access to scholarly information raise questions about copyright and the ownership of
intellectual property, examine these tools as they become available. For instance, a tool such as Google Scholar will direct you
to academic sources and scholarly papers on a topic—exactly
the kind of material you want to use in term papers or reports.
As an experiment, compare the hits you get on a topic with a
regular Google search with those that turn up when you select
the Scholar option: You'll find the Scholar items more serious
and technical—and also more difficult to access. In some cases,
you may see only an abstract of a journal article or the first page
of the item. Yet the materials you locate may be worth a trip to
the library to retrieve in their entirety.

Resources to Consult When Conducting Academic Research

SOURCE	WHAT IT PROVIDES	USEFULNESS	WHERE TO FIND IT
Scholarly Books	Fully documented and detailed primary research and analyses by scholars	Highly useful if not too high-level or technical	Library, Google Scholar
Scholarly Journals	Carefully documented primary research by scientists and scholars	Highly useful if not too high-level or technical	Library, databases
Newspapers	Accounts of current events	Useful as starting point	Library, microfilm, databases (*LexisNexis*), Internet
Magazines	Wide topic range, usually based on secondary research; written for popular audience	Useful if magazine has serious reputation	Libraries, newsstands, databases (*EBSCOhost, InfoTrac*), Internet
Encyclopedias (General or Discipline Specific)	Brief articles	Useful as a starting point	Libraries, Internet
Wikipedia	Open-source encyclopedia: entries written/edited by online contributors	Not considered reliable for academic projects	Internet: www.wikipedia.org

Resources to Consult When Conducting Academic Research *(continued)*

SOURCE	WHAT IT PROVIDES	USEFULNESS	WHERE TO FIND IT
Special Collections	Materials such as maps, paintings, artifacts, etc.	Highly useful for specialized projects	Libraries, museums; images available via Internet
Government, Academic, or Organization Web Sites	Vast data compilations of varying quality, some of it reviewed	Highly useful	Internet sites with URLs ending in *.gov, .edu,* or *.org*
Commercial Web Sites	Information on many subjects; quality varies	Useful if possible biases are known	Internet sites
Blogs	Controlled, often highly partisan discussions of specialized topics	Useful when affiliated with reputable sources such as newspapers	Internet
Personal Web Sites	Often idiosyncratic information	Rarely useful; content varies widely	Internet

Seek Expert Advice

Forget about *expert* as an intimidating word. When you need help with your writing, especially with finding sources and developing ideas, get advice from people who either know more about your subject than you do or have more experience developing such a project. The more individuals you talk to, the better. Experts can get you on track quickly, confirming the merit of your topic ideas, cutting through issues irrelevant to your work, and directing you to the best resources.

Always begin by talking with your instructor. Don't be timid. Instructors hold office hours to answer your questions, especially about readings and assignments. Save yourself time and, perhaps, much grief by getting early feedback on a project. (It's better to learn that your thesis is hopeless before you compose a first draft.) Your instructor might also help you appreciate aspects of a reading you hadn't noticed or direct you to key sources. You shouldn't write papers only to please instructors, but you'd be foolish to ignore their counsel.

Your instructor is a valuable resource.

Take your ideas to the campus writing center, too, if you can. Many writers mistakenly believe that these facilities are only for drafts on life support. In fact, writing center tutors would rather not be EMTs, and so they're eager to offer advice at the start of a project, when you're still developing a topic or looking for materials. They may not be experts on your subject, but tutors have seen enough bad project ideas to offer sensible advice for focusing a subject, choosing reliable sources, or adapting a paper to an audience. They also recognize when you're so clueless that you better talk with your instructor pronto.

Use the writing center.

Consider, too, whether any people in your campus community might know something about your subject. Campuses in particular are teeming with knowledgeable people—and that doesn't just mean faculty in their disciplines. Staff, administrative personnel, technicians, and coaches at your school can advise you on everything from trends in college admissions to local crime statistics. Don't bother them for information you could find easily yourself in the library or online: Save human contacts for when you need serious help on a major writing project—a senior thesis, an important story for a campus periodical, a public presentation on a controversial subject.

Finally, have you considered talking about your work with peers? They aren't really experts, but an honest classroom conversation among fellow students can be an eye-opening experience. (Remember Chapter 11?) You'll likely encounter a spectrum of opinions (if the discussion is frank) and even be surprised when people raise solid objections to your ideas or potential sources. ("MSNBC? You've got to be kidding!") Peers often have an amazing range of knowledge and, if the group is diverse, your friends will bring their varied life experiences to the table.

Consult your peers.

> **YOUR TURN**
>
> **45.** In school, you likely spend much time searching library databases and browsing titles to find useful material. Open a comprehensive scholarly database such as *Academic Search Complete* or *Academic OneFile* and search a keyword that identifies a concept, issue, or reading that you are currently studying in class. Survey the language of the first twenty or

thirty titles that come up. What do the titles alone tell you about your subject—its scope, dimensions, and complexity? Which titles do you find helpful and approachable? Which are too technical for you to use? Can you tell the difference between highly academic pieces and those that might be accessible to readers who are not specialists?

46. Identify a reading or general topic or topic area that interests you. Then explore that subject by using one of the "research guide" sources identified in this chapter on page 188. When you are done, compile a brief report describing the features and usefulness of the guide you have used. What kinds of information did it provide? Was it easy to use? Well organized? Helpful to someone from outside of the institution sponsoring it?

47. If you were asked to identify yourself as an expert on a subject, what would it be? Don't consider academic subjects only. Think about any areas or activities about which you could confidently offer authoritative and reliable advice. Make a list, share it with classmates, and remember who is an authority on what subjects. This information will come in handy throughout college when you need expert opinions.

16

. . . if you happen to be an intellectual,
you are what you quote.

— JOSEPH EPSTEIN

Frame Ideas
and Quotations

Joseph Epstein is right. Authors routinely shape their work in response to the words and ideas of others. Throughout this book, and especially in Part Two, we have examined strategies writers use to weave those borrowed notions and words into their own texts. When managed well, this integration of materials seems effortless, but it's a great balancing act for novices — like riding a unicycle, with every screw-up glaringly obvious and potentially painful.

The basic principles are simple. Readers always need to know who or what you've introduced into your own work, why they are there, and what exactly they've accomplished or said to make them noteworthy. That's true whether you are summarizing material you have read or quoting from it. The last point is important. Most college writers know that they need to place quotation marks and maybe a *he said* or *she said* in the vicinity of borrowed words, but to acknowledge summarized or paraphrased ideas just seems fussy. Yet that courtesy is one of the keys to successful academic writing — and not just because crediting sources helps you to evade charges of plagiarism (which it does).

Acknowledge experts and their ideas in your work.

When you incorporate sources into your work cogently, you give readers information they need to appraise the thinking you've done. They discover what you've read and learned and how much purchase you have on ideas. The give-and-take between you and these raw materials creates a topographical map of your thinking and prepares you to introduce ideas of your own. If the territory you describe seems dull, flat, and under-populated, no one will stay long; instead, readers will steer toward more interesting texts full of possibilities.

Yet introducing quotations and ideas into a paper is far from intuitive. Even students who read a lot don't always nail these landings. So you want to watch how experienced writers present the materials they borrow. You also want to learn how to merge quotations into neighboring passages without a rip-ple — no problems with clarity, verb tense, subject or pronoun references, and so on.

Mimic how authors introduce sources.

Use Frames to Give Credit

Here's the challenge then: Readers always need to know what words and ideas are yours in a paper and what you've imported from others. So give them a signal whenever borrowed material becomes part of your own text. Think of it as *framing* these sup-porting elements. Typically, all that's required for a frame is a brief phrase that identifies the author, title, or source you are drawing on. Frames can introduce, interrupt, follow, or even surround the words or ideas taken from sources. The following list shows several examples of frames in action, giving credit to other people's ideas.

EXACT WORDS

Michelle Obama **argued** on *The View* **that** ". . . [quotation]."

"[Quotation] . . . ," **says** Jack Welch, former CEO of General Elec-tric, **pointing out that** ". . . [more quotation]."

SUMMARIZED FACTS

According to a report in *Scientific American* (October 2012), the Mars rover *Curiosity* will soon . . . [your own words].

PARAPHRASED IDEA

Can a person talk intelligently about books even without read-ing them? Pierre Bayard, for one, **suggests that** . . . [your own words].

YOUR SUMMARY WITH QUOTATION

In *Encounters with the Archdruid*, author John McPhee **introduces** readers to conservationist David Brower, whom he **credits** with [your own words], **calling him** ". . . [quotation]."

As you see, most such frames include a "verb of attribution" or "signal verb" that characterizes a source's contribution or, per-haps, its perspective and attitude. The default choice is often an innocuous, yet adequate, "says" or "said." But you have an almost endless list of choices that ensures that your frame can be an exact fit. Consider the vast difference in meaning and connotation, for instance, between *said* and *snarled*; *reported* and *claimed*; *stated* and *implied*. In general, you'll employ neutral signal verbs in reports and use more descriptive attributions in arguments. By MLA convention, verbs of attribution are usually in the present tense when talking about current work or ideas. In APA style, these verbs are generally in the past tense or present perfect tense.

Frames signal which ideas are yours — and which aren't.

Selected Verbs of Attribution

NEUTRAL	DESCRIPTIVE	SLANTED
adds	acknowledges	admits
explains	argues	charges
finds	asserts	confesses
notes	believes	confuses
observes	claims	derides
offers	confirms	disputes
says	disagrees	evades
shows	responds	impugns
states	reveals	pretends
writes	suggests	smears

Of course, there's far more to framing material than just giving credit to other writers or using verbs of attribution. Framing is a way of setting ideas and authors into complex relationships. You can use frames to provide background information on borrowed material; to introduce, explain, or amplify evidence; to present contrasts; to highlight disagreements; and, naturally, to enter the discussion yourself. Frames even provide structure for many paragraphs or entire sections in longer works.

Use Frames to Connect Ideas

One of the most common uses of frames is to accumulate evidence in support of an idea or claim, connecting one source to another to reach a persuasive critical mass. Consider William Patry, the author of *Moral Panics and the Copyright Wars*. He believes that contemporary notions of copyright are far more restrictive than they were in the past, when authors borrowed freely and creatively from each other. To support this claim, he assembles a paragraph by connecting authorities that illustrate an older, more liberal view of intellectual property (footnotes omitted). The frames (underlined) show readers exactly how the different sources connect:

First authority sets context.

Patry's claim

Second authority confirms claim.

Third authority supports the claim.

The author of Kohelet (Ecclesiastes) wrote around 250 B.C.E.: "That which has been is what will be, and that which has been done is that which will be done; and there is nothing new under the sun." Whether the author meant this sentiment to apply to his own statement is perhaps paradoxical, but all authors not only build on the works of past authors, those works exist only in context with past and present authors and culture: readers can only understand contextually; that is, within shared communal understandings. This is what Hans-Georg Gadamer meant when he wrote: "Understanding is to be thought of less as a subjective act than as participating in an event of tradition, a process of transmission in which the past and present are constantly mediated." T. S. Eliot made the same point more eloquently in his essay "Tradition and the Individual Talent": "The historical generation compels a man to write not merely with his own generation in his bones, but with a feeling that the whole of literature from Homer and within it the whole literature of his own country has a simultaneous existence and composes a simultaneous order."

Even if readers don't follow every nuance of this paragraph, they appreciate how carefully Patry has assembled his evidence. He identifies three heavyweight supporters of his position and presents them as all singing the same tune.

Frames help readers follow arguments across much longer sections of a work. For example, in the "Afterword" to *The Immortal Life of Henrietta Lacks*, author Rebecca Skloot outlines the legal nuances within the controversy that has been the subject of her book—whether people like the late Henrietta Lacks should have control over tissues taken from their bodies. The full passage runs about a dozen pages, much too long to reproduce here, but the frames Skloot uses tell much of the story, connecting the people and groups involved in the dispute. Here's a sampling:

When I tell people the story of Henrietta Lacks and her cells, their first question is usually *Wasn't it illegal for doctors to take Henrietta's cells without her knowledge? Don't doctors have to tell you when they use your cells in research?* . . .

Frames connect the players and controversies.

Kathy Hudson, who has discussed focus groups about the public's feelings on the tissue issue, says she believes that tissue rights have the potential to become a bona fide movement. . . .

Supporters of the status quo argue that passing new, tissue-specific legislation isn't necessary and the current oversight practices are enough. . . .

. . . some tissue-rights advocates believe donors should have the right to say, for example, that they don't want their tissues used for . . .

Various policy analysts, scientists, philosophers, and ethicists have suggested ways to compensate tissue donors. . . .

Experts on both sides of the debate worry that compensating patients would lead to profit-seekers inhibiting science by insisting on unrealistic financial agreements. . . .

The debate over the commercialization of human biological material always comes back to one fundamental point: like it or not, we live in a market-driven society. . . .

Thanks to the frames, readers can easily follow the complex story that Skloot tells.

Use Frames to Synthesize Ideas

When writers have completed reading and note taking on specific topics, they often need to sort out the relationships between the ideas and authors they've encountered: Are they *similar, different, congruent, divergent, consistent, wildly varying, essential,* or *unremarkable,* and how so? Not surprisingly, this process of "synthesizing" ideas relies heavily on frames to express all these variables. You'll find syntheses at the beginnings of many books or articles, the material sometimes labeled as a "review of literature."

Increasingly, college students are asked to prepare formal synthesis papers to hone their skills as researchers and to prepare them to write longer reports and arguments. These are, in fact, exercises in framing ideas and sources. They typically begin with summarizing and paraphrasing a range of sources (see Chapter 10) and then follow up with an overall assessment of a controversy. Following is a truncated example that highlights the frames used to position the opinions of nine different writers with varying opinions about the merit of digital media, a subject mentioned not a few times in this book. Notice how many different ways authors are introduced as their ideas are either quoted or summarized:

Time to Adapt?

Synthesis topic is introduced.

There is considerable agreement that the Internet and other electronic media are changing the way people read, write, think, and behave. Scholars such as **Sven Birkerts** report that

Frames identify a complaint . . .

their students do not seem to read printed materials anymore, a fact confirmed by fifteen-year-old intern **Matthew Robson**, when asked by his employer Morgan Stanley to describe the media habits of teenagers in England: "No teenager that I know

. . . and lead to a direct quote.

of regularly reads a newspaper, as most do not have the time and cannot be bothered to read pages and pages of text."

But the changes we are experiencing may be more significant than just students abandoning the printed word.

Frame introduces speculation.

Working with an iPad, for instance, makes **Verlyn Klinkenborg** wonder whether reading on a screen may actually be a different and less perceptive experience than reading on paper. More worrisome, **Nicholas Carr** points to a growing body of research suggesting that the cognitive abilities of those who use media frequently may actually be degraded, weakening their comprehension and concentration.

Yet, according to **Clay Shirky**, the Internet is increasing our ability to communicate immeasurably, and so we simply have to deal with whatever consequences follow from such a major shift in technology. Thinkers like Shirky argue that we do not,

Frames identify a shift in the thinking.

in fact, have any choice but to adapt to such changes. Even **Christine Rosen**, a critic of technology, acknowledges that people will likely have to adjust to their diminished attention spans (110). After all, are there really any alternatives to the speed, convenience, and power of the new technologies when we have become what **Kevin Kelly** describes as "people of the screen" and are no more likely to return to paper for reading than we are to vinyl for music recordings?

Fears of the Internet may be overblown, too. **Peter Suderman** observes that changes in media allow us to do vastly more than we can with print alone. Moreover, because the sheer amount of knowledge is increasing so quickly, **Steven Pinker** argues that we absolutely need the new ways of communicating: "these technologies are the only things that will keep us smart."

We cannot, however, ignore voices of caution. The differences Carr describes between habits of deep reading and skimming are especially troubling because so many users of the Web have experienced them. And who can doubt the loss of seriousness in our public and political discussions these days? Maybe Rosen *is* right when she worries that our culture is trading wisdom for a glut of information. But it seems more likely that society will be better off trying to fix the problems electronic media are causing than imagining that we can return to simpler technologies that have already just about vanished.

Author of the synthesis offers opinion.

Works Cited

Birkerts, Sven. "Reading in a Digital Age." *The American Scholar.* Phi Beta Kappa, Spring 2010. Web. 10 Sept. 2010.

Carr, Nicholas. "Does the Internet Make You Dumber?" *Wall Street Journal.* Wall Street Journal, 5 June 2010. Web. 9 Sept. 2010.

Kelly, Kevin. "Reading in a Whole New Way." *Smithsonian.com.* Smithsonian, Aug. 2010. Web. 13 Sept. 2010.

Klinkenborg, Verlyn. "Further Thoughts of a Novice E-Reader." *New York Times.* New York Times, 28 May 2010. Web. 12 Sept. 2010.

Pinker, Steven. "Mind over Mass Media." *New York Times.* New York Times, 10 June 2010. Web. 12 Sept. 2010.

Robson, Matthew. "How Teenagers Consume Media." *Guardian. co.uk.* Guardian News and Media, 13 July 2009. Web. 14 Sept. 2010.

Rosen, Christine. "The Myth of Multitasking." *The New Atlantis* 20 (Spring 2008): 105–110. Print.

Shirky, Clay. "Does the Internet Make You Smarter?" *Wall Street Journal.* Wall Street Journal, 4 June 2010. Web. 9 Sept. 2010.

Suderman, Peter. "Don't Fear the E-Reader." *Reason.com.* Reason Magazine, 23 Mar. 2010. Web. 11 Sept. 2010.

Even this shortened example of a synthesis shows how frames enable a writer to position authors and sources, exposing, in the process, the salient issues of a controversy. The writer of the synthesis is left, at the end of the exercise, with a well-informed thesis that might support a full paper on its own: *[It] seems more likely that society will be better off trying to fix the problems electronic media are causing than imagining that we can return to simpler technologies that have already just about vanished.*

Use Frames to Join the Conversation

Finally, there is the matter of framing ideas and words to join an academic conversation yourself, whether you do it impersonally from a third-person point of view (*he, she, it, they*) or enter the fray directly by using first-person *I*. We'll present both possible strategies while having you imagine that you're composing a review of a book by Professor Pierre Bayard entitled, appropriately, *How to Talk about Books You Haven't Read*. Yes, you read that right. Now just play along.

By this point, I'll assume you know what an opening paragraph requires: You have to get readers interested. So why not compare one famous book on reading with another? You also need to set the context for your review, and so you should offer some details about the book you're reviewing. Your introductory paragraph might even close with an observation that functions *somewhat* like a thesis. But don't tip your hand yet; keep readers guessing about your opinion of the book. How's this?

Explains subject and gives context

Not everyone is as committed to slow and purposeful reading as Mortimer Adler, author of the classic *How to Read a Book* (1940). Pierre Bayard, a professor of literature at the University of Paris, offers a completely different perspective on reading in a more recent work—half serious, half playful—entitled *How to Talk about Books You Haven't Read* (2007). Bayard suggests that it is possible for people to engage in profitable discussions of books they barely know. In fact, he goes even further, stating in his preface that "it is sometimes easier to do justice to a book if you haven't read it in its entirety—or even opened it." Professor Bayard draws upon literary figures from Paul Valéry and Umberto Eco to Michel de Montaigne and Oscar Wilde to support his ironic and theoretical argument. Yet people who value reading may find that Bayard has it exactly backwards.

Summarizes Bayard's argument and quotes him

Suggests a point of view, but doesn't judge—yet

Notice how the opening paragraph is written entirely from a third-person perspective. You haven't entered the discussion yet.

Your second paragraph continues in this vein, summarizing Bayard and quoting him. You use transitional words and phrases (*True; Nor; And yet*) that sound critical and make some readers think they hear your voice. But your frames are still mostly unbiased and third person:

> True, some of Bayard's claims about reading are undeniable. It is humbling to realize, as Bayard points out, that no matter how many books we examine, we encounter only a minute fraction of all possible texts in a lifetime. Nor would most readers dispute his observations about how little even careful readers recall of the books they examine. As Bayard explains, "Reading is not just acquainting ourselves with a text or acquiring knowledge; it is also, from its first moments, an inevitable process of forgetting" (47). And yet Bayard is probably signaling his audience not to take him entirely seriously when he asserts, for example, that "it is not at all necessary to be familiar with what you're talking about in order to talk about it accurately" (19). Throughout *How to Talk about Books You Haven't Read*, it is clear that its author has spent plenty of time in libraries.

Transitions signal your presence.

Frames clarify and interpret Bayard's positions.

You could continue in this third-person mode throughout the review and readers *would* ordinarily expect you to be consistent. Such a point of view makes you sound serious and judicious, in control of your material. That's an advantage in academic writing.

But a more direct and personal approach also has advantages: If you present a credible and sympathetic ethos, readers will pay attention. So let's see what happens in this imaginary review if you switch to first-person frames and enter the argument yourself. The following paragraph, for example, could just as easily open "Still, what is surprising is . . . " But, instead, let's try *Still, what I find surprising* and go from there:

> Still, what I find surprising is how attractive Bayard can make the process of faking our way through books we haven't read seem. For him, encounters with authors and texts are part of a social process. This social process happens outside those handful of books most people only vaguely remember: "For a true reader, one who cares about being able to reflect on literature, it is not any specific book that counts, but the totality of all books" (30). Instead of being stifled by individual works that challenge our individual creativity, Bayard claims that only

Reacts to Bayard

Summarizes and quotes Bayard to set up point

in separating ourselves from books will we find opportunities to become writers ourselves (180). So when *Professor* Bayard deplores the fact that students are not taught "the art of talking about books they haven't read" (183), I find myself actually smiling and imagining what such a course might look like.

Notice that most of the frames here still focus on what Bayard has to say about reading because that's the consequential issue in the review. But when you enter the discussion ("I find myself actually smiling"), some readers may be comforted that you, like they, find Bayard's radical idea oddly appealing. That's because using "I" encourages readers to identify with you and your opinions. And that's one choice that framing offers: You can keep your distance from readers and sound highbrow and serious or you can come closer and encourage them to connect with you.

So why not finish this review now by stating your views clearly and personally? Sounds good. Let's imagine that you finally reject Bayard's approach to reading and explain why. You even find yourself briefly in a conversation with Bayard, trading points of view. Because you're smart (having read most of *this* book), you even draw upon a credible authority to land the final punches:

Even if Bayard scores points when he points out how easily people manage to get by without doing much more than skimming books, I doubt that he will convince dedicated readers to abandon their favorite pastime. Serious or not, he seems to value reading largely as a means to display cultural sophistication at parties. There, people can interact comfortably

with others who have read as little as they have. All that is required from such "creative" readers is that they understand what Bayard describes as the "location" of a work they wish to talk about, that is, "how it is situated in relation to other books" (11). But what I believe Bayard ignores throughout his own short work is the pleasure people take from the process of reading itself. Critic Sam Anderson captures my objection perfectly in his own review of Bayard's book in *New York Magazine* (October 21, 2007): "Real reading is not just hoarding fodder for cocktail chatter, it's crawling, phrase by phrase, through a text and finding yourself surprised or disappointed or ruined or bored with every other line." People who read treasure the experience itself, not just what they do with it afterwards.

It's probably important to mention that using *I* this way is increasingly accepted in academic writing, a strategy employed by too many serious writers and researchers to ignore. But always check with your instructor before using first-person frames, especially in research essays and term papers.

Handle Quotations Correctly

We'll close this chapter with a few housekeeping chores, essential to handling quotations.

First of all, learn to handle ellipsis marks [. . .]. They make it possible for you to do something quite practical: shorten lengthy quotations. When quoting a source in a paper, you don't need to use every word or sentence, as long as the cuts you make don't distort the meaning of the original material. An ellipsis mark, formed by those familiar three spaced periods, shows exactly where words, phrases, full sentences, or more have been removed from a quotation. However, the mark doesn't replace punctuation within a sentence. Thus, you might see a period or a comma immediately followed by an ellipsis mark.

ORIGINAL PASSAGE

Although gift giving has been a pillar of Hopi society, trade has also flourished in Hopi towns since prehistory, with a network that extended from the Great Plains to the Pacific Coast, and from the Great Basin, centered on present-day Nevada and Utah, to the Valley of Mexico. Manufactured goods, raw materials, and gems drove the trade, supplemented by exotic items such as parrots. The Hopis were producers as well, manufacturing large quantities of cotton cloth and ceramics for the trade. To this day, interhousehold trade and barter, especially for items of traditional manufacture for ceremonial use (such as basketry, bows, cloth, moccasins, pottery, and rattles), remain vigorous.

Words to be deleted from the quotation are underlined.

—Peter M. Whiteley, "Ties That Bind: Hopi Gift Culture and Its First Encounter with the United States"

PASSAGE WITH ELLIPSES

Whiteley has characterized Hopi economic practices this way:

> Although gift giving has been a pillar of Hopi society, trade has also flourished in Hopi towns since prehistory. . . . Manufactured goods, raw materials, and gems drove the trade, supplemented by exotic items such as parrots. The Hopis were producers as well, manufacturing large quantities of cotton cloth and ceramics for the trade. To this day, interhousehold trade and barter, especially for items of traditional manufacture for ceremonial use . . . , remain vigorous. (26)

Ellipses inserted where words have been deleted.

One useful point: You don't need ellipses at the beginning of a quotation to indicate that you have broken into a sentence someplace other than the beginning. The lowercase letter at the beginning of the quotation already signals that.

> Whitely notes that Hopi trade "extended from the Great Plains to the Pacific Coast."

You need an initial ellipsis only in rare cases when a capital letter at the beginning of quoted material might give readers a mistaken impression that you are citing a complete sentence when you actually aren't. Confused? Check a writing handbook for how exactly to position ellipsis marks within sentences and how to punctuate around them. The details are, depending upon your constitution, either maddening or fascinating.

What do you do when you need to insert explanatory details into a quotation? Do it with brackets [ ]. By convention, readers understand that the bracketed words are not part of the original material.

Brackets [ ] insert explanations into quotations.

> Writing in the *London Review of Books* (January 26, 2006), John Lancaster describes the fears of publishers: "At the moment Google says they have no intention of providing access to this content [scanned books still under copyright]; but why should anybody believe them?"

You can also use ellipsis marks, brackets, and other devices to make quoted materials fit the grammar of your sentences. Sometimes, sentences you want to quote won't quite match the point of view, verb tense, parallel structure, or other technical aspects of your own surrounding prose. In these situations, remember that you don't have to use a quote in its entirety or exactly as presented. If necessary, divide up a borrowed passage to slip appropriate sections into your own sentence. You may also delete words and phrases (using ellipses if necessary), or use brackets to signal changes in wording.

ORIGINAL PASSAGE

Baking soda also has many other interesting uses aside from cleaning, cooking, and first aid. These include extinguishing fires, making crack cocaine, and causing things to explode. Just about every kid can recall an elementary school science fair for which he/she made a papier-mâché volcano. And as everyone should know, baking soda mixed with vinegar is the recipe for an eye-popping explosion that simulates a real-life lava flow. If you happen to be that one in a hundred kid who has never created a volcano, I insist you spend an afternoon experiencing everyone's favorite use of baking soda.

—STEFAN CASSO, "THE MAGIC WHITE POWDER"

Words to be quoted

Words to be quoted

MATERIAL AS QUOTED

Stefan Casso reminds readers that baking soda has uses well beyond "cleaning, cooking, and first aid." One of those is making simulated volcanic explosions. He even recommends that people who have "never created a volcano . . . spend an afternoon experiencing everyone's favorite use of baking soda."

Borrows a phrase rather than an entire sentence

Note the ellipsis

On the rare occasions when you find an obvious error in quoted materials, use *[sic]* to signal the blunder. You don't want readers to blame a mistake on you, and yet you are obligated to reproduce a quotation exactly—including mistakes in the original. Simply insert *sic* (the Latin word for "thus") in brackets immediately following the mistake. The device says, in effect, that this is the way you found it.

The late Senator Edward Kennedy once took Supreme Court nominee Samuel Alito to task for his record: "In an era when America is still too divided by race and riches, Judge Alioto [sic] has not written one single opinion on the merits in favor of a person of color alleging race discrimination on the job."

Use [sic] to signal an error in quoted text.

48. As the chapter has suggested, find a research essay or well-sourced magazine article and highlight all the framing devices used to set ideas or quoted passages into contexts readers will understand.

49. Choose a feature article or editorial from a recent newspaper or news magazine and write a brief report about it, using the following techniques for integrating sources:

- Quote from the source at least four times, being certain to include appropriate signal phrases and verbs of attribution. At least one of the signal phrases should not appear at the beginning of the quoted material.
- Introduce ideas borrowed from the article at least twice, acknowledging the borrowing, but not quoting from the material directly. Be sure readers realize that you are crediting a source.
- Include an ellipsis mark in at least one of the quotations to shorten it. Cite a lengthy passage and pare it down carefully to make it more useful to readers.
- Use brackets to add pertinent information to a quotation. You might add a date, an author's first name, an explanatory phrase, and so on.
- If you find an error in the essay (unlikely, we hope), point it out using *[sic]*.

50. All the sources on page 201, from which the sample synthesis paper is assembled, are available online. Choose two or three of them and write a more detailed synthesis of their full positions, being sure to frame the similarities and/or differences you find carefully. You might even highlight your own frames so they stand out. For this exercise, you need not offer a position of your own, nor should you criticize or slant your presentation of the source material. Keep your analysis as neutral and objective as you can, especially if you find yourself taking sides. When you are done, a reader should have some sense of the overall media controversy that the pieces you chose address, but have no idea where you might stand.

17

When you write, you lay out a line of words.

— Annie Dillard

Style

I suspect that many of us have better ears for music than for words. Even people with no musical training instantly recognize musical genres they love, applaud performers with distinctive styles, and argue passionately about favorite songs and artists. But sentences strung together? No music there. To most folks, prose just all sounds the same (in a word *prosaic*)—except that it isn't.

Think about it. Though you might be clueless to explain why one paragraph grabs your attention and another seems flat as day-old soda, you do know what you like to read. You probably pay more attention when writing feels precise and energetic and nod off when it rambles. You find yourself drawn to particular writers and bloggers as much for how they express themselves as for what they say. And don't you know instinctively—in just a few sentences or paragraphs—whether you're going to connect with a book or article?

When we respond to language in this impulsive way, we're being seduced by the melding of voice, tone, rhythm, and texture some call *style*. And when "you lay out a line of words" yourself, to borrow a phrase from writer Annie Dillard, the choices you make matter a great deal to potential readers. With every word, sentence, and piece of punctuation, you create a voice and send signals to audiences: I am a friendly author; I'm a gnarly rogue; I am a trustworthy writer; I'm sorta new at this; I am precise and careful; I'm a windbag and, hey, pleez don't check my spelling.

Style is voice, tone, rhythm, and texture.

So choose wisely, prose writer.

High, Middle, and Low Style

In fact, there are as many styles of writing as of dress. In most cases, language that is clear, active, and taut will do the job. But even such a bedrock style has variations. Since the time of the ancient Greeks, writers have imagined a "high" or formal style at one end of a scale and a "low" or colloquial style at the other, bracketing a just-right porridge in the middle. Style is more complex than that, but keeping the full range in mind reveals all your mix-and-match options.

High Style

Reserve high style for formal, scientific, and scholarly writing. This is the choice of writers in professional journals, scholarly books, legal briefs, formal speeches, many newspaper editorials, some types of technical writing, and even traditional wedding invitations. Use it yourself when a lot is at stake—in a scholarship application, for example, or a job letter, term paper, or thesis. High style is signaled by some combination of the following features, all of which vary:

- Serious or professional subjects
- Knowledgeable or professional audiences
- Impersonal point of view signaled by dominant, though not exclusive, third-person (*he, she, it, they*) pronouns
- Relatively complex and self-consciously patterned sentences (that display *parallelism, balance, repetition, alliteration,* or other rhetorical devices)
- Sophisticated or professional vocabulary, sometimes abstract or technical
- Few contractions, colloquial expressions, or nonstandard forms in grammar or vocabulary
- Conventional grammar and punctuation; standard document design
- Formal documentation, when required, often with notes and a bibliography

The following example is from a scholarly journal. The article uses a formal scientific style, appropriate when an expert in a field is writing for an audience of his or her peers:

Technical term introduced and defined

Temperament is a construct closely related to personality. In human research, temperament has been defined by some researchers as the inherited, early appearing tendencies that continue throughout life and serve as the foundation for personality (A. H. Buss, 1995; Goldsmith et al., 1987). Although this definition is not adopted uniformly by human researchers (McCrae et al., 2000), animal researchers agree even less about how to define temperament (Budaev, 2000). In some cases, the word *temperament* appears to be used purely to avoid using the word *personality*, which some animal researchers associate with anthropomorphism. Thus, to ensure that my review captured all potentially relevant reports, I searched for studies that examined either personality or temperament.

— SAMUEL D. GOSLING, "FROM MICE
TO MEN: WHAT CAN WE LEARN ABOUT
PERSONALITY FROM ANIMAL RESEARCH?"

Sources documented

Impersonal perspective — even with the use of the pronoun I

The following *New York Times* editorial also uses a formal style, though it sounds different because the piece is argumentative. The style in this situation signals that the paper's editorial board is dealing with serious political and social issues.

Haiti, founded two centuries ago by ex-slaves who fought to regain their freedom, has again become a hub of human trafficking.

Tone is sober and direct.

Today, tens of thousands of Haitian children live lives of modern-day bondage. Under the system known as *restavek*, a Creole word meaning "stay with," these children work for wealthier families in exchange for education and shelter. They frequently end up cruelly overworked, physically or sexually abused, and without access to education.

Key term defined

The most effective way to root out this deeply oppressive but deeply ingrained system would be to attack the conditions that sustain it — chiefly, impoverished, environmentally unsustainable agriculture and a severe shortage of rural schools.

Diction: the formal voice of the New York Times.

This is an area in which America can and should help. Washington has been quick to respond to political turmoil in Haiti, with its accompanying fears of uncontrollable refugee flows. But the frenzied flurries of international crisis management that follow typically leave no lasting results.

A wiser, more promising alternative would be to help create long-term economic options by improving access to schools and creating sustainable agriculture. Meanwhile, the United

Alliteration for emphasis: repeats (f) sound

Technical language

States should work with nongovernmental organizations to battle the resigned acceptance by many Haitians of the restavek system. They could, for example, help local radio stations broadcast programs of open dialogue about how damaging the system is, and include restavek survivors or human-rights experts.

The primary responsibility for eliminating the restavek system lies with the Haitian people and their government. After years of political crisis, there is a new democratically elected government. Eradicating the restavek system should be one of its top priorities, combining law enforcement efforts with attacks on the root social and economic causes.

Emotional conclusion supports a call to action.

The former slaves who won Haiti's freedom two hundred years ago dreamed of something better for their children than restavek bondage. The time is overdue for helping those dreams become reality.

— "The Lost Children of Haiti"

Middle Style

Use middle style for personal, argumentative, and some academic writing. This kind of prose, perhaps the most common of all, falls between the extremes and, like the other styles, varies enormously. It is the language of journalism, popular books and magazines, professional memos and nonscientific reports, instructional guides and manuals, and most commercial Web sites. Use this style in position papers, letters to the editor, personal statements, and business e-mails and memos—even in some business and professional work, once you are comfortable with the people to whom you are writing. Middle style doesn't so much claim features of its own as walk a path between formal and everyday language. It may combine some of the following characteristics:

- Full range of topics, from serious to humorous
- General audiences
- Range of perspectives, including first-person (*I*) and second-person (*you*) points of view
- Typically, a personal rather than an institutional voice
- Sentences in active voice that vary in complexity and length

- General vocabulary, more specific than abstract, with concrete nouns and action verbs, and with unfamiliar terms or concepts routinely defined
- Informal expressions, occasional dialogue, slang, and contractions, when appropriate to the subject or audience
- Conventional grammar and reasonably correct formats
- Informal documentation, usually without notes

In the following excerpt from an article that appeared in the popular magazine *Psychology Today*, Ellen McGrath illustrates a conversational but serious middle style used to present scientific information to a general audience:

Families often inherit a negative thinking style that carries the germ of depression. Typically it is a legacy passed from one generation to the next, a pattern of pessimism invoked to protect loved ones from disappointment or stress. But in fact, negative thinking patterns do just the opposite, eroding the mental health of all exposed. *[Sophisticated but not technical vocabulary]*

When Dad consistently expresses his disappointment in Josh for bringing home a B minus in chemistry although all the other grades are A's, he is exhibiting a kind of cognitive distortion that children learn to deploy on themselves—a mental filtering that screens out positive experience from consideration. *[Familiar example illustrates technical term.]*

Or perhaps the father envisions catastrophe, seeing such grades as foreclosing the possibility of a top college, thus dooming his son's future. It is their repetition over time that gives these events power to shape a person's belief system. *[Clear style conveys serious ideas.]*

> —ELLEN MCGRATH, "IS DEPRESSION CONTAGIOUS?"

Like McGrath, Stefan Casso, a student in a college writing course, employs a middle style to share research findings in a report. However his subject—the manifold uses of baking soda—has a comic edge, and so Casso's version of middle style is several notches more familiar and colloquial than McGrath's, illustrating how these styles may vary.

Arm & Hammer's website claims 94 different uses for the resourceful substance. Some of the more eye-catching include cutting through shower grime, erasing carpet stains, polishing *[Clear style for a general audience]*

Vocabulary
item from pop
culture

silver, treating swimming pools, and de-funkifizing sneakers. In each of these specific uses of baking soda, its cleansing ability seems to be a common theme. Fittingly, Arm & Hammer's slogan is "The Standard of Purity."

Being a substitute for chemical cleaners isn't the only job this white powder is good for. Another use for baking soda

Readers
addressed
directly

is — you guessed it — baking. It's commonly found in cakes and bread because of its leavening ability. As the heat turns up, baking soda releases carbon dioxide, causing the batter or dough to rise and fluff. And if by chance your cake causes you heartburn, you can use baking soda as an antacid as well (Breyer).

Major claims
documented

Baking soda has a multitude of medical applications in addition to neutralizing your stomach's acidity. Baking soda treats burns, insect bites, and even acne (Breyer). In the 1920s, baking soda was even a popular remedy for the common cold. According to a Dr. Cheney, an early 20th century physician, patients who took baking soda at the first sign of a cold were able to recover twice as fast as those who did not ("Overlooked"). Baking soda's ability to fight off the infectious disease is unsubstantiated, but many people

Paragraph ends
informally

still believe in its curative powers. And why not? It seems baking soda fixes just about anything aside from cancer. Oh wait —

— Stefan Casso, "The Magic White
Powder"

Low Style

Use a low style for personal, informal, and even playful writing. Don't think of "low" here in a negative sense: A colloquial or informal style is fine on occasions when you want or need to sound more at ease and open. Low style can be right for your personal e-mails and instant messaging, of course, as well as in many blogs, advertisements, magazines trying to be hip, personal narratives, and humor writing. Low style has many of the following features:

- Everyday or off-the-wall subjects, often humorous or parodic
- In-group or specialized readers

- Highly personal and idiosyncratic points of view; lots of *I, me, you, us,* and even some dialogue
- Shorter sentences and irregular constructions, especially fragments
- Vocabulary from pop culture and the street—idiomatic, allusive, and obscure to outsiders
- Colloquial expressions resembling speech
- Unconventional grammar and mechanics and alternative formats
- No systematic acknowledgment of sources

While low style may seem best suited to everyday subjects and situations, that doesn't mean it cannot explore serious themes. In the following passage, Arnold, the teenaged narrator of Sherman Alexie's *The Absolutely True Diary of a Part-Time Indian,* reacts to a white teacher who has just told him that his sister had died. His language is colloquial, but his feelings are not diminished by his style:

> **Low style can explore weighty topics.**

"Miss Warren," I said, "I want to wait outside."

"But it's snowing," she said.

"Well, that would make it perfect, then, wouldn't it?" I said.

It was a rhetorical question, meaning there <u>wasn't supposed to be an answer, right?</u> But poor Miss Warren, she answered my rhetorical question.

> **Readers addressed directly**

"No, I don't think it's a good idea to wait in the snow," she said. "You're very vulnerable now."

<u>VULNERABLE!</u> She told me I was <u>vulnerable</u>. My big sister was dead. Of course I was <u>vulnerable</u>. I was a reservation Indian attending an all-white school and my sister had just died a horrible death. I was <u>the most vulnerable kid in the United States</u>. Miss Warren was obviously trying to win <u>the Captain Obvious Award</u>.

> **"Vulnerable" repeated for emphasis**

> **Hyperbolic teen sarcasm**

"I'm waiting outside," I said.

"I'll wait with you," she said.

"<u>Kiss my ass</u>," I said and ran.

> **Timely profanity**

Miss Warren tried to run after me. But she was wearing heels and she was crying and she was absolutely <u>freaked out</u> by my reaction to the bad news. <u>By my cursing.</u> She was nice. <u>Too nice to deal with death.</u> So she just ran a few feet before she stopped and slumped against the wall.

> **Simple, emotive sentences and fragments**

Inclusive and Culturally Sensitive Style

Remember Polish jokes? I hope not, and that's a good thing. Slowly, we're all learning to avoid offensive racial, ethnic, and gender stereotypes in our public life and the bigoted language that propagated them. Thanks to electronic media, the world is smaller and more diverse today: When you compose any document electronically, it may sail quickly around the Web, conveying not only ideas but also your attitudes and prejudices. You won't ever please every reader in this vast potential audience, but you can at least write respectfully, accurately, and, yes, honestly. Language that is both inclusive and culturally sensitive can and should have these qualities.

It goes without saying that expressions that stereotype genders or sexual orientations don't belong in your prose. Largely purged from contemporary English usage, for instance, are job titles that suggest that they are occupied exclusively by men or women. Gone are *stewardess* and *poetess*, *policeman* and *chairman*, *male nurse* and *woman scientist*. When referring to professions, even those still dominated by one gender or another, avoid using a gendered pronoun. But don't strain sense to be politically correct. *Nun* and *NFL quarterback* are still gendered, as are *witch* and *warlock*—and *surrogate mother*. Here are some easy solutions.

Avoid stereotyping

STEREOTYPED

The **postman** came up the walk.

INCLUSIVE

The **letter carrier** came up the walk.

STEREOTYPED

Among all **her** other tasks, a **nurse** must also stay up-to-date on **her** medical education.

INCLUSIVE

Among all **their** other tasks, **nurses** must also stay up-to-date on **their** medical education.

You should similarly eliminate from your work expressions that stereotype races, ethnic groups, or religious groups. Deliberate racial slurs these days tend to be rare in professional discourse. But it is still not unusual to find clueless writers (and politicians) noting how "hardworking," "articulate," "athletic," "well-groomed," or "ambitious" members of minority and religious groups are. The praise rings hollow because it draws on demeaning stereotypes. You have an obligation to learn the history and nature of such ethnic caricatures and grow beyond them. It's part of your education, no matter what group or groups you belong to.

Avoid language and sentiments that carry prejudices.

OUTDATED TERMS	ALTERNATIVES
fireman	firefighter
mankind	humankind, people, humans
congressman	congressional representative
chairman	chair
policewoman	police officer
stewardess	flight attendant
actress, poetess	actor, poet

When in doubt about how to refer to a people or group, pay attention to the terminology used by serious and respected publications, understanding that many racial and ethnic terms remain contested: African American, black (or Black), Negro, people of color, Asian American, Hispanic, Latino, Mexican American, Cuban American, Native American, Indian, Inuit, Anglo, white (or White). Even the ancient group of American Indians once called Anasazi now go by the more culturally and historically accurate Native Puebloans. While shifts of this sort may seem fussy or politically correct to some, it costs little to address people as they prefer, acknowledging both their humanity and our differences.

Be aware, too, that being from an ethnic or racial group usually gives you license to say things about its members not open to outsiders. Chris Rock, George Lopez, and Margaret Cho can joke about topics Jimmy Fallon can't touch, using racial and gender epithets that would cost the late-night talk show host his job. In academic and professional settings, show similar discretion in your language. But sensitivities of language should not become an excuse for avoiding open debate, or a weapon to chill it. In the following table are suggestions for inclusive, culturally sensitive terms.

OUTDATED TERMS	ALTERNATIVES
Eskimo	Inuit
Oriental	Asian American (better to specify country of origin)
Hispanic	Specify: Mexican, Cuban, Nicaraguan, and so on
Negro (acceptable to some)	African American, black
colored	people of color
a gay, the gays	gay, lesbian, gays and lesbians, LGBT community
cancer victim	cancer survivor
boys, girls (to refer to young adults)	men, women, teens, teenagers, youth

Your goal should be to treat people with dignity, a policy that makes sense in all writing. Some slights may not be intended—against the elderly, for example. But remarking casually that someone "drives like an old woman" manages to offend two groups. The bottom line is that writing that is respectful will itself be treated with respect.

Finally, avoid sensational or obscene language in your academic work. Believe me, every semester, especially in first-year courses, one or more students will ask whether it's okay to use **Skip the four-letter words.** four-letter words in academic papers. Some instructors tolerate them in narratives when the subject matter demands frankness, but it is difficult to make a case for the expressions in academic reports, research papers, or position papers unless they are part of quoted material—as they may be in writing about contemporary life and literature. Frankly, four-letter expletives just sound juvenile.

> **YOUR TURN**
>
> **51.** Over the next day, look for three pieces of writing that seem to you to represent examples of high, middle, and low style. Then study several paragraphs or a section of each in detail, paying attention to the features listed in the checklists for the three styles. How well do the pieces actually conform to the descriptions of high, middle, and low style? Where would you place your three examples on a continuum that

moves from high to low? Do the pieces share some stylistic features? Do you find any variations of style within the individual passages you examined?

52. Write a paragraph or two about any pet peeve you may have with language use. Your problem may address a serious issue like insensitivities in naming your ethnicity, community, or beliefs. Or you may just be tired of a friend insisting that you describe Sweetie Pie as your "animal companion" rather than use that demeaning and hegemonic term "pet." You'll surely want to share your paragraph and also read what others have written.

18

The shorter and the plainer the better.
— BEATRIX POTTER

Clarity and Economy

Ordinarily, tips and tricks don't do much to enhance a writer's skills. And so, for seventeen chapters, I've mostly avoided numbered checklists. But a few suggestions, applied sensibly, can improve the power of sentences and paragraphs noticeably. (You simply *will* sound more professional, for example, when every word and phrase you write pulls its weight.) So following is a baker's dozen of suggestions to make your prose work better. In applying the tips, be sure to work with whole paragraphs and pages, not just individual sentences. Remember, too, that these are guidelines, not rules. Ignore them when good sense and particular situations suggest better alternatives.

Thirteen Suggestions to Improve Your Writing

1. Build sentences around clear subjects and objects.
Scholar Richard Lanham famously advised writers troubled by tangled sentences to ask, "*Who is kicking who?*" on the principle that readers shouldn't have to puzzle over what they read. They are less likely to be confused when they can identify the people or things in a sentence that act upon other people and things. Answering Professor Lanham's question often leads to stronger verbs and tighter sentences as well.

CONFUSING

Current tax policies necessitate congressional reform if the **reoccurrence of a recession** is to be avoided.

BETTER

Congress needs to reform current tax policies to avoid another recession.

CONFUSING

In the Prohibition era, **tuning cars** enabled the bootleggers to turn ordinary automobiles into speed machines for the transportation of illegal alcohol by simply altering certain components of the cars.

BETTER

In the Prohibition era, **bootleggers** modified their cars to turn them into speed machines for transporting illegal alcohol.

Both of the confusing sentences here work better with subjects capable of action: *Congress* and *bootleggers*. Once identified, these subjects make it easy to simplify the sentences, giving them more power.

2. Prefer specific nouns and noun phrases to abstract ones. The advice to use concrete expressions rather than abstract ones depends very much on context. You need abstractions—and plenty of them—in philosophy papers, theoretical analyses, and many other kinds of writing. But in most cases, specific terms create clearer, more memorable images for readers and so they have more impact.

ABSTRACT	SPECIFIC
bird	roadrunner
cactus	prickly pear
breakfast cereal	Cheerios
threatening bug	venomous scorpion
academic institution	school
current fiscal pressure	budget cuts

Many writers are fond of abstract words and the impenetrable phrases they inspire because they sound serious and sophisticated (see the introductory section in Chapter 12). But such language can be hard to figure out or even suggest a cover-up. What better way to hide an inconvenient truth than to bury it in words? So revise those ugly, unreadable, inhuman sentences.

ABSTRACT

All of the separate constituencies at this academic institution must be invited to participate in the decision-making process **under the current fiscal pressures we face.**

BETTER

Faculty, students, and staff at this school must all have a say during **this current budget crunch**.

There's an expression for using abstract and inflated language simply to sound impressive or intimidating—and it begins with "slinging."

Ironically, terms that are highly specific can be as impenetrable as abstractions when they are too specialized for general readers. You experience the problem the moment you run into people who know more about a subject than you do and they begin using the technical language, acronyms, or foreign expressions common to that field.

TECHNICAL	GENERAL
Geococcyx californianus	roadrunner
Opuntia megasperma	prickly pear
super PAC	political group
fiscal outlays	spending
MMORPG	role-playing game
Weltanschauung	worldview

Highly specific or specialized terminology makes sense for audiences familiar with it. It's shorthand for them—but Greek to the rest of us. Again, you make the call what form of language works in a given assignment or paper.

3. Avoid sprawling phrases. These constructions give readers fits, especially when they thicken, sentence by sentence, like lime scale or sludge. Be concerned whenever your prose regularly shows any combination of the following features:

- Strings of prepositional phrases
- Verbs turned into nouns via endings such as *-ation* (*implement* becomes *implementation*)
- Lots of articles (*the, a*)
- Lots of heavily modified verbals

Such expressions aren't inaccurate or wrong—just tedious because they make readers work hard for no good reason. Fortunately, they're remarkably easy to chip away once you notice the accumulation.

WORDY

members of the student body at Arizona State

BETTER

students at Arizona State

WORDY

the manufacturing of products **made up of** steel

BETTER

making steel products

WORDY

the prioritization of decisions for policies of the student government

BETTER

the student government's **priorities**

4. Avoid sentences with slow windups. The more stuff you pile up ahead of the main verb, the more readers have to remember. Very skillful writers can pull off complex sentences of this kind because they know how to build interest and manage clauses. But a safer strategy in academic and professional writing is to get to the point of your sentences quickly. Here's a sentence from the Internal Revenue Service Web site that keeps readers waiting far too long for a verb. Yet it's easy to fix once its problem is diagnosed.

ORIGINAL

A new scam e-mail that appears to be a solicitation from the IRS and U.S. government asking for contributions to victims of the recent Southern California wildfires has been making the rounds.

REVISED

A new e-mail scam making the rounds asks for charitable contributions for victims of the recent Southern California wildfires. Though the message appears to be from the IRS and the U.S. government, it is a fake.

Watch out, too, for slow-moving expressions such as *it is* and *there is/are*. These expressions, called expletives, are fine when they are conventional: How else would you phrase the following sentences?

It is a fake.

It was her first Oscar.

There is a tide in the affairs of men.

There's no exit.

But don't default to easy expletives at the beginning of every other sentence. Your prose will seem dull and plodding. Fortunately, revision is easy.

SLOW

It is necessary that we simplify admissions policies.

BETTER

We need to simplify admissions policies.

SLOW

There are many internships offered by the business school to its students.

BETTER

The business school offers students many internships.

Expletives in a sentence often attract other wordy constructions and vague expressions. Then language swells like a blister. Imagine having to read paragraph after paragraph of prose like that in the following sentence.

SLOW

It is quite evident that **an argument Annette Lareau supports** is that **it is important** to find the balance between authoritarian and indulgent styles of parenting because **it** contributes to successful child development.

BETTER

Clearly, Annette Lareau believes that balancing authoritarian and indulgent styles of parenting contributes to successful child development.

5. Favor simple, active verbs. When a sentence, even a short one, stumbles, consider whether the problem might be a nebulous, strung-out, or unimaginative verb. Replace it with a verb that does something.

WORDY VERB PHRASE

We must **make a determination** soon.

BETTER

We must **decide** soon.

WORDY VERB PHRASE

Students **are absolutely reliant** on federal loans.

BETTER

Students **need** federal loans.

WORDY VERB PHRASE

Engineers **proceeded to reinforce** the levee.

BETTER

Engineers **reinforced** the levee.

You'll be a better writer the moment you apply this guideline.

6. Keep pronouns on a tight leash. A pronoun should re-fer back clearly to a noun or pronoun (its *antecedent*), usually the one nearest to it that matches it in number and, when nec-essary, gender.

Consumers will buy a **Rolex** because **they** covet **its** snob appeal.

Nancy Pelosi spoke instead of **Harry Reid** because **she** had more interest in the legislation than **he** did.

Readers will struggle with your style if they can't figure out exactly who is doing what to whom. So revise any sentences (or lengthier passages) in which connections between pronouns and their antecedents wobble. Multiple revisions are usually possible, depending on how the confusing sentence could be interpreted.

CONFUSING

The **batter** collided with the **first baseman**, but **he** wasn't injured.

BETTER

The batter collided with the **first baseman**, **who** wasn't injured.

BETTER

The **batter** wasn't injured by **his** collision with the first baseman.

Also make sure a pronoun has a plausible antecedent. Sometimes the problem is that the antecedent doesn't actually exist—it is only implied. In these cases, either reconsider the antecedent/pronoun relationship or replace the pronoun with a noun.

CONFUSING

Grandmother had hip-replacement surgery two months ago, and **it** is already fully healed.

In the prior sentence, the implied antecedent for *it* is *hip*, but the noun *hip* isn't in the sentence (*hip-replacement* is an adjective describing *surgery*).

BETTER
Grandmother had **her hip** replaced two months ago, and **she** is already fully healed.

BETTER
Grandmother had hip-replacement surgery two months ago, and **her hip** is already fully healed.

Finally, be certain that the antecedent of the pronouns *this, that,* or *which* is perfectly clear, not vague or ambiguous. In the following example, a humble *this* is asked to shoulder the burden of a writer who hasn't quite figured out how to pull together all the ideas raised in the preceding sentence. What exactly might the antecedent for *this* be? It doesn't exist. To fix the problem, the writer needs to replace *this* with a more thoughtful analysis.

VAGUE FINAL SENTENCE
The university staff is underpaid, the labs are short on equipment, and campus maintenance is neglected. Moreover, we need two or three new parking garages to make up for the lots lost because of recent construction projects. Yet students cannot be expected to shoulder additional costs because tuition and fees are high already. **This** is a problem that must be solved.

CLARIFIED FINAL SENTENCE
The problem is **how to fund both academic and infrastructure needs without increasing students' costs**.

7. Avoid tedious strings of prepositional phrases. Prepositional phrases are simple structures, consisting of prepositions and their objects and an occasional modifier: *from the beginning, under the spreading chestnut tree, between you and me, in the line of duty, over the rainbow.* You can't write much without prepositional phrases. But use more than two or, rarely, three in a row and they drain the energy from a sentence. When that's the case, try turning the prepositions into more compact modifiers or moving them into different positions within the sentence. Sometimes you may need to revise the sentence more substantially.

TOO MANY PHRASES

We stood **in line at the observatory on the top of a hill in the mountains** to look **in a huge telescope at the moons of Saturn.**

BETTER

We lined up **at the mountaintop observatory** to view Saturn's moons **through a huge telescope.**

TOO MANY PHRASES

To help first-year students **in their adjustment to the rigors of college life,** the Faculty Council voted **for the creation of a new midterm break during the third week of October.**

BETTER

To help first-year students adjust better **to college life,** the Faculty Council endorsed a new break **in mid-October.**

8. Don't repeat key words close together. You can often improve the style of a passage just by making sure you haven't used a particular word or phrase too often—unless you repeat it deliberately for effect (government of the *people*, by the *people*, for the *people*). Your sentences will sound fresher after you have eliminated unintentional or pointless repetition; they also may end up shorter.

REPETITIVE

Students in **writing** courses are often assigned common **readings**, which they are expected to **read** to prepare for various **student writing** projects.

BETTER

Students in writing courses are often assigned common readings to prepare them for projects.

This is a guideline to apply sensibly: Sometimes—especially in technical writing—you simply must repeat key nouns and verbs sentence after sentence to be clear. Looking for synonyms is pointless:

The *New Horizons* payload is incredibly power efficient, with the instruments collectively drawing only about 28 watts. The payload consists of three optical instruments, two plasma instruments, a dust sensor, and a radio science receiver/ radiometer.

—NASA, "*New Horizons* Spacecraft Ready for Flight"

9. Avoid doublings. In speech, we tend to repeat ourselves or say things two or three different ways to be sure listeners get the point. Such repetitions are natural, even appreciated. But in writing, habitual redundancies or doublings can irritate readers. And it *is* very much a habit, backed by a long literary tradition comfortable with pairings such as *home and hearth, friend and colleague, tried and true, clean and sober, neat and tidy,* and so on.

Sometimes, writers will add an extra noun or two to be sure they have covered the bases: *colleges and universities, books and articles, ideas and opinions.* There may be good reasons for listing a second (or third) item. But frequently, the doubling is just baggage that slows down the train. Leave it at the station.

The same goes for redundant expressions. For the most part they go unnoticed, except by readers who crawl up walls when someone writes *young **in age**, bold **in character**, **totally** dead, **basically** unhappy, **current** fashion, **empty** hole, **extremely** outraged, later **in time**, mix **together**, reply **back**,* and so on. (In each case, the expressions in boldface restate what is already obvious.) People precise enough to care about details deserve respect: They land rovers on Mars. Cut the dumb redundancies. (Is *dumb* unnecessary here?)

10. Turn clauses into more direct modifiers. If you are fond of *that, which,* and *who* clauses, be sure you need them. You can sometimes save a word or two by pulling the modifiers out of the expressions and moving them directly ahead of the words they explain. Or you may be able to tighten a sentence just by cutting *that, which,* or *who.*

WORDY

Our football coach, **who is nationally renowned**, expected a raise.

BETTER

Our **nationally renowned** football coach expected a raise.

WORDY

Our football coach, **who is nationally renowned and already rich**, still expected a raise.

BETTER

Our football coach, **nationally renowned and already rich**, still expected a raise.

11. Vary sentence lengths and structures. As we noted in Chapter 17, sentences, like music, have rhythm. If all your sentences run about the same length or rarely vary from a predictable subject-verb-object pattern, readers will grow bored without knowing why. Every so often, surprise them with an unexpectedly short statement. Or open with a longer-than-usual introductory phrase. Or try compound subjects or verbs, or attach a series of parallel modifiers to the verb or object. Or let a sentence roll toward a grand conclusion, as in the following example:

> [Carl] Newman is a singing encyclopedia of pop power. He has identified, cultured, and cloned the most buoyant elements of his favorite Squeeze, Raspberries, Supertramp, and Sparks records, and he's pretty pathological about making sure there's something unpredictable and catchy happening in a New Pornographers song every couple of seconds—a stereo flurry of *ooohs*, an extra beat or two bubbling up unexpectedly.
>
> —DOUGLAS WOLK, "SOMETHING TO TALK ABOUT"

12. Read what you have written aloud. Then fix any words or phrases that cause you to pause or stumble and rethink sentences that feel *awkward*—a notoriously vague reaction that should still be taken seriously. Reading drafts aloud is a great way to find problems. After all, if you can't move smoothly through your own writing, a reader won't be able to either. Better yet, persuade a friend or roommate to read your draft to you. Take notes.

Understand, though, that prose never sounds quite like spoken language—and thank goodness for that. Accurate transcripts of dialogue are almost unreadable, full of gaps, disconnected phrases, pauses, repetitions, and the occasional obscenity. And yet written language, especially in the middle style, should create a reasonable facsimile of an idealized human voice, all its cadences and rhythms pulling readers along, making them want to read more.

13. Cut a first draft by 25 percent—or more. If you tend to be wordy, try to cut your first drafts by at least one-quarter. Put all your thoughts down on the page when drafting a paper. But when editing, cut every unnecessary word.

Think of it as a competition. However, don't eliminate any important ideas and facts. If possible, ask an honest friend to read your work and point out where you might tighten your language.

If you ~~are aware that you~~ tend to be wordy, ~~and say more than you need to in your writing, then get in the habit of~~ trying to cut your ~~the~~ first drafts ~~that you have written~~ by at least one-quarter. ~~There may be good reasons for you to p~~Put all your thoughts ~~and ideas~~ down on the page when ~~you are in the process of~~ drafting a paper ~~or project~~. But when ~~you are in the process of~~ editing, ~~you should be sure to~~ cut every unnecessary word. ~~that is not needed or necessary. You may find it advantageous to t~~Think of it as a competition. ~~or a game.~~ However, ~~In making your cuts, it is important that you~~ don't eliminate any important ideas ~~that may be essential~~ and facts. ~~that may be important.~~ If ~~you find it~~ possible, ~~you might consider~~ asking an honest friend ~~whom you trust~~ to read your work ~~writing~~ and ~~ask them to~~ point out ~~those places in your writing~~ where you might tighten your language.

YOUR TURN

53. Even if you think your prose is as light as hydrogen, take a first draft you have written and reduce it by 25 percent. Count the words in the original (or let your software do it) and then prune until you are under quota. And, while at it, turn abstract nouns and strung-out verbs into livelier expressions, and eliminate long windups and boring chains of prepositional phrases. When done, read the revised version aloud—and then revise again.

APPENDIX

Style Guides
Used in Various
Disciplines

FIELD OR DISCIPLINE	DOCUMENTATION AND STYLE GUIDES
Anthropology	*AAA Style Guide* (2009) *Chicago Manual of Style* (16th ed., 2010)
Biology	*Scientific Style and Format: The CSE Manual for Authors, Editors, and Publishers* (7th ed., 2006)
Business and management	*The Business Style Handbook: An A-to-Z Guide for Writing on the Job* (2nd ed., 2012)
Chemistry	*The ACS Style Guide: Effective Communication of Scientific Information* (3rd ed., 2006)
Earth sciences	*Geowriting: A Guide to Writing, Editing, and Printing in Earth Science* (Rev. ed., 2004)
Engineering	Varies by area; *IEEE Standards Style Manual* (online)
Federal government	*United States Government Printing Office Manual,* (30th ed., 2008)
History	*Chicago Manual of Style* (16th ed., 2010)
Humanities	*MLA Handbook for Writers of Research Papers* (7th ed., 2009)
Journalism	*The Associated Press Stylebook and Briefing on Media Law* (2013); *UPI Stylebook and Guide to Newswriting* (4th ed., 2004)
Law	*The Bluebook: A Uniform System of Citation* (19th ed., 2010)
Mathematics	*A Manual for Authors of Mathematical Papers* (8th ed., 1990)

(continued on next page)

FIELD OR DISCIPLINE	DOCUMENTATION AND STYLE GUIDES
Music	*Writing about Music: An Introductory Guide* (4th ed., 2008)
Nursing	*Writing for Publication in Nursing* (2nd ed., 2010)
Political science	*The Style Manual for Political Science* (2006)
Psychology	*Publication Manual of the American Psychological Association* (6th ed., 2010)
Sociology	*American Sociological Association Style Guide* (4th ed., 2010)

B

MLA and
APA Basics

MLA Documentation and Format

The style of the Modern Language Association (MLA) is used in many humanities disciplines. For complete details about MLA style, consult the *MLA Handbook for Writers of Research Papers*, 7th ed. (2009). The basic details for documenting sources and formatting research papers in MLA style are presented below.

DOCUMENT SOURCES ACCORDING TO CONVENTION.

When you use sources in a research paper, you are required to cite the source, letting readers know that the information has been borrowed from somewhere else, and showing them how to find the original material if they would like to study it further. An MLA-style citation includes two parts: a brief in-text citation and a more detailed works cited entry to be included in a list at the end of your paper.

In-text citations must include the author's name as well as the number of the page where the borrowed material can be found. The author's name (underlined) is generally included in the signal phrase that introduces the passage, and the page number (also underlined) is included in parentheses after the borrowed text.

> Frazier points out that the Wetherill-sponsored expedition to explore Chaco Canyon was roundly criticized (43).

Alternatively, the author's name can be included in parentheses along with the page number.

> The Wetherill-sponsored expedition to explore Chaco Canyon was roundly criticized (Frazier 43).

At the end of the paper, in the works cited list, a more detailed citation includes the author's name as well as the title and publication information about the source.

> Frasier, Kendrick. *People of Chaco: A Canyon and Its Culture.* Rev. ed. New York: Norton, 1999. Print.

Both in-text citations and works cited entries can vary greatly depending on the type of source cited (book, periodical, Web site, etc.). The following pages give specific examples of how to cite a range of sources in MLA style.

MLA In-Text Citation

1. AUTHOR NAMED IN SIGNAL PHRASE

Include the author's name in the signal phrase that introduces the borrowed material. Follow the borrowed material with the page number of the source in parentheses. Note that the period comes after the parentheses.

> According to Seabrook, "astronomy was a vital and practical form of knowledge" for the ancient Greeks (98).

2. AUTHOR NAMED IN PARENTHESES

Follow the borrowed material with the author and page number of the source in parentheses, and end with a period.

> For the ancient Greeks, "astronomy was a vital and practical form of knowledge" (Seabrook 98).

Works Cited

General Guidelines for MLA Works Cited Entries

AUTHOR NAMES

- Authors listed at the start of an entry should be listed last name first and should end with a period.
- Subsequent author names, or the names of authors or editors listed in the middle of the entry, should be listed first name first.

DATES

- Dates should be formatted day month year: 27 May 2007.
- Use abbreviations for all months except for May, June, and July, which are short enough to spell out: Jan., Feb., Mar., Apr., Aug., Sept., Oct., Nov., Dec. (Months should always be spelled out in the text of your paper.)

TITLES

- Titles of long works — such as books, plays, periodicals, entire Web sites, and films — should be italicized. (Underlining is an acceptable alternative to italics, but note that whichever format you choose, you should be consistent throughout your paper.)
- Titles of short works — such as essays, articles, poems, and songs — should be placed in quotation marks.

PUBLICATION INFORMATION

- Include only the city name.
- Abbreviate familiar words such as "University" ("U") and "Press" ("P") in the publisher's name. Leave out terms such as "Inc." and "Corp."
- Include the medium of publication for each entry ("Print," "Web," "DVD," "Radio," etc.).

1. SINGLE AUTHOR

Author's Last Name, First Name. *Book Title*. Publication City: Publisher, Year of Publication. Medium.

> Will, George. *Men at Work: The Craft of Baseball*. New York: Macmillan, 1990. Print.

2. BOOK: BASIC FORMAT

The example here is the basic format for a book with one author. After listing the author's name, include the title (and subtitle, if any) of the book, italicized. Next give the publication city, publisher's name, and year. End with the medium of publication.

> Author's Last Name, First Name. *Book Title: Book Subtitle*. Publication City: Publisher, Publication Year. Medium.

> Mah, Adeline Yen. *Falling Leaves: The True Story of an Unwanted Chinese Daughter*. New York: Wiley, 1997. Print.

3. MAGAZINE ARTICLE

Include the date of publication rather than volume and issue numbers. If page numbers are not consecutive, add "+" after the initial page.

> Author's Last Name, First Name. "Title of Article." *Title of Magazine* Date of Publication: Page Numbers. Medium.

> Fredenburg, Peter. "Mekong Harvests: Balancing Shrimp and Rice Farming in Vietnam." *World and I* Mar. 2002: 204+. Print.

4. SHORT WORK FROM A WEB SITE

> Short Work Author's Last Name, First Name. "Title of Short Work." *Title of Web Site.* Name of Sponsoring Organization, Date of Publication or Most Recent Update. Medium. Date of Access.

> McFee, Gord. "Why 'Revisionism' Isn't." *The Holocaust History Project.* Holocaust Hist. Project, 15 May 1999. Web. 10 Sept. 2011.

Format an MLA Paper Correctly

You can now find software to format your academic papers in MLA style, but the key alignments for such documents are usually simple enough for you to manage on your own.

- Set up a header on the right-hand side of each page, one-half inch from the top. The header should include your last name and the page number.
- In the upper left on the first — or title — page, include your name, the instructor's name, the course title and/or number, and the date.
- Center the title above the first line of text.
- Use one-inch margins on all sides of the paper.
- Double-space the entire paper (including your name and the course information, the title, and any block quotations).
- Indent paragraphs one-half inch.
- Use block quotations for quoted material of four or more lines. Indent block quotations one inch from the left margin.
- Do not include a separate title page unless your instructor requires one.
- When you document using MLA style, you'll need to create an alphabetically arranged works cited page at the end of the paper so that readers have a convenient list of all the books, articles, and other data you have used.

Works Cited

Chae, Seung-jun. Personal interview. 8 Mar. 2010.

Cho, Eun-saem. Personal interview. 7 Mar. 2010.

Cummings, William K. "Human Resource Development: The   **Essay in**
J-Model." *The Challenge of Eastern Asian Education: Implications*   **an edited**
for America. Ed. William K. Cummings and Philip G. Altbach.   **collection**
Albany: State U of New York P, 1997. Print.

Ferris, Dana, and John S. Hedgcock. *Teaching ESL Composition:*
Purpose, Process, and Practice. Mahwah: Erlbaum, 1998. Print.

Feuerbacher, Kellie, et al. "The ESL Experience in the Writing Center."   **Online scholarly**
Praxis: A Writing Center Journal 2 (2005). Web. 10 Mar. 2010.   **journal/article**

Kim, Ki-joong. Personal communication. 14 Apr 2010.

Lee, Albert H. *East Asian Higher Education: Traditions and*   **A book**
Transformations. Oxford: IAU P, 1995. Print.

Planty, M., et al. *The Condition of Education 2009.* National Center   **Government**
for Education Statistics, Institute of Education Sciences, U.S.   **report**
Department of Education, June 2009. Web. 10 Mar. 2010.

APA Documentation and Format

APA (American Psychological Association) style is used in many social science disciplines. For full details about APA style and documentation, consult the *Publication Manual of the American Psychological Association,* 6th ed. (2010). The basic details for documenting sources and formatting research papers in APA style are presented below.

DOCUMENT SOURCES ACCORDING TO CONVENTION.

When you use sources in a research paper, you are required to cite the source, letting readers know that the information has been borrowed from somewhere else and showing them how to find the original material if they would like to study it further. Like MLA style, APA includes two parts: a brief in-text citation and a more detailed reference entry.

In-text citations should include the author's name, the year the material was published, and the page number(s) that the borrowed material can be found on. The author's name and year of publication are generally included in a signal phrase that introduces the passage, and the page number is included in parentheses after the borrowed text. Note that for APA style, the verb in the signal phrase should be in the past tense (*reported*) or present perfect tense (*has reported*).

> Millman (2007) reported that college students around the country are participating in Harry Potter discussion groups, sports activities, and even courses for college credit (p. A4).

Alternatively, the author's name and year can be included in parentheses with the page number.

> College students around the country are participating in Harry Potter discussion groups, sports activities, and even courses for college credit (Millman, 2007, p. A4).

The list of references at the end of the paper contains a more detailed citation that repeats the author's name and publication year and includes the title and additional publication information about the source. Inclusive page numbers are included for periodical articles and parts of books.

> Millman, S. (2007). Generation hex. *The Chronicle of Higher Education, 53*(46), A4.

Both in-text citations and reference entries can vary greatly depending on the type of source cited (book, periodical, Web site, etc.). The following pages give specific examples of how to cite a range of sources in APA style.

APA In-Text Citation

General Guidelines for In-Text Citations in APA Style

AUTHOR NAMES

- Give last names only, unless two authors have the same last name or if the source is a personal communication. In these cases, include the first initial before the last name ("J. Smith").

DATES

- Give only the year in the in-text citation. The one exception to this rule is personal communications, which should include a full date.
- Months and days for periodical publications should not be given with the year in in-text citations; this information will

---

be provided as needed in the reference entry at the end of your paper.

- If you have two or more works by the same author in the same year, include letters after the year to distinguish the works (2005a, 2005b).
- If you can't locate a date for your source, include the abbreviation "n.d." (for "no date") in place of the date in parentheses.

TITLES
- Titles of works generally do not need to be given in in-text citations. Exceptions include works with no author and two or more works by the same author.

PAGE NUMBERS
- Include page numbers whenever possible in parentheses after borrowed material. Put "p." (or "pp.") before the page number(s).
- When you have a range of pages, list the full first and last page numbers (for example, "311–324"). If the borrowed material isn't printed on consecutive pages, list all the pages it appears on (for example, "A1, A4–A6").
- If page numbers are not available, use section names and/or paragraph (written as "para.") numbers when available to help a reader locate a specific quotation.

1. AUTHOR NAMED IN SIGNAL PHRASE

Doyle (2005) asserted that "Although some immigrants are a burden on the welfare system, as a group they pay far more in taxes than they receive in government benefits, such as public education and social services" (p. 25).

2. AUTHOR NAMED IN PARENTHESES

"Although some immigrants are a burden on the welfare system, as a group they pay far more in taxes than they receive in government benefits, such as public education and social services" (Doyle, 2005, p. 25).

3. TWO AUTHORS

Note that if you name the authors in the parentheses, connect them with an ampersand (&).

Sharpe and Young (2005) reported that new understandings about tooth development, along with advances in stem cell technology, have brought researchers closer to the possibility of producing replacement teeth from human tissue (p. 36).

New understandings about tooth development, along with advances in stem cell technology, have brought researchers closer to the possibility of producing replacement teeth from human tissue (Sharpe & Young, 2005, p. 36).

4. THREE TO FIVE AUTHORS

The first time you cite a source with three to five authors, list all their names in either the signal phrase or parentheses. If you cite the same source again in your paper, use just the first author's name followed by "et al."

Swain, Scahill, Lombroso, King, and Leckman (2007) pointed out that "[a]lthough no ideal treatment for tics has been established, randomized clinical trials have clarified the short-term benefits of a number of agents" (p. 947).

Swain et al. (2007) claimed that "[m]any tics are often under partial voluntary control, evidenced by patients' capacity to suppress them for brief periods of time" (p. 948).

5. SIX OR MORE AUTHORS

List the first author's name only, followed by "et al."

Grossoehme et al. (2007) examined the disparity between the number of pediatricians who claim that religion and spirituality are important factors in treating patients and those who actually use religion and spirituality in their practice (p. 968).

List of References

General Guidelines for Reference Entries in APA Style

AUTHOR NAMES

- When an author's name appears *before* the title of the work, list it by last name followed by a comma and first initial followed by a period. (Middle initials may also be included.)
- If an author, editor, or other name is listed *after* the title, then the initial(s) precede the last name.

- When multiple authors are listed, their names should be separated by commas, and an ampersand (&) should precede the final author.

DATES

- For scholarly journals, include only the year (2007).
- For monthly magazines, include the year followed by a comma and the month (2007, May).
- For newspapers and weekly magazines, include the year, followed by a comma and the month and the day (2007, May 27).
- Access dates for electronic documents use the month-day-year format: "Retrieved May 27, 2007."
- Months should not be abbreviated.
- If a date is not available, use "n.d." (for "no date") in parentheses.

TITLES

- Titles of periodicals should be italicized, and all major words capitalized (*Psychology Today; Journal of Archaeological Research*).
- Titles of books, Web sites, and other non-periodical long works should be italicized. Capitalize the first word of the title (and subtitle, if any) and proper nouns only (*Legacy of ashes: The history of the CIA*).
- For short works such as essays, articles, and chapters, capitalize the first word of the title (and subtitle, if any) and proper nouns only (The black sites: A rare look inside the CIA's secret interrogation program).

PAGE NUMBERS / DOI

- Reference entries for periodical articles and sections of books should include the range of pages: "245–257." For material in parentheses, include the abbreviation "p." or "pp." before the page numbers ("pp. A4–A5").
- If the pages are not continuous, list all the pages separated by commas: "245, 249, 301–306."
- Many articles published electronically now have a DOI (digital object identifier) — that is, a unique number that helps to locate it (for example, doi:10.1503/cmaj.109-3003). Include the DOI at the end of an entry instead of a URL. No period follows the DOI.

References

Online source

Campbell, D., Carlin M., Justen, J., III, & Baird, S. (2004). Cri-du-chat syndrome: A topical overview. Retrieved from http://fivepminus.org/online.htm

Journal article with no DOI

Denny, M., Marchand-Martella, N., Martella, R., Reilly, J. R., & Reilly, J. F. (2000). Using parent-delivered graduated guidance to teach functional living skills to a child with cri du chat syndrome. *Education & Treatment of Children, 23*(4), 441.

Journal article with DOI

Erlenkamp, S., & Kristoffersen, E. K. (2010). Sign communication in cri du chat syndrome. *Journal of Communication Disorders, 43,* 225–251. doi:10.1016/j.jcomdis.2010.03.002

Online source with group author

Five P Minus Society. (n.d.). *About 5p- syndrome.* Retrieved from http://www.fivepminus.org/about.htm

Kugler, M. (2006). Cri-du-chat syndrome: Distinctive kitten-like cry in infancy. Retrieved from http://rarediseases.about.com/cs/criduchatsynd/a/010704.htm

Part of a Web site

Sondheimer, N. (2005). Cri du chat syndrome. In *MedLinePlus medical encyclopedia.* Retrieved from http://www.nlm.nih.gov/medlineplus/ency/article/001593.htm

BIBLIOGRAPHY

of works quoted or discussed

The following books and published articles are quoted or discussed in *A Reader's Guide to College Writing*.

Alexie, Sherman. *The Absolutely True Diary of a Part-Time Indian*. New York: Little, Brown, 2007. (narrative)

Aynajian, Pegor, et al. "Visualizing Heavy Fermions Emerging in a Quantum Critical Kondo Lattice." *Nature* 486 (June 14, 2012): 201–6. doi: 10.1038/nature11204 (report)

Bauerlein, Mark, ed. *The Digital Divide: Arguments for and against Facebook, Google, Texting, and the Age of Social Networking*. New York: Jeremy P. Tarcher / Penguin, 2011. (report)

Bayard, Pierre. *How to Talk about Books You Haven't Read*. Trans. Jeffrey Mehlman. New York: Bloomsbury, 2007. (report/argument)

Carr, Nicholas. "Is Google Making Us Stupid?" In *The Digital Divide*, edited by Mark Bauerlein, 63–75. New York: Jeremy P. Tarcher / Penguin, 2011. Originally published in *Atlantic Monthly*, July/August 2008. (argument)

Charles, Ron. "On Campus, Vampires Are Besting the Beats." *Washington Post*, March 8, 2009. (argument)

Cleave, Chris. *Little Bee*. New York: Simon & Schuster, 2008. (narrative)

Eggers, Dave. *Zeitoun*. San Francisco: McSweeney's Books, 2009. (narrative/report/argument)

Ehrenreich, Barbara. *Nickel and Dimed: On (Not) Getting By in America*. New York: Holt, 2001. (report/argument)

Fish, Stanley. "Rhetoric." In *Doing What Comes Naturally: Change, Rhetoric, and the Practice of Theory in Literary and Legal Studies*. Durham, NC: Duke University Press, 1989. (report/analysis)

Foer, Jonathan Safran. *Eating Animals*. New York: Little, Brown, 2009. (argument)

Frazier, Ian. *On the Rez*. New York: Picador, 2000. (narrative)

Friedman, Thomas L. *Hot, Flat, and Crowded: Why We Need a Green Revolution—and How It Can Renew America*. New York: Farrar, Straus, and Giroux, 2008. (report/argument)

Gillmor, Alison. "It's a Dog's Life: They're Not Just Pets Anymore." *The Walrus*, April 2007. (argument)

Gladwell, Malcolm. *Outliers: The Story of Success.* New York: Little, Brown, 2008. (report/argument)

———. "Troublemakers." *New Yorker,* February 6, 2006. (report)

Gosling, Samuel D. "From Mice to Men: What Can We Learn about Personality from Animal Research?" *Psychological Bulletin* 127 (2001). (report)

Hayde, Michael J. *My Name's Friday: The Unauthorized but True Story of Dragnet and the Films of Jack Webb.* Nashville: Cumberland, 2001. (report)

Helprin, Mark. *Digital Barbarism: A Writer's Manifesto.* New York: HarperCollins, 2009. (argument)

Johnson, Michael B. "Systemic Model of Doping Behavior." *American Journal of Psychology* (Summer 2011): 151+. (report)

Johnson, Steven. *Everything Bad Is Good for You.* New York: Riverhead, 2005. (argument/analysis)

Kagan, Donald. "What Is a Liberal Education?" In *Reconstructing History,* edited by Elizabeth Fox-Genovese and Elizabeth Lasch-Quinn. New York: Routledge, 1999. (report/argument)

Keyes, Scott. "Stop Asking Me My Major." Commentary, *Chronicle of Higher Education* (January 10, 2010). (argument)

Kidder, Tracy. *Strength in What Remains: A Journey of Remembrance and Forgiveness.* New York: Random House, 2009. (narrative)

Kleinfeld, Andrew, and Judith Kleinfeld. "Go Ahead, Call Us Cowboys." *Wall Street Journal,* July 19, 2004. (argument)

Krakauer, Jon. *Into the Wild.* New York: Villard, 1996. (narrative)

———. *Three Cups of Deceit.* New York: Anchor Books, 2011. (argument)

Lareau, Annette. *Unequal Childhoods: Class, Race, and Family Life.* 2nd ed. Berkeley: University of California Press, 2011. (report)

Larson, Erik. *The Devil in the White City: Murder, Magic, and Madness at the Fair That Changed America.* New York: Vintage Books, 2004. (narrative)

LePatner, Barry B. *Too Big to Fall: America's Failing Infrastructure and the Way Forward.* New York: Foster, 2010. (argument)

Levitt, Steven D., and Stephen J. Dubner. *Freakonomics: A Rogue Economist Explores the Hidden Side of Everything.* New York: William Morrow, 2005. (report)

Lindberg, Sara M.; Janet Shipley Hyde, Jennifer L. Petersen, and Marcia C. Linn. "New Trends in Gender and Mathematics Performance: A Meta-Analysis." *Psychological Bulletin* 136, no. 6 (2010). (report)

"The Lost Children of Haiti." Editorial, *New York Times*, September 5, 2006. (argument)

Luey, Beth. *Expanding the American Mind: Books and the Popularization of Knowledge*. Amherst: University of Massachusetts Press, 2010. (report)

Mann, Charles C. *1491: New Revelations of the Americas before Columbus*. New York: Vintage Books, 2006. (report)

McGrath, Ellen. "Is Depression Contagious?" *Psychology Today* (July/August 2003). (report)

Menchú Tum, Rigoberta. *I, Rigoberta Menchú*. London: Versa, 1984.

Michaels, Walter Benn. *The Trouble with Diversity: How We Learned to Love Identity and Ignore Inequality*. New York: Metropolitan Books, 2006. (argument)

Mill, John Stuart. *On Liberty*. London: Longman, 1869. (argument)

Morgenson, Gretchen, and Joshua Rosner. *Reckles$ Endangerment: How Outsized Ambition, Greed, and Corruption Led to Economic Armageddon*. New York: Times Books / Henry Holt, 2011. (argument)

Mortenson, Greg, and David Oliver Relin. *Three Cups of Tea*. London: Penguin, 2006. (narrative/report)

Naylor, Gloria. "The Love of Books." In *The Writing Life: A Collection of Essays and Interviews*. New York: Random House, 1995. (narrative)

Nicolson, Adam. *God's Secretaries: The Making of the King James Bible*. New York: HarperCollins, 2003. (narrative/report)

O'Hanlon, Redmond. *Into the Heart of Borneo*. New York: Random House, 1984. (narrative)

Patry, William. *Moral Panics and the Copyright Wars*. New York: Oxford University Press, 2009. (argument)

Pennebaker, James W., and Amy Gonzales. "Making History: Social and Psychological Processes Underlying Collective Memory." In Pascal Boyer and James V. Wertsch, *Memory in Mind and Culture*. Cambridge, MA: Cambridge University Press, 2009. (report)

Prensky, Marc. "Digital Natives, Digital Immigrants." In *The Digital Divide*, edited by Mark Bauerlein, 3–11. New York: Jeremy P. Tarcher / Penguin, 2011. (argument)

———. "Do They Really Think Differently?" In *The Digital Divide*, edited by Mark Bauerlein, 12–25. New York: Jeremy P. Tarcher / Penguin, 2011. (argument)

Rank, Mark Robert. *One Nation, Underprivileged: Why American Poverty Affects Us All*. New York: Oxford University Press, 2005. (argument)

Ravitch, Diane. *The Death and Life of the Great American School System: How Testing and Choice Are Undermining Education*. New York: Basic Books, 2010. (report/argument)

Reynolds, David West. *Apollo: The Epic Journey to the Moon*. New York: Harcourt, 2002. (narrative)

Riddle, J. A. "Brave New Beef: Animal Cloning and Its Impacts." *Brown Journal of World Affairs* 14.1 (2007): 111–19. (report)

Rivoli, Pietra. *The Travels of a T-Shirt in the Global Economy: An Economist Examines the Markets, Power, and Politics of World Trade*. Hoboken, NJ: Wiley, 2005. (report)

Ryan, Maureen. "*Dallas* Review: J.R. Is Back but Can the Next Generation Compete?" *Huffington Post* (blog), June 12, 2012. (argument)

"Sanity 101." Editorial, *USA Today*, January 19, 2006, A10. (argument)

Schlosser, Eric. *Fast Food Nation*. New York: Harper-Perennial, 2002. (argument)

Siegel, Lee. "A Dream Come True" from *Against the Machine: How the Web Is Reshaping Culture and Commerce—And Why It Matters* (2008). Chapter reprinted in *The Digital Divide*, edited by Mark Bauerlein, 295–306. New York: Jeremy P. Tarcher / Penguin, 2011. (argument)

Silko, Leslie Marmon. *Ceremony*. New York: Viking Press, 1977. (narrative)

Skloot, Rebecca. *The Immortal Life of Henrietta Lacks*. New York: Broadway, 2010. (narrative/report)

Sword, Helen. "Inoculating against Jargonitis." Chronicle Review, *Chronicle of Higher Education* (June 3, 2012). (argument)

Urrea, Luis Alberto. *The Devil's Highway: A True Story*. New York: Back Bay Books, 2004. (narrative/argument)

Vanderbilt, Tom. *Traffic: Why We Drive the Way We Do (and What It Says about Us)*. New York: Knopf, 2008. (report)

Waldfogel, Joel. "Short End: Tall People Earn More Because They're Smarter." *Slate*, September 1, 2006. (report)

West, Michael, and Myron Silberstein. "The Controversial Eloquence of Shakespeare's Coriolanus: An Anti-Ciceronian Orator?" *Modern Philology* 102, no. 3 (February 2005). (argument)

Whiteley, Peter M. "Ties That Bind: Hopi Gift Culture and Its First Encounter with the United States." *Natural History* 113.9 (2004): 26–31. (report)

Wolk, Douglas. "Something to Talk About: Can Music Be a Conversation?" *Spin*, August 2005. (argument)

Wood, Peter. "How to Ask a Question." *Chronicle of Higher Education* (March 30, 2012). (report)

Acknowledgments (continued from p. ii)

Sherman Alexie. From *The Absolutely True Diary of a Part-Time Indian* by Sherman Alexie. Copyright © 2007 by Sherman Alexie. By permission of Little, Brown and Company. All rights reserved.

Pegor Aynajian, et al. "Visualizing heavy fermions emerging in a quantum critical Kondo lattice." Copyright © 2012, Rights Managed by Nature Publishing Group.

Nicholas Carr. "Is Google Making Us Stupid?" from *The Digital Divide.* © 2008 The Atlantic Media Co., as first published in *The Atlantic Magazine.* All rights reserved. Distributed by Tribune Media Services.

Ron Charles. "On Campus, Vampires are Besting the Beats." © 2009 *Washington Post.* Reprinted by permission of *Washington Post.*

Thomas L. Friedman. Excerpts from *Hot, Flat, and Crowded: Why We Need a Green Revolution — and How it Can Renew America* by Thomas L. Friedman. Copyright © 2008 by Thomas L. Friedman. Reprinted by permission of Farrar, Straus and Giroux, LLC.

Alison Gillmor. "It's a Dog's Life: They're Not Just Pets Anymore." Reprinted by permission of the author.

Scott Keyes. "Stop Asking Me My Major." Reprinted by permission of the author.

Ellen McGrath. "Is Depression Contagious?" Reprinted by permission of the author.

Walter Benn Michaels. Excerpts from pages 15, 16, 178, 179, and 180 from the book *The Trouble with Diversity: How We Learned to Love Identity and Ignore Inequality* by Walter Benn Michaels. Copyright © 2006 by Walter Benn Michaels. Used by permission of Henry Holt and Company, LLC. All rights reserved.

The New York Times. "The Lost Children of Haiti." From *The New York Times,* September 5, 2006. © 2006 *The New York Times.* All rights reserved. Used by permission and protected by the Copyright Laws of the United States. The printing, copying, redistribution, or retransmission of this Content without express written permission is prohibited.

Marc Prensky. From "Digital Natives, Digital Immigrants" by Marc Prensky (*On the Horizon,* October 2001). © Emerald Group Publishing.

Diane Ravitch. "The Death and Life of the Great American School System: How Testing and Choice Are Undermining Education" by Ravitch, Diane. Reproduced with permission of Basic Books in the format Republish in a book via Copyright Clearance Center.

Maureen Ryan. "*Dallas* Review: J. R. Is Back But Can the Next Generation Compete?" From *The Huffington Post,* June 12, 2012. © 2012

INDEX